PENT[illegible]

of the GODS

A Pilgrimage into the Heart of Tibet and the Sacred City of Lhasa

By

THEOS BERNARD

CHARLES SCRIBNER'S SONS · NEW YORK

CHARLES SCRIBNER'S SONS · LTD · LONDON

1939

To

VIOLA

CONTENTS.

ILLUSTRATIONS

Illustrations

Illustrations

Illustrations

PENTHOUSE
OF THE GODS

CHAPTER I

ECSTASY

I

LIFE began to stir in the middle of the night, as preparations were being made for the great ceremony. With the dawn I was awakened by the rhythmic beating of drums, the ceaseless drone of sixteen-foot trumpets and the vibrant chanting of thousands of Lamas, as they filed their way to the slab-paved courtyard of the famous temple.

For an instant I was startled, wondering where I was that I should experience such strange sensations. Then I remembered. This was the presaging for me of the day of days: I was to appear before the T'ri Rimpoche, the highest Lama of Tibet, who was to instal me with my vestments after this ultimate ritual initiation. For months this divine soul had been the unforeseen guide of my destiny; it was he who had prepared me for this final step.

These great ceremonial initiations might be compared to our own festive occasions at graduation, when the diploma is presented to the student, confirming the bestowal upon the candidate of certain knowledge which for a period he has been receiving. As one attains the more advanced stages, the ritual assumes a less formal tone; in the final mystical initiation the initiate merely sits in silent meditation with his mentor, who endows him with an inner revelation by the means of thought transference.

There was unusual significance to this particular initiation. The fact is, I, the person about to be initiated into Tibetan sacred mysteries, was no native, no Tibetan, not even an Oriental, but an American, hailing from Arizona. And here, at the end of the ceremony, I would become a full-fledged Buddhist monk, a Lama.

The servants had brought my early morning buttered tea, which it is customary to take upon awakening. They appeared to be more excited than I over this historic event; never before had an American been accepted. It was, indeed, not as a stranger that I was being permitted to receive this divine benediction; I had been accepted as one of their own, as a reincarnation of one of their celebrated Saints. Fate had brought it about that I should be reborn in the Western world that I might learn of its forms and customs, and now the same fate had restored me to my homeland that I might have my inner consciousness reawakened, and thus become mindful of that old soul that was silently guiding the footsteps of this physical form into which it had passed for its further development.

This was how they interpreted my action in leaving America and in coming to them. So it was not a mystery to them how I came always to do the right thing when passing through these various esoteric initiations, and why it was possible for me to possess such a deep comprehension of all their teachings. My subconscious self had directed my thoughts and guided my desires so that I simply had to come to them, and each successive initiation was no more than a reawakening of my true self. Otherwise, it would have been scarcely possible for me to advance so rapidly. They explained that often a man will have to experience many existences before it is possible for him to be sufficiently prepared to receive the next initiation, and here I had prepared myself for the final initiation within the incredible space of a few months.

My emotions ran high; little time was wasted in preparing to descend to the temple room. Dressing for the event was a relatively simple task. I donned a golden silken robe with a sash around the waist; the garment was cut on lines very much like those worn by the Chinese. My boys insisted on an immaculate appearance; they almost irritated me with the pains they took in arranging each separate fold, where the material is doubled back, so that all might be smooth in front. The long silken sash around my waist had been especially pressed for the occasion. Altogether, I felt almost too prim to bend, or sit. This self-conscious moment went as quickly as it came; soon I was lost again in the excitement of the event.

While waiting for the summons, I stood by the small open window to fill my lungs with that fresh rarefied air which envelops this monastery hidden away in the arms of heaven at an elevation of sixteen thousand feet. The distant horizon was still veiled in the early morning mist, which was rapidly evaporating with the increase of daylight. All nature was astir, even as was every cell in my body. I could hardly wait; had I not spent years in actual preparation of this event? Until now it had only been a secret dream, and even at this moment I almost feared to trust my own feelings; was this event really going to take place? At all times I had held fast to my faith in the old teaching that one should never contemplate the end, but ever be about the task of preparing oneself, secure in the knowledge that when one was ready the teacher would appear. And now the truth of this saying was manifesting itself; so I mulled over the thought that I must not lose myself in the torrent of emotions which this event would release, but content myself with the knowledge that it was to be only another step and that I should accept it only as part of my whole training, as a preparation for a yet greater goal.

2

At last the summons came, and we made haste to the temple room. The attendant Lamas carried the long silk scarves known as *kata*, which are used as offerings before all shrines when we ask for the blessings and protection of their unending pantheon of Holy Hosts.

One of the beautiful things about the Tibetan is his seeming irrelevance in mixing up the external forms with the details of existence which has its place behind the scene. Thus, for example, our descent to the temple led us through the immense kitchens, where great vats in which the tea is made could be seen steaming, as the workmen lifted the covers to see if it was ready. These huge kettles, some of them four feet deep and eight feet in diameter, made of heavy metal cast in Tibet, repose on high brick ovens, beneath which large quantities of yak dung are stoked, filling the rooms with soot. This soot has been collecting on the walls for centuries, and, in consequence, the place is darker than a coal mine. The workmen are attired in rags, which shine with an accumulation of grease. They take great pride in this attire, and when a new garment comes their way, which is perhaps once in a lifetime, they promptly cover it with grease as a foundation coat for the encrustations of grease in the years to come. Their faces are even blacker than the walls, and only lighted up with a smile; for they are a cheerful lot, taking inordinate pride in their work. The tea for the T'ri Rimpoche is made separate from the rest. His tea is not only a superior quality, but the butter with which it is made is infinitely fresher; the tea of the others is often made with butter several years old. Again, a supervision is maintained against the possibility of any attempt to poison this deified mortal.

We traversed this chamber of toil, holding our skirts high to protect them from the grease and filth on the floors. We left one cell of dark oblivion only to enter another and another, until at last we emerged in a court leading to the main temple; the windows were few and far between. The slab-paved pavilion was packed with countless mounds of holiness, as the Lamas sat in silent prayer, waiting for the rising sun. From beneath their bowed heads I could detect the young acolytes furtively watching out of the corners of their eyes: Were they human? To discover this, I would smile at them in passing, and was usually rewarded with a smile. The high throne upon which I was to remain in silence with the coming sun was waiting for me; a well-disciplined escort urged me to make haste, for the golden rays of light were already beginning to bathe the heavens.

The impressive silence of the morning was being rent with the low muffled sounds of those long sixteen-foot trumpets, and their vibrant volume swelled by the chants of the Lamas filled the air with a strange ecstasy. Life was born again, and each soul lived for a new beginning. Once the sun had passed above the horizon visible to man, all lapsed quietly into the peace of the morning, and listened to the awakening soul within.

The time had come for all to file into the large temple room. Military discipline made this a simple task; it was a matter of only a few minutes, and I returned to a complete awareness of the events of the morning. The courtyard had been made clean from end to end; within the temple I could hear the preparations being made for the ceremony. I approached the immense door, which was guarded by one who waited until I had recited my *mantras* (mystic sounds), this in order to purify myself before entering the holy sanctuary, in which I was to receive a divine dispensation. For an instant I hesitated: I did not know why the door was closed, and, as if there were another person within me, and advised by him, I paused on the threshold, my head bowed, while I uttered a silent prayer. The bolted barrier slowly swung open.

The great temple room is without windows. Its sole source of light is from the opening above the first story roof of the building, where the inner nave extends beyond; this is covered over with a long drapery of woven yak hair, in order to keep the rains and the snows from beating down into the temple room, which might prove ruinous to the elaborate wall paintings.

As I stepped across the sanctified threshold, I found myself enveloped in a stream of sunlight flowing in from above. I promptly prostrated myself in that cascade of sunbeams, and, while lying there in humble devotion, bathed by the golden light, I dived for a fleeting instant into the innermost depths of human consciousness. An overwhelming emotion filled me, and I understood the wonder which held the faithful to this ancient cult.

I rose to my feet, and stood aside, while others in my party were finishing their three devotional prostrations. The great hall was vibrant with the prayers chanted by countless Lamas seated cross-legged, heads bowed, upon raised flat benches placed in endless rows. Draped from the shoulders with garnet capes of rags, they formed parallel aisles of holiness, all merging into a single mass as they receded into the remote darkness of the opposite end of the nave. The massive pillars of wood urged one's eyes to the ceiling, from which descended long paintings on canvas, bordered with three colors of silk. Some of these *thangkas*—for thus these sacred paintings are called—were fifteen feet in length, and their broad edges of costly silk added to their expanse. They told the story of Tibetan religious leaders and saints.

The flickering of a thousand and more butter lamps lighted the way for us as we advanced slowly toward the high throne of the T'ri Rimpoche, and it was as if I were being borne along on the waves created by the tremulous murmurings of the chanting Lamas. The dais upon which *he*, the T'ri Rimpoche, sat was some twelve feet above the floor; and it was needful to perform many cleansing rites before the altars below, upon which stood the deities moulded in gold and

gleaming in the yellow light of the sacred offerings of the eternal light of knowledge. But it is scarcely possible to crystallize such emotions as were experienced there into the frozen form of words.

3

Hours went by in these devotional rites. This is hardly astonishing, for no detail could or had been overlooked in the intensive preparation of my consciousness for the experience yet ahead of me. Their teaching is that there are no gaps in nature. Everything unfolds according to a divine rule. The individual can do no more than hasten this process, which is slow at best. They have a saying here: a seed can never pop into a tree. It must pass through each of its several stages, even as does the worm that eventually becomes a beautiful butterfly. Thus, also, was it essential that plenty of time be allotted for each of these rites to take effect within the depths of my inner self. If one tried to skip a single phase of spiritual maturation, he would be sure to find himself in the blind alley of delusion. The planting of the seed is the first step, and this was being done by the repetition of the *mantras* given me by my unforeseen mentor. While I was reciting these mystic syllables the lamaist choir went on with its heavy bombardment of monotonous chants, occasionally broken by the tinkling of thousands of tiny bells used as a part of their mystic rites. The mere movement of their hands and twisting of their fingers, as they went from one *mudra* (mystic posture) to another, symbolic of certain attitudes of the imagination, acted as a hypnotic spur.

Finally I was conducted into the black chamber of horrors, hidden away behind bolted doors, whose locks required keys as large as automobile cranks in order to open them. A young acolyte guided our footsteps with a small butter light, which he held close to the floor that the way might be seen, until I entered a chamber, one foot sliding after the other in order to be certain of my footing, all of which recalled to my mind an experience of childhood, when I used to wander through the mines with the aid of a candle. We could see only a brief distance ahead, and for the moment all that was visible was the glowing light of a large butter lamp, which held sufficient fuel to burn several months without replenishment.

We sighted an altar. Above it reposed a symbol which represented the destructive aspect of that great creative force within, on the verge of release. This enormous demon stood in an array of flames, crushing beneath his feet the bodies of human beings, while from the great mound upon which he rested there trickled endless rivulets of blood. He possesses many arms, each carrying a weapon of destruction, thereby revealing the many avenues the human being is offered for self-destruction, which he may escape only by understanding. The same chamber harbored other fiends, standing in sexual embrace with their deified consorts, draped with necklaces of human skulls, intended to convey the transitoriness of human existence with its fleeting passions of the senses. Each is symbolic of a stage in the development of human consciousness in its earthly evolution. It is taught here that there is only one force in life, but that it has an infinite number of manifestations; only through knowledge is it possible to direct this force. To the initiate this knowledge is essential, since it stimulates his imagination and provides him with the key for the release of the internal power of man.

This vast chamber is always kept under guard and under lock and key, so that the uninstructed may not have the opportunity to see these hideous forms; there is too much danger of their being interpreted literally and not in their symbolic form. It is argued that the revelation they offer is eso-

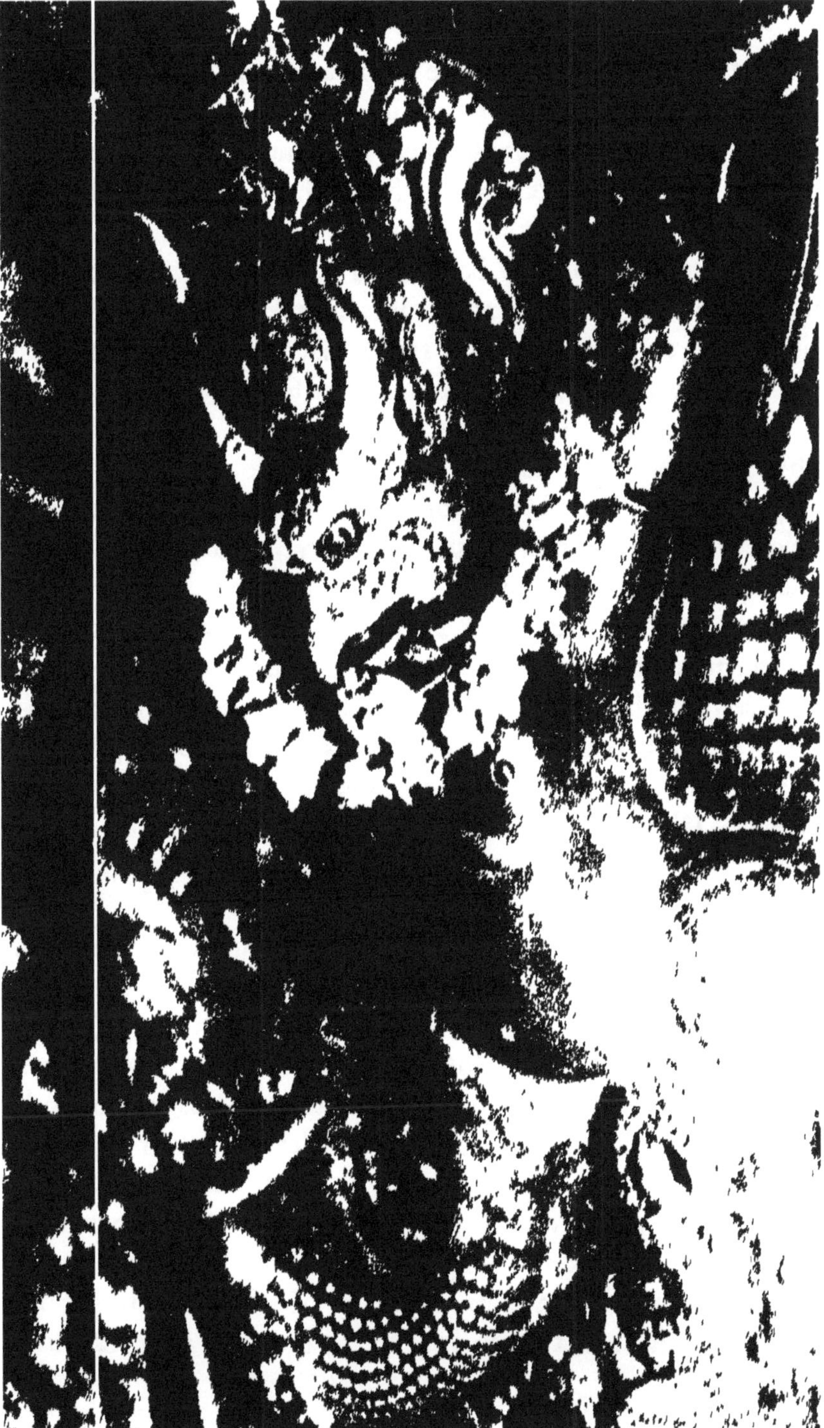

teric, and that it is impossible to pass on knowledge until the consciousness of the individual is prepared to receive it. The individual will never grasp their meaning merely by reading all the books and imbibing all the teachings. He must be prepared, and in this he must follow the processes of nature herself; there are things to be learned only through sorrow and misfortune. This preparation usually takes a great deal of time, and until the pupil is ready, a contemplation of these can only be productive of considerable harm.

We seated ourselves below the altar which pedestalled this objective representation of the destructive channels of the stream of life. The *khorlo*, or circle, was headed by the high priest who has the power over this esoteric knowledge. Awakened by the solemn darkness of the sanctuary, I first heard the low rumbling drone of his chants, which he repeated for the purpose of preparing us. Then his assistants slowly joined, intensifying the vibrant echoes of this dungeon of holiness. Soon I began to repeat the *mantras* which had been provided me, until my entire being felt like the buzzing wings of a bumble-bee. I knew that I had to control this and to direct the energy which was being stirred up through the channels of the sympathetic nervous system. My months of training in the Yoga practices were useful here, even essential. The test was yet to come, and it was whether or not I had developed sufficient power of control to direct that energy so as to contact the hidden reservoirs of the imagination in the subconscious. With each succeeding step the internal pressures of the body became more fierce, and I began to understand their power of destruction. It was only by sheer will power that I was able to hold on, fully aware as I was that here was the opportunity for which I had been so long preparing; this experience was a conscious dip into the eternal flow of life. The agony became terrifying, and had I given vent to the thoughts of fears which were beginning to beset me I should have burst forth screaming and not stopped running until I either went mad or touched the borderline of madness. But I had come to do or die. I had grown weary of reading what others had to say about what these esoteric rites might reveal to me, and I had long ago decided that it was for me to dedicate my life to being a spiritual guinea-pig that I might give others the benefit of my experience. It was for me to hold on. I was reminded of the days when I stopped on the banks of a lake while a friend who was a strong swimmer trod water, imploring me to jump in and assuring me that he would save me. He spent days expatiating on the joys of swimming. Fear, however, restrained me; until one day some one came along and pushed me in. And thus I learned to swim. At this moment, girding myself with the teachings of the ancient sages, I felt infusions of faith, and was ready to go the limit.

I observed an assistant speaking to the officiating high priest. Then the vibrations were changed, and a new *mantra* was being repeated, and another was given me. Slowly I began to read it, repeating it after my mentor. Each line was the same, but a different syllable was stressed at the end of each phrase. The entire internal rhythm was changing, ever swelling. The walls almost seemed to sway with the ever increasing drone of beating drums, blaring horns and clashing cymbals. My imagination was beginning to run wild. I had learned by now how to sit apart and watch the inner-self function. Yet I was in constant fear of being swept away by these mystical rites, which utilize every known emotional phenomenon.

In the midst of this spiritual storm, everything suddenly seemed dispelled as by some mysterious magic; the tinkling bells could be felt, when all receded, and we meditated in the dead silence of darkness. It will never be possible for me to express in words what actually took place. It was something beyond the realm of the mind and, therefore, beyond the expression of name and form.

Moreover, the philosophical instructions which appertain to these ritualistic forms would take up several volumes. It is not within the province of this record to do more than to treat of some of the broader aspects of universal experience interpreted in the light of the customs to be found in the Penthouse of the Gods.

4

The ceremony was over, and a new world had been opened to me. Now it was for me to remain and reflect upon this volcano of subconscious power in the light of the teachings which had been previously given me, of which these fiendish plastic forms were some of the symbols. Beginning with the first chief image which had caught my eye before entering into the ceremony, I was deliberately to study each and to interpret its inner meaning. Not until then did I fully realize the wisdom of those who had created these hideous forms of devastation. Before me—so it had seemed to me at first—had stood a fiend of destruction; but now it had become a symbol of the greatest force of nature, that creative flow of nature in the eternal battle to penetrate its way from the subconscious into the conscious, giving intelligent guidance to each separate personality.

I had no way of telling how many hours had passed since I first entered this hell, or heaven—call it what you will—for I was in a world in which the phenomenon of time did not exist. It was as if I had come back for a rebirth, memory of my past lives assisting me in my new orientation, with the prospect of future experiences; since this was merely the beginning of that for which I was being prepared. It was, indeed, a test.

And now to find out if I had passed.

I was conducted to the altar below the dais, upon which sat the T'ri Rimpoche, shut away from the vision of all yet in full command of every one within this vast temple chamber.

The officiating Lama turned from the altar with a silver jar of holy water. This he poured into my hands, from which I sipped, placing the remainder on my head. Then he who had been conducting me through the ceremonies returned with a small image of Buddha, a Tibetan book and a sacred scarf, symbolic of the eternal truth, knowledge and the divine knot of life. This told me that I was to be accepted and permitted to receive his blessing; for in some mysterious way he knew that I had gained the inner realization.

Prior to ascending the stairway, I was taken before the golden image of Buddha; here I was to meditate on the meaning of each of the symbols as they were being mystically prepared for the offering. As soon as, by the means of certain *mantras*, everything was firmly fixed in my mind and my consciousness so arrested that I was wholly oblivious to everything else, lost in the spiritual intoxication of the mystic chants, my mentor beckoned to me to follow. Slowly we ascended the stairways, and it seemed as if I were about to climb into the attic of Heaven, taking this bodily form with me; for the consciousness was no longer that of the personality who had first entered this great temple room. With each step my vision grew increasingly obscure, until complete darkness encompassed me. What was the meaning of this? Was I to be deprived of the glory of seeing him after all this arduous ritualistic ordeal?

Even in the midst of this reflection I caught a glimpse of a ray of light. I did not know whence it came, but after I had climbed high enough for my eyes to fall above the floor of his throne I looked up, and I saw his radiant face silhouetted against a tiny beam of sun that filtered through the thick darkness from a removed panel in the upper wall of his sanctuary.

Promptly I paid my deep respects with the three customary prostrations before him, after which I took my place on a low raised platform set apart for me. What was I to do next, and what was going to happen to me? Was some astonishing miracle about to be worked? I let an inner hand guide my actions, while I tried to tuck away conscious notes, so that I might be able to relive the experience again in memory.

Soon his hands began to move slowly in the air as they gracefully formed different *mudras*, before proceeding to the reading of different prayers, to which I responded. To this day I wonder how I knew what to say, though I do not now remember what I did say. It was as if I were a member of an orchestra, and the conductor turned to me with his baton, from which emanated his subconscious feelings, and I responded in kind, naturally and automatically, without consciousness other than that of being an integral part of this spiritual symphony. Three assistants stood in front of him, holding the objects which had been so carefully prepared for the offering.

Acting upon a prompting within, I rose from my cross-legged posture, and as I stood up before him a strange feeling crept over me; I suddenly realized that I was about to receive from him the power and authority to pass on what had been given me to others.

As I offered each symbolic object to him I felt the warm pressure of his fingers and his forehead touching my head; something was generously released in me when, finally, his divine hands formed a spiritual cap over my head. No one spoke; words were, indeed, superfluous here. When the ceremony was over, I had the feeling that I had been talking with him for a lifetime and had spent years studying under his guidance. A torrent of thoughts poured through my mind, as I reviewed every year of my life; yet they appeared to have nothing to do with me as I had known myself. And, again, this was an inexpressible experience, which left an indelible impression beyond the power of words.

5

After a blessing from the T'ri Rimpoche, I left his presence, overflowing with the energy which he had caused to be released from my subconscious. It yet remained to me to make a devotional tour of the sacred shrines and temples of the monastery and to circumambulate the monastery walls, before he would install me with my vestments and give me my last instructions prior to taking the vows and being clothed with the power and authority to pass on the teachings to others.

Cautiously we descended to the world of name and form, symbolized by the endless rituals performed in the temple room below, where the Lamas were still repeating their chants. The acolytes were waiting for us at the foot of the stairs, with their small butter lamps to guide us through the long narrow passages leading to the innermost sanctuaries of the monastery.

We began the tour by visiting the tomb of the founder of this religious sect. I have heard it said that every few years the tomb is opened and the body dressed, this procedure having been followed through the centuries. It has been further said that the skin is still in perfect condition and that the nails and hair of this honored saint are still growing, making it necessary to give him a periodical hair-cut, according to the custom of this order of monks. The entrance to the tomb is protected by a large shrine, containing a large image of a protecting deity. Within the room, on each side of the entrance, there hung from the ceiling a number of large stuffed yaks; while just over the doorway there was a large stuffed tiger. In the middle of this outer room was an enormous yak which, according to legend, was the one which the founder of the monastery used to ride to the valley four thousand feet below, and back. The other yaks were reputed to be those which had been used in carrying the rock employed in the construction of this series of vast structures, situated nearly sixteen thousand feet above sea-level, remote from the turmoil of an agitated, materialistic world of men. The tiger had been sent as a gift to the head Lama, thus bestowing upon it the privilege of gathering dust in this lofty shelter of the Gods.

Before the image, and hanging from the four walls, were weapons in endless variety. These had been used in the defence of the faith in the early centuries, after Buddhism first began to filter into the country, which was in the seventh century. They consisted mostly of spears, shields, armor plate, metal lace jackets, bows and arrows, swords, and the crude Tibetan musket. One was expected to inspect these historical souvenirs with the same measure of devotion as that of worshipping before a shrine. A door of this antechamber opened on a large room in which was built the *chorten*—the sacred cairn containing the body of the honored saint. Before its altars I offered the sacred scarf, then walked through the dark pathway bordering round the tomb, taking holy water from the officiating Lama before leaving this cell of sanctity.

By now the Lama assigned to the task of escorting us around the monastery walls arrived on the scene. He led us through the narrow canyons of holiness which served as the streets of the monastery; these consisted of the confined passageways left between the huge stone buildings.

The trail led to a narrow ledge on the brim of nowhere, so that it was possible for us to get around the cliff which formed the back wall of this spiritual superstructure nestled in the shelter of a Himalayan wing of rock. The effort to gain altitude was deemed the greatest test of one's spiritual sincerity, because the first physical reaction was the inclination to lie down, and the attitude of mind that went with it was the questioning as to what was to be gained from the circumambulation of the monastery other than the vision of this indescribable canyon of the Gods. It was not for me to settle the doubts raised, for the next step was the one for which I had really been working; this was the mystical initiation, free from all ritualistic formalism. The deeper one penetrates in this journey into the subconscious, the less ritual one encounters.

It is the Tibetan teaching that the world in which we live is one purely of name and form—in other words, one of mind. Hence, it is essential for the mind to have something tangible to grasp in order that it may function effectively, its inherent nature being that of activity. It is argued that if the individual fails to provide it with food for thought, the mind will function in vacuum, conjuring up an infinite variety of ideas having no real direction, or many directions. Therefore, the individual must give it these concrete external forms to serve as symbols on which it can reflect. Yet as a child soon learns to read without running its finger along after each word and mumbling with its lips, so the individual must develop his faculties for inner penetration and learn to do without such external factors. It is the Tibetan contention that man must first learn of his own incapacities, and at that point begins his discipline, and through the arduous process of continuous repetitions he can attain the more subtle ways, until he can deal direct with the subconscious. Here, however, the mind comes into its own. The mind, indeed, is a tool serving the individual in gathering in the facts through his different senses, and equally as an instrument for the personal expression of his inner self. Everything must pass through the mind, which is not only the tool of consciousness but also the most highly specialized tool of precision that man has for his own destruction.

The mystical initiation still before me was one in which there was no ritual whatsoever; for the previous initiations were supposed to have prepared the initiate to receive direct from his spiritual mentor the power that he wished to transfer to him, even while both sat as still, and as attuned to each other, as two wireless towers in the heart of Death Valley.

We had proceeded but a few hundred yards, when our guide began to point out the places about which the moss of religious tradition had gathered. Almost every crack and crevice of the hillside had some story connected with it. In some places there was moss, whereupon the guide would stop to explain to me that their great saint had once thrown the cuttings from his hair to the winds and they, having landed here, had been growing ever since. There were many places where the Precious One had come for an hour's reflection. And, indeed, at these points I did receive considerable inspiration; the vistas alone were enough to make any one gasp in mystical awe, to say nothing of the Truths of Life taught by him and which must have come to him precisely during the brief pauses on this marvellous way.

Well did I realize that in order to sound such depths of human understanding it was first necessary to establish a flow between the personal and the universal aspects of the individual, so that it would be possible to direct those torrents of the racial subconscious of man into the conscious aspect of this mortal self. Meditating upon this, I accepted each of these pauses as an opportunity for filling my mind with thoughts of fortitude, that I might be strong enough to endure the preparation for this final of initiations, which was to reveal to me the keenly guarded teachings of the sages of ageless Asia. One of the essential Tibetan teachings is that the motivating factor of this endless chain of rebirths is that of ideas; so that our only escape from the "Wheel of Life" is by storing the consciousness with the right ideas, which come from true understanding. Once a subconscious flickering becomes crystallized into an idea, the individual is ready to take off in a flight of action, but until that moment comes he will merely sit around and bask in the intoxicating radiance of his own flickerings.

We came to a place where we were shown the water level to be reached by the next great flood; the monastery was insured safety by being built on the crags above. Likewise was it indicated to us how high the flames will reach when the world is destroyed by fire.

These tales have their own interest, because they reveal how their highly symbolistic teachings are accepted and believed literally by the less informed. At times the superstitions of the ignorant believers are incredible. But the great teachers deem this an essential beginning, in much the same way that among us the belief in Santa Claus is supposed to help small children in doing the right thing. There are no idle superstitions in the world. If one should investigate them he would find that they serve a useful function for the common mass, permitting social development, which, in its own turn, holds the individual in harness until he is able to proceed alone with his inner evolution, which is the purpose of his existence.

Now on the downhill grade of our devotional tour, which consisted of about a mile in all, we next stopped at the tiny meditative chamber, chiselled into a cliff of solid rock. It was built at some distance from the main part of the monastery, so that the Precious One could be left wholly undisturbed; and it was cut into the ground to allow him to get away from all the vibratory effects which are continually subjecting the surface of the earth. When a person is thoroughly prepared to enter such a cell of solitary confinement, he is already highly sensitized to the vibrations of the world, even as is the radio, which is the mechanical manifestation of something those of the East professed countless centuries ago. An individual may spend a lifetime in the effort to prepare himself to undergo the experience of solitary confinement as the final step in the ultimate initiation. For here no one feels that everything must be done during one's lifetime. The great Wheel of Life will continue through eternity, and until they gain "understanding" they are forever bound to this sequence of endless deaths and rebirths. Life is filled with pain and suffering. Hence, they strive to advance at least a single step during this lifetime, regardless of how infinitesimal this advance might be. They do not try for the golden ideal and fail at everything. The first instruction to be imparted to the student is never to be concerned about the end. One step at a time, the next will inevitably follow—even without a teacher, who can only be a guide. The accomplishment is up to the individual.

The mentally impoverished will often go insane in a cell of solitary confinement; so extreme caution is used in permitting one to undertake this preparation. The length of time to be spent in the cell depends largely upon the individual and the measure of his development. Has he the fortitude? To what depths can he dive into the subconscious? There alone can he find the needful guidance.

6

The most interesting part of the visit to this cell was the contemplation of the vast richness of Tsong-Khapa, who had been able to find such joy in a spot so isolated from the rest of the world. He did not have any of the things deemed so vital to human happiness in the West. Indeed, at the time of his life, the United States had not even come into existence. It would be a strange world if only the people of a particular century and of a particular country of this vast globe could find that which has been termed salvation. Here is a people wholly isolated from all that the West thinks so essential for development. It has reached the conclusion that inner growth may be attained regardless of externals, save for shelter and enough food to protect the body, which is primarily an instrument for the maturation of the soul. According to this people's tenets, if one were given the knowledge of these truths, it would be possible for him to fulfill his purpose during this existence regardless of circumstance, and thereby be liberated from all desires which only seem necessary.

These are real questions, and it was to answer them that the mystical initiation was designed. The mere realization of this in itself provided me with sufficient fortitude to face the approaching ordeal, yes, even to the point of death, so eager was I to receive the ultimate understanding that I was seeking.

The guide of this devotional tour appeared somewhat restless, and, sensible of the fact that there yet remained a great deal to be done, I checked the inner flow and continued my way on to the monastery, where a repast was awaiting me. With all their holiness they seemed to be fully aware of the demands of the flesh, and at the same time cognizant of just how long the food for the soul might sustain the body. The saving grace of the Tibetan is his habit of drinking tea. Tea goes on being served throughout the day; it seems to be brewing almost round every corner; it has been served to me in the most unheard-of places. On entering the monastery, we went to the division which always took charge of non-Tibetans. Upon my sitting down to partake of refreshment, preliminary to another visit to the T'ri Rimpoche, who would give me final commandments on taking my last vows, the room assumed an air of bustle, as the attendant Lamas hurried from all directions to join in the real meal which was being rushed from the distant kitchens to this hidden dining room. It was good to rest the weary feet, which had been lugging around Tibetan boots over that sky-high thoroughfare of devotion. Only a couple of minutes elapsed before a large tray arrived with an endless variety of tasty native tidbits, at which I soon nibbled with chopsticks. Throughout the meal butter tea was repeatedly served, and at the conclusion of the meal still greater quantities of tea were graciously offered, and the politeness of the custom calls for the development of a capacity for its consumption.

Once I had been served, my retinue of attendants were taken care of, while I relaxed to the tune of their munching rhythm of complete gustative satisfaction, which could be heard several rooms away.

7

Soon after our repast word came that everything was ready for my installation. There was need to hurry; our walk apparently had exceeded the time allotted to it. The room, however, in which the formal ceremony was to take place, was quite near; so in quick time we ducked through the narrow hallways until we reached the appointed spot.

The vestments were brought, and no time was lost in being folded into the flowing Lamaist robes of garnet homespun, each robe having symbolic significance. Having "taken the veil," so to speak, I directed my footsteps to the temple of my monastic division, to worship there before appearing in the private chamber of the T'ri Rimpoche.

The summons came. The T'ri Rimpoche's chamber was tiny and simple. It contained only a small altar and a couple of very plain Tibetan banners. One banner was that of the founder of this religious sect, the other of the Lord Buddha. What impressed me most was the profundity of happiness manifested by the radiant face of Tibet's highest Lama. Not for him the wealth and grandeur within his reach. Pilgrims from every corner of Asia brought him gifts, and asked for his blessing. All this wealth was promptly turned over to the monastery; it was used to feed the inmate, the surplus was converted into sacred images. His entire empire is made up of his personal conquests of the soul, and he is ever willing to guide others over the same arduous path. The Tibetans teach that there are no short cuts to heaven; they remind the pilgrim and the disciple of the inevitable chain of continual deaths and continual rebirths in the Wheel of Life.

A signal honor was paid me in that I was permitted to sit on a seat placed next to the T'ri Rimpoche. This gave me some indication of how they felt toward me, and how far I had advanced in my innermost soul. Yet, as he explained later, I was one of their famous saints who had been reborn in the Western world, and that this was the reason that I had to come to Tibet and had been able to pass through all Tibetan ritualistic rites. It was merely a case of regaining lost memories, and I should presently be able to recall my past existences. And, actually, though at that moment I could not give an exact accounting of material details of any existence beyond this one, I did feel wholly at home in this land of mystery, and no experience I had undergone these past several months had revealed to me anything which seemed absolutely new. The mood was rather one of recalling things. The T'ri Rimpoche also told me that it was because of the old soul contained in this bodily form that it was possible for me to make this inner contact so rapidly and so easily. Nevertheless, I was still trying, as it were, to keep one foot on the ground; for my training had taught me that there were no mysteries, that every phenomenon in this world of name and form could be explained; moreover, that if a single untenability in any system could be found, then the whole system had to be discarded and a new beginning made. Hence, it was essential fully to comprehend the system, and in this instant it meant the complete awakening of the subconscious.

We recited various prayers, and I took the vows, after which

I was invited to ask the T'ri Rimpoche any questions I might wish to have answered before he prepared my imagination to face the coming ordeal of the cell of solitary confinement. Had this opportunity been granted me before this day, I should have availed myself of it with an endless stream of questions; but coming as it did, after the initiation, I had nothing to ask, but merely to implore that the great privilege of confinement in a solitary cell be granted me promptly.

8

After a prolonged philosophical discussion I bade my holy host good-bye, and followed my escort to the small rock sanctuary which had been made ready for me.

Even while I was to sit in my solitary cell meditating, my guide and teacher was also to shut himself away and spend his time in silent meditation, maintaining some sort of psychic communication with my inner self, even though I might be unaware of it. This seems to be the way in which it is possible for him to determine if I have been fully able to sound the depths and still the mind, so that it might become receptive to that power which is to pass on to me.

The view from the rock sanctuary is one of the most magnificent in the world. A vast perspective spread out before me, valleys of verdure against snow-clad peaks and tempestuous clouds. My chief attendant was deeply moved with fear, we were impelled to pause for a consoling talk before I crossed the threshold of perpetual silence. These Tibetans had vivid pictures in mind of the dangers faced by any one who accepted this vow, and by now they had a strong attachment for me. It was not that they lacked confidence, but they were reluctant to give up the intimate association we had enjoyed, even though it was among their duties to fetch me one meal a day and keep watch, should anything happen.

At the very moment I crossed the threshold a strange feeling came over me. It was as if only then did I realize what it meant from that instant not to see or speak to another living soul, and I wondered whether by now I had a sufficiently rich soul to sustain me. Could it stand the test? Would I emerge victor? I promptly consoled myself with the knowledge that I had been thoroughly prepared—physically, mentally, and consciously; so there need be no fear on my part. This was to be an adventure in the subsconscious, and had I not spent years in grasping the fundamental principles, and months in learning and developing the essential practices, which logically and inevitably led to this, the final test?

I must go back a little. Just before I crossed the threshold of the solitary cell, there had been a brief pause for silent prayer, and the Lamas with me repeated certain chants which were supposed to give me the needful strength to accomplish the purpose of this experience. At the same time the Lamas in the main temple were finishing the repetition of the prayers which they had begun at daybreak. The precise number of repetitions was 108,000. Every soul in the monastery was with me in thought at this moment, and I somehow sensed the strength of their complete confidence. My last thought before entering was to try and retain a memory of myself as I was, as I knew it would not be the same individual to emerge from that cell.

Never shall I forget the joys of ecstasy which swept over me like a stream of ripples as I bade every one good-bye and stepped into the tomb of holiness. The sun had long left the slope of the mountain. There was no light at all in the tiny anteroom in which the attendants were to leave my food each day. The door opening from this into my cave was far too small to enable me to enter upright. Indeed, the cave itself only permitted me to stand erect provided that I kept my legs apart. There was only a very narrow slit in the side of the rock wall, which had been built up to form this cave; the light which it allowed to enter was not enough to read by; not that there was anything to read. The only reason for the opening was to permit an infusion of fresh air, and not too much of that; for, according to their standards, very little is needed, just enough to keep the lungs filled for the sake of health.

The room was bare of everything but a *thangka* of the Lord Buddha and the Wheel of Life, which I could use to help me in my meditations on the cause and purpose of this endless chain of existence. Facing the door was the small Tibetan sitting box, in which I was to sit; for at no time was I to lie down to sleep. It was quite legitimate to doze off whenever the mind grew too weary, but the teachings forbade one to lie down to sleep during such meditations.

9

For once in my life there was no rush. All I had to do was to sit and think, and there was no one around who would feel that I was wasting precious time. The fact is, here it was believed that I was making the best use of my time. No one could interfere with me, no telephone could ring, no fire could distract my attention. As I reflected upon the discipline to which I was subjecting myself I realized how numerous were our distractions, not because they are necessary, but chiefly because we have so little within us that we must see to it that they exist, in order to keep us occupied. All the externals of life were for once wholly banished but the inner life went on, the mind was still active, the body continued to function—so now what to do? And noise itself ceased to exist. There was nothing left to do but to bring the mind under control, to delve into self, and live there deep in the subconscious. I was, of course, able to use physical and breathing practices devised to banish automatically the desires of the body and the uncontrolled wanderings of the mind; at the same time these practices made it possible to use the mind to gain consciousness over my inner self. It becomes a sort of receiving set of the racial subconscious of man, as it flows through the subconscious of the individual.

The discipline which I arranged allowed ample time for reflection. I went back to my earliest conscious memory, and reviewed every detail of my life up to the present moment. By the mere evocation of these pictures, they tended to vanish, enabling the mind to pass on to others, until the mind can rest from satiation, even as it begins to receive the flow from within. The principle is that if the mind is not under control it must be active, and if it fails to receive food for thought from without it will seek it within, the purpose of this experience being to remove all its external stimuli.

It was impossible to jump right into the middle of things. I first had to let the impressions of the day fully settle before considering anything new. I spent whole hours in doing absolutely nothing but watching the mind wander as the thoughts continued to pour into my consciousness. With no timepiece at hand, I had yet to become subconsciously aware of the phases of the day and night, in order to establish my discipline which called for specific practices at the four quarters of the twenty-four hours. I entertained no concern about making haste, since I had all the time in the world in which to banish non-essentials.

Most important of all was that I should become attuned to the rhythm of nature, rather than strive to set up a rhythm of my own. This attitude served to dispel all barriers, and instantly I was overcome with the desire to get into action, which is the law of life. Deliberately, at the beginning, I stayed far within conservative bounds with my practices, adding a little to my discipline as I gained inner strength; for I did not want to suffer defeat by making a false start, which is often the case. Never once did I lose sight of the instruction that there were no short cuts to a goal, that it all must be done step by step.

It is not possible here to go into the nature of these practices, which had taken so much of my time under the supervision of native specialists; improper training can result in injury.

The periods between my practices, which had to be done at sunup and at sundown and at midnight and at noon, were allotted to reflection. I went back to the earliest recollections of childhood and reviewed every detail of that early memory in the steady effort to find a stimulus which would permit me to delve even deeper into the past. Once I had reviewed all the facts, I tried to gain some insight into the meaning behind the facts; this was to enable me to look into the workings of the law of Karma, which was motivating this life.

CHAPTER II

THE QUEST

I

As I sat in that solitary cell my mind travelled back to my beginnings. What was happening to me in Tibet was, after all, only my early childhood's dreams come into their reality. I shall limit my narrative to the essential facts: why and how I came to Tibet, what happened to me *en route* to Lhasa, what happened in the sacred city itself, and what I saw, felt, and experienced during the entire pilgrimage, which was to culminate in the ecstasy of mystical initiation, already recorded.

I was born of parents who had been following the teachings of the East throughout their life. They had personal contact with a great teacher in India, having studied under him. Thus, the foundation was laid at the very beginning. But it was not their design that I should follow the code of the wandering ascetic. They felt that I was born in America and should be trained to the code of American success. Hence, I was provided with the usual background of education and religious instruction, such as are given to what I suppose may be called the typical American boy. It must be admitted, however, that these were in some measure tainted by being interpreted in the light of Eastern philosophical teachings.

In any event, my education was directed to making a lawyer of me. A few years after finishing law school I arrived at the decision that the legal profession was not for me. The readings I had done in my spare time during those early years had turned my mind in another direction. I could not see any purpose in material success, and there was a growing yearning in me for inner development. I was sure that my greatest happiness was to be found in striving toward that goal. By now I had a surfeit of literature to be found in our libraries dealing with Buddhist teachings. No author but gave them the highest praise and contrasted them with those of the Western world to the disadvantage of the latter. Then and there I resolved to dedicate my life to a personal quest, I would test the claims made for these teachings by putting myself through the required training. This meant that I must obtain a full grounding of Western teachings, and follow it with a similar grounding of Eastern teachings as revealed in the best available books on the subject. After that I would try the practices. The first half of the program was simple enough. I merely returned to school, proceeding to obtain a Ph.D. on the subject from Columbia University. The second half, however, demanded that I go to the Orient and seek out a teacher capable of guiding me. In my case our family connections stood me in good stead.

On my arrival in India I sent word to the home of the family *guru* (spiritual teacher), but received a message that he had passed away. This was a profound disappointment, for I had many years looked forward to meeting him again and had hoped to have the privilege of becoming his disciple. I had other contacts, however, but before proceeding with my training under some one else I toured the length and breadth of India, from Bengal to Bombay, and from Kashmir to Ceylon, stopping off to visit all of the important temples and shrines and out-of-the-way holy spots, and interviewing every holy man and Yogi who happened my way; thus I went on incessantly adding to my increasing store of information on their practices.

Eventually the moment had come for taking up the practices, which required the close guidance of a teacher. So I went to the jungle retreat of a disciple of the family *guru*. He was about to have his seventy-first birthday, yet was far more vital than I; he never slept more than two hours a day and appeared to be in the finest physical condition. He had an exceptionally keen and active mind. He gave me tasks, demanding that I dig up everything for myself. Philosophical teachings were given me at times; they were never forthcoming until I asked the questions, and then only if the questions were correctly framed. A new practice came only after I had perfected the previous one. My mentor always stressed the fundamental purpose or essence of life; the illusions or transitory phenomena of this material existence did not interest him.

As soon as I was initiated as a *tantrik** I was instructed to go to a point on the border of Tibet, where a certain personage would give further introductions. I was aflame with excitement. Here seemed to be the opportunity of a lifetime. Yet never did I dream that I would be sitting in a sacred Himalayan cave, reviewing an incredible spiritual adventure.

When I left for the border of Tibet I had only the rudiments of my new education. I knew the practices, of course. But I had also spent no little time in the study of Buddhist psychology and mental attitudes. This involved such details as how long was a thought, how many repetitions were necessary to have a thought made a memory impression, how many of these were needed to store it in the subconscious, and the proper hours of

**Tantrik*—one grounded in doctrine. The *Tantras* were the encyclopedias of the knowledge of their time, for they dealt with nearly every subject, from the doctrine of the origin of the world to the laws which govern societies, and have always been considered as the repository of esoteric beliefs and practices, particularly those of the Spiritual Science, Yoga, the key to which has always been with the initiate and only passed on by word of mouth. Generically speaking, it is the term for the writings of various traditions which express the whole culture of a certain epoch in the ancient history of India.

the day to make them take effect. I was also taught the diet which should be followed during such training, and the precise practices essential to the achievement of desired results.

All Yoga training demands the maintenance of a high heat within the body. I was directed to a hermit who lived among the Himalayan snows in northern Sikkim, bordering on Tibet. He was reputed to possess the knowledge of the art of Tummo of raising the body heat. This permitted these people to live in such high altitudes without fire or clothes.

2

I arrived at Gangtok, the capital of the Sikkim, at the beginning of winter.

Sikkim reminded me of the lovely valleys of Kashmir. When it is better known, the world will come to this beautiful valley 5,000 feet above the sea. The melting snows. seem to leap from the sky, forming a mist that bathes the dense jungles below as it rushes on to the torrents. It is a land of contrasts. A verdant jungle is hemmed in by perpetual snows. Nowhere else on earth can one sit under an orange tree, eating bananas, and feast one's eyes on orchids beneath a peak 29,000 feet high. But that is Sikkim.

I recall having a most enjoyable Christmas dinner at the home of Mr. and Mrs. C. E. Dudley. Mr. Dudley was headmaster of the school. With his friendly assistance, as well as that of Birmiok and Renock Kazi—the secretary and the treasurer, respectively, of the Maharajah of Sikkim, then on his deathbed—I was enabled to make hurried arrangements for the hundred-mile trek to the abode of the mystic hermit. My initiation as a *tantrik* acted as an *open sesame;* he undertook to pass his secret art on to me. It was my plan to settle in a small Tibetan border town on the historical Pekin-to-India trade route and take up the study of Tibetan literature. He gave me a long list of rare manuscripts which contained the teachings I was seeking. So now I was faced with two problems: that of learning the language, and of obtaining the manuscripts. I was ambitious to conquer both.

At Kalimpong I secured the services of Tharchin, a Tibetan who had been raised on the border and was well qualified to act as my mentor; he was to remain with me throughout my entire pilgrimage. I was extremely fortunate in my choice.

It was my ambition to translate the Life of Padma Sambhava, the founder of Lamaism in Tibet, reputed to have been the greatest *tantrik* of India during his time, as well as the Lives of the Saints of the Kargyupa sect, which still adhered to his teachings. At this time I was making many valuable contacts. David Macdonald, who is so very well known and loved by all the Tibetans because of his intimate friendship with the late Dalai and Tashi Lamas, was always most gracious in introducing me to his many friends, who visited him on their pilgrimages to the birthplace of Lord Buddha in India. I could not have been in a more ideal place, as Tharchin, likewise, had a host of friends in Lhasa and a wide acquaintance among the Lamas from the large monasteries.

After a rather strenuous period of discipline, I felt the need of a change, especially when the monsoon came. If the British would give me permission, I decided to go to Gyantsé, 250 miles into Tibet. This would enable me to gain a first-hand experience of their culture and be the very best way for me to develop the colloquial language. I had heard that the British did not particularly like to have visitors go up and down the Trade route, but they sometimes made an exception. There was nothing to be done until Mr. J. B. Gould, the Political Officer at Sikkim, returned from Lhasa. It was a great event in my life when I finally had a talk with him at the home of Mr. and Mrs. A. N. Odling in Kalimpong and he said that he would wire a recommendation to the Government of India. All such permissions must come from this authority, but only with the consent of the Political Officer in charge.

Immediately preparations were started for what I felt was to be the greatest experience of my life. Had it not been for the enthusiastic assistance of Mr. Frank Perry, who had spent several years as an officer at Gyantsé, it would have never been possible for me to get my outfit in time to arrive in Gyantsé on *Dawa Shu nyma chu naga*, or the 15th day of the fourth month according to the Tibetan calendar briefly known as *Sa-kar-dawa*. This is the Tibetan equivalent for our Easter. He promptly got the weavers started on my Tibetan blanket, and the native carpenters planing down the boards from the logs brought direct from the jungle in order to make my transport boxes. Thus, by working day and night, the workers had everything ready for me within a few days.

3

The day of days had arrived. The mules were there at eight in order to start with my pack outfit for Gangtok, where I was to join them for the long trail over the hill, which happens to be a small knoll of snow and ice resting among storm clouds about 15,000 feet above sea-level. The *tinwalla* (tin-smith) had arrived at six in order to finish labelling a couple of extra boxes that had to be secured at the last moment to take the miscellaneous odds and ends that seemed to be continually cropping up. By now I had decided to take a large portion of my library, so that I might set up my study in any place in which I happened to be lingering for an extra day or so. I had little inclination to waste any time during my trek through Tibet; along with my personal experience, I was writing my Columbia Ph.D. dissertation on *tantrik* Yoga. After seeing the mules were on their way, I took off in a small Austin for Gangtok.

Several hours were wasted in the Tista valley as we tried to win a losing race with a leaking tire. Every few miles we had to stop and pump it up again, until finally we were forced to stop and repair it in typical Indian fashion, which is identical with no attempt at repair. Toward the end of the trip the driver certainly tried to make up for lost time, almost skipping a few of the intricate curves by which the road followed the Tista.

It was late in the afternoon, after a hot, dry, and dusty ride, that I arrived at the Residency in Gangtok. Here the spring was just bursting into bloom, throwing splashes of gorgeous color over the entire hillside.

In India I had spent considerable time in the jungles with my *guru,* and for some months before I left for Tibet I had been closely following the instructions of the hermit among the Himalayan snows. During this period I had to be content with a single small meal a day and only a few hours' sleep. At the same time I was forced to maintain a vigorous mental discipline, directed for the most part to the study of the Tibetan tongue. In consequence, I had lost something like thirty-five pounds, which meant that I was far from being a Bernarr Macfadden star, and, really, it would have been comforting to be one, as I thought of negotiating that little knoll behind Gangtok rising some 15,000 feet and leading into Tibet. Yet I knew that the body was strong enough to endure anything that should come, provided I could adjust the stomach to accepting sufficient food, for it had shrunk considerably and was averse to rough foods; my diet, indeed, had been reduced to liquids. I had only a little over a week for reconditioning; this meant I had to be rather careful for a while, and this was very difficult when being entertained so royally at the Residency.

On the day the transport was due to arrive I strolled down to the bungalow shortly after tea to see that everything was in order for our departure on the following morning. The animals were feeding, the men were busy around the kitchen. But there was no sign of Tharchin, who was supposed to have driven up from Kalimpong. I learned by telegraph that the Governor of Bengal, John Anderson, had come to Kalimpong for the day. This meant that all roads were cleared until he had passed, which made it impossible for Tharchin to leave before evening. There was a typical Sikkim downpour, which meant heavy snow on the pass. Unless one has experienced jungle rains of the monsoon it is almost impossible to imagine the amount of water which can come down from a clear sky within a couple of hours.

Dinner that night was a very festive occasion and as chic as if it had been served at the Ritz. It made me acutely aware that it was my parting meal with Western civilization. Once I entered Tibet there would be a radical change in my diet. Mr. Gould and a friend and I all dressed in evening clothes. I must admit it was a treat to eat again from a table covered with fine linen and set with silver that glistened in the candlelight. It was a meal of delicious food and many jests. In the drawing room over our coffee we started a learned discussion on the value of the classics. About all I could do was to indicate how much Greek and Latin I had forgotten; however, it eventually led the conversation around to the beginnings of Buddhism and to the Eastern philosophy in general. Apparently my host was only familiar with the popular conception of the *tantras* which meant that he, like many others, considered them to be the undermining influence in all Buddhism. It had been this attitude which I constantly encountered in literature that had fired my imagination to the point where I decided to make a personal investigation of their teachings and practices and see for myself if they were degenerate.

We finally broke up the discussion about eleven and I retired to my room to complete my packing. I had left orders for the men to be there at five sharp. At four-thirty I hopped out of bed with an upset stomach. I had ordered an early breakfast and didn't want to disappoint them by not eating, so I stuffed it in, but not for long. There was no alternative but to go on a complete fast which is hardly the thing when one takes off to cross the Himalayan ridges.

About nine o'clock we were ready to set out for Changu, twenty-three miles up the hill. Another party had already made reservations for the bungalow at Karponang, which is situated about half-way; consequently we had to do a double stage. These bungalows were first established when the Younghusband Expedition of 1904 forged its way into Tibet with a large army under the command of General Sir Ronald Macdonald. They have been constantly improved, and today the British maintain an excellent chain of rock-constructed bungalows.

4

As soon as the transport of fifteen mules laden with packs had left, Tharchin and I rode to the Residency to bid farewell, though it was already nine o'clock and we were behind the schedule. Henceforth, Tharchin was to be my almost inseparable companion. He was a smallish man, with a figure inclined to plumpness. He had a little fat face with a tiny moustache, and he was dressed in plus-fours and a rather loud English tweed coat. He usually held his cigarette within the palm of a closed fist, and it scarcely touched his lips. What is more important is that, a Tibetan who had been raised on the border, he had a full knowledge of the literature of his country and he had been in Lhasa many times, and had devoted many years to study. He was exceptionally competent.

For the first several miles we wound our way round the mountain-side, rising up from the jungles of Sikkim and re-

Lake among the clouds

vealing a magnificent view of the pass that we were to cross the following day. We were about 8000 feet above sea-level, and there it was looming about another 7000 feet above us, seeming treacherously near. In the morning it seemed as if we should reach the top within a few hours, but by night we began to wonder if we had moved at all. The weather was threatening, a downpour seemed imminent. At first I thought it might be wise to spare the horses, and I contemplated walking in the steeper places of this craggy stairway. But as I attained a couple of thousand feet closer to heaven I gave up the idea, because my legs began to vibrate like bow strings at every step forward.

We reached Karponang about one-thirty. I immediately collapsed, but left imperative orders to be awakened within an hour. At the moment I felt that I should die right then and there, but regained consciousness when called. In the midst of a heavy hail and rain storm, wrapped in an Abercrombie & Fitch watch-pocket raincoat, I took off for Changu, another twelve miles up the stairway of patience moulded by nature. We were at this time at the bottom of the snow line, an indication that with each ascending mile it would be colder and colder; moreover, we were heading into the tempest above us. Immense clouds were already speeding past us, and at an elevation of 13,000 feet they formed a white billowy stormy lake. As the transport had already left before we arrived, there was no alternative but to push on.

My only salvation was to go to sleep on the pony and pray that I did not lose my balance in going over one of those man-made ledges built on the sheer face of a cliff overhanging space. I must confess that it was something of a joy when I would open my eyes and see ridges and canyons generously ablaze with towering rhododenron trees, from fifty to seventy feet high, blooming amidst the snow. Elsewhere, lost among the foliage, tiny shoots of flowers might be seen forcing their way through the snow, only the pink and red blooms being visible above the submerged stems. The trail wound its way for miles along such ridges, over streams and beneath roaring waterfalls, whose spray was worse than the rain storm itself. The rain poured steadily for three hours; a fish would have been in its element here. It was, indeed, something more than rain alone; for we were actually in the heart of vast rain clouds, which sooner or later would break and pour their copious contents on the country below. There was a likelihood of snow on the morrow, when we were to cross the Nathu Pass at an elevation of a little over a thousand feet above us.

Tharchin and I stumbled along over the boulders which lie scattered over the trail, to protect it from being washed away. Now and then we would come upon a rude boulevard, much like the Roman roads, except that it is less than half the width. It did ease our travelling no little, as it was usually possible here to judge my position when the pony took the next step; this meant much to me who was having, more or less, to keep my eyes closed because of the corrupted condition of my innards. My constant thought was, how would I ever live to make the next step; but it somehow happened, with me none the worse for it. As we were mounting over the highest ridge of the day, all I could do to greet the most beautiful lake among the clouds that I had ever seen was vomiting all that I had eaten about twenty-four hours previously. It was something of a compensation that at this point we could see our destination at the other end of the heart-shaped lake, gleaming like a gun-metalled crystal, and reflecting tenfold the beauty of the cloud-clad mountain that hemmed us in. It was fabulous grandeur.

At last, the bungalow. More quickly than my feet hit the ground my head hit the bed which had been prepared with solicitude by the boys who had gone ahead with the transport, and there I remained until six the next morning, when I awoke, feeling perfect but for a slight weakness due to the thirty-six-hour fast which I had just completed. The comfortable circumstances of my slumber were in no small measure due to Tharchin and the two "boys" who, apart from looking after my pack mules, acted as my servants. They were strong, good-natured fellows, patient and loyal as they make them. The older of the pair, Norphel, was thirty-two years old and was attired in native clothes and earrings. The younger, Lhare, was about twenty-three; he had had wider experience, and was dressed as a European. Their solicitude was, indeed, touching. Yet notwithstanding a *Puk-sha* (a fur-lined Tibetan robe), and a doubled *Cha-tuk* (a heavy Tibetan woven blanket), I felt as cold as though it was ten below zero. In the end the chills left me, and I relaxed for the night, to meet the new day with a better spirit.

A heavy snow had fallen in the night; so I clad myself warm. I could not risk a chill in my weakened condition. I put on "Gilgit-boots" (heavy knee boots of thick felt), and an extra heavy Tibetan *Pak-sha,* which goes round one a couple of times; its front pocket is capable of holding an unlimited quantity of useful things. The weather, however, soon moderated, and it was now a question of how to keep cool. All the morning, while we were packing, the clouds were racing up the gorge as if they were trying to reach some Fair in Heaven.

It is only ten miles to Chumbi Tang, the next bungalow, a couple of miles on the other side of the Nathu Pass, but under prevailing weather conditions it meant an all-day trip. Often the traders make less than a mile an hour in negotiating this pass. We did a trifle better, for we were on the trail only nine hours, though we must have been some fifty pounds heavier, soaked as we were to the skin as we waded through the mud and the slush of melting snow under a downpour of rain and sleet. Much time, too, was lost in picking up fallen mules and horses. There was no crust on the snow, and every time that a foot slipped off the narrow trail there was no stopping one from sinking until belly-deep.

My companions gave expression to glee upon reaching the summit, for it meant they were now in their native land, Tibet. They added some stones to the accumulating stone-mound, in accordance with the traveller's custom—a better custom, it seems to me, than our own, that of carving our initials—and gave vent to what would be analogous to our three cheers. On this stone pile countless "prayer-flags" are to be seen, an offering to the spirit of the mountain. If a Tibetan wants to offer a certain prayer, he may take several of these tiny flags and inscribe on them the desired prayer; these he erects then on the mound in the pass, and every time they wave in the wind his prayer is automatically repeated for him, conferring favor upon him with the Gods. The summit, by the way, is not a plateau, but a real summit, limited in space, and only permitting to walk along the narrow ridge round the stone pile.

From this point the journey was considerably simplified, for the trail wound its way around the side of the mountain almost on a level hundreds of feet above the rushing streams, of which we could catch passing glimpses through the moss-clad firs and rhododenrons. There was one alarming moment when I was negotiating one of the plank bridges that crossed the many little streams. These bridges are made of only large logs flattened on one side and thrown across the gap. About half a dozen logs are used, and where the crevices between the logs happen to be too large they are filled in with loose rocks, which roll about in perfect unison with the logs. At one point my pony lost the rhythm, swaying now to the right now to the left, leaving me to figure out which would be his choice, so that I might fall in the direction which left me more leeway for safety. I did not relish the idea of falling twenty feet or so into a torrent of molten ice.

As it was, I did not feel any too well. Luckily for me, the syce happened to be near, and he grasped at the horse's head just in time to enable him to regain his footing and save me a spill. It was a very uncomfortable moment.

Presently, we settled for the night at Chumbi Tang. The boys brought me a nice bowl of Van Camp's tomato soup, diluted with an equal quantity of yak's milk, to which I was slowly becoming accustomed.

5

The next morning I was up at three o'clock. I found the boys had already fed the animals and packed. We were soon on our way to the Kargyupa Monastery, which is at the end of the Chumbi valley. This is the abode of the Red sects of the Tibetans who follow the living teachings of the *tantras*. I was especially eager to make this step, as the head Lama was reputed to be well schooled in these teachings and possessed of great power.

The sun was not yet up, so we had a lantern to guide us. The trail was a very steep and narrow ridge, with chiselled pockets in the rock made by the animals' hooves. Parts of it were so treacherous as to force one to dismount and walk. The monastery perched on a rocky promontory became visible. My excitement increased. Yet I was becoming exhausted, and by the time we reached the monastery I hadn't a desire for anything but water. My tongue felt thick, my mouth seemed to be filled with cotton.

Tharchin having sent on word of our visit ahead, we were met by a friendly party of monks in reddish-brown robes and with shaven heads. One of them promptly began to show us around. The entrance to the courtyard was lined with prayer-wheels. Around the inside ran a porch, the walls of which were decorated with the important deities in the customary colorful manner. We were directly led into the monastery proper. The nave was nothing but a huge barren barn with a few *thangkas* hung about the walls. At the other end the boys opened a door into another room, situated where the altar should have been. Within were their deities.

Still I had had no water, and I was rapidly becoming sick.

They had already heard of my work and of my interest in their teachings, so there was nothing I could do but offer a scarf to the Lord Buddha, as is the custom of the country when visiting holy shrines. It was really the last thing I wanted to do at the moment. I knew I should be feeling no better afterwards, and probably much worse. But when in Tibet one must do as the Tibetans do. I tried to collect myself and made the offering by trying to throw the scarf into the hands of the enormous image.

Next came a tour of inspection. I tried to hurry it, as I didn't know if I could last out. When it was over, I rushed for a door, but was called back to see yet another Buddha. By then I could scarcely stand, but it was worth the effort. They had a Buddha about forty feet high with his disciples, all hand-carved and beautifully painted. I again rushed to the door—only to find it led to one of the hidden antechambers in the upper stories of the monastery, where the head Lama awaited us. After winding our way up the shaky staircase and through narrow hallways we reached an extraordinary little shrine with Guru Rimpoche as the chief deity. He is also known by the sanskrit name of Padma Sambhava and is believed to be the founder of Lamaism in Tibet, as well as the greatest *tantrik* in India in his time. His life and teaching were naturally of the greatest importance to me. But I was forced to make straight for a chair, which had been drawn up to the table for tea. Monks were coming in from all directions, and I became confused and ill. The head Lama came in adorned with a crackling robe of gold. His face glowed from ear to ear with a toothless smile. Somehow or other I sum-

moned enough strength to go through with the ceremony of exchanging sacred scarves, which is a token of friendship and goodwill, a sort of Tibetan calling-card.

Once this was over, I could hold out no longer. I begged for a place to rest. Immediately there was a helter-skelter, a scurrying of willing feet, and, as if by magic, beautiful embroidered cushions appeared, with a leopard skin to cover them. But I had held out as long as I could. I now implored them to take me rapidly to some other place, lest I defile this inner sanctuary of the esoteric Tibetan faith. The boys started to run, and so did I. Unexpectedly I found a pan being held under my chin. It was just what was needed. After that I returned to the cushions and slept three hours, awaking much refreshed.

Tharchin and the head Lama were still in the room talking. I propped up my head by rolling the blanket into a pillow and joined in a most interesting and illuminating discussion which occupied the rest of the day. We talked of Tibetan literature, and when I asked where I could find teachers to prepare me for initiation and similar questions to which I desired answers on guidance, it was always the same response:

"Whenever you are ready for it, the answer will always come to you."

From the head Lama I got a much clearer impression of the *tantrik* works written by Padma Sambhava and of the teachings which came down from Tilopa, through Naropa, Marpa, Mila and Tarpa. In the biography of Guru Rimpoche, which I had just finished translating, I had learned of a set of eighteen volumes which were supposed to contain his complete works. One of the purposes of my journey into Tibet was to obtain this set of books. We discussed among other things the scope of the *tantras* that are found in the Kangyur and Tengyur in contrast with the *tantras* that make up the scriptures of this sect.

Before taking our departure, our friend, who wore a coil of

hair some twenty feet long on his head as a symbol of his rank and power, took us for another short tour of inspection. Above all I enjoyed our visit to the inner shrines which exhibited deities in various sexual embraces, portraying the several aspects of the *tantrik* teachings in the universal phases rather than the fleeting and transitory which we are able to embrace in this bodily consciousness. When we brought our visit to a close, plans were made for a prolonged stay on my return.

6

When I reached Yatung I was ready to call a halt and stay over a day to let nature catch up with our pace. This ended my upset state, and afterwards I never had even as much as a headache. Indeed, I never felt better in my entire life from that day until I reached New York City.

While I lay around in the bungalow resting, Tharchin made calls on his many Tibetan friends in the village. They no sooner heard that he had arrived than a steady human stream was coming and going, which meant that an endless quantity of tea was consumed. In Tibet all time is Tea Time. It matters little what time of day or night you visit a Tibetan, there will be tea served immediately upon your arrival. One of Tharchin's friends came to see me, and we had a long talk about the products and activities of the Chumbi valley, which captivated me. This valley is nearly 10,000 feet above sea level and, with its profusion of pines, dark firs, apple, peach and apricot orchards in bloom, it is as beautiful as any of the famous spots in Switzerland.

Yak seems to be the favorite meat; it is eaten raw in a dried form. Mutton is subjected to the same treatment. The Tibetan has little inclination toward chicken, for so many have to be killed and it is his religious belief that it is wrong to kill. A little killing has to be done to survive. Hence, it is thought better to choose the life of an animal whose flesh will feed many persons. Potatoes, as well as other vegetables, grow in great abundance. Wild mountain sheep are still plentiful. Fine agricultural country, its air is pure and bracing; it is likely that some day it will be opened up and exploited as a health resort. It really reminded me of those beautiful hidden valleys of our great Rocky Mountains, where everything grows in abundance and wild life is everywhere. Today, there is no entrance except over the Nathu Pass (14,394 feet), but it is not at all impossible to construct as scenic a boulevard as there is in the world following the Amo River out into India. For sport, there is fishing in great quantities at the head of the valley near what is known as the Lingmo Plain.

We had to obtain fresh animals at Yatung, so an early start was doubtful; the natives here never show up within two hours of the time they are told to be ready. The delay, however, enabled me to take a couple of snaps of the tiny village on the banks of the foaming Amo, "milk river." There seems to be a practice here to hold down the roofs with rocks, to protect them against the heavy wind storms that visit the country. Another safety measure is to build a roof several feet above the house itself, thereby allowing ample space for the wind to have its way without doing damage to the house or the roof.

The first six or seven miles in the narrow valley followed the rapids up to the Lingmo Plain, a gentle grass-covered plateau hemmed in by crumbling barriers of rock. Throughout the morning we passed long pack-trains of wool coming from Central Tibet. This slowed down our progress, as difficulties often arose in efforts to pass one another on the narrow trails, when the animals on either side could not decide whether they should keep to the middle path or scramble up the steep mountainside.

From the next village we could see the Tung Kara (White

Concha) monastery perched on the top of the distant ridge; several thousand feet above it, along the ridge of the other side of the valley, could be seen another *gompa* (monastery), which had been used as a meditation retreat for the Geshe Rimpoche, who was in charge of the Tung Kara Gompa. Our trail was now beginning to rise from the valley and wind its way up the mountainside, gaining elevation rapidly from the Lingmo Plain, which was two or three miles away; for we were now at the upper end of the Chumbi valley, which was one vast garden of rhododendrons. Just before reaching the plain we climbed up alongside of the waterfall, into the valley bordered on each side with high swaying pines over the rhododendrons.

The contrast betwen the ruggedness of the narrow valley and the pastoral peace of the plain was very impressive. As far as we could see there was this flat grass-covered tableland surrounded by almost perpendicular walls of fallen rock for thousands of feet, far into the snow-line among the clouds. How could such a paradise have come about? I was told that at the end of summer the grass is several feet high and reminiscent of a quiet lake when the wind blows. The entire area was dotted over with small nomad tents and yaks grazing. Our trail wound its way along the edge to the opposite end. At this point, however, we left our transport and clambered up the mountainside to visit the monastery which had been our guiding-star for the past several hours.

It was almost a perpendicular ascent, but the grandeur was well worth the effort. The head Lama had died last winter; so there was a little difficulty at first. Once our purpose was ascertained, we were given entry to all the shrines. On our arrival in the courtyard we were immediately escorted among growling unchained mastiffs to a place before the entrance to the temple, where we seated ourselves to enjoy the inevitable tea. Abundant victuals came with the tea, and they looked appetizing to my

My transport winding its way up the Lhasa Valley

half-starved eyes. They consisted of Tibetan bread piled up a foot and a half high, enough for two persons. This bread is a thin flat pastry-like substance rolled up on a side to form a trough to be filled with knick-knacks of cookies and dried fruit. My eyes strayed from the repast before me to the greasiest looking cancerous specimen of syphilitic humanity that I have ever seen. I was hungry and thirsty, so why not make the best of it? I reckoned, however, without my host, for after several efforts to break off a piece of bread I was forced to desist—might as well try to break concrete. At my other elbow was another chap with his teapot urging me to drink. I never thought at the time that I should live to tell the story, but it is such minor trifles, I suppose, that toughen up the system.

After some nourishment I was rescued by a monk, who conducted us into the temple, the floor of which was so highly polished that I hesitated to step on it lest I soil it. How these human animals can preserve such beauty as met my eyes is sometimes beyond me, for the interior was by far the finest æsthetic expression of Tibetan Buddhism that I had yet seen. The entire grandeur of this *gompa* is attributed to the effort of the late Geshe Rimpoche, for whose body they were at this time erecting a *chorten* (shrine) on the monastery grounds. This monastic gem, hidden away on the top of a Himalayan rockpile, is one of the sanctuaries of the Gelupa sect (yellow hats), which is the ruling sect of the country today. The chief deity here is the Coming Buddha, a carved figure of recent date, whose crown is adorned with studded rubies and turquoises. Its freshness is perhaps one of the reasons of its impressiveness; for after hundreds of butter lamps have been burning for years, its color will no longer be visible through that veil of grease which time will slowly cast over it. The artist who was doing the wall decorations followed us about, filled up with pride over our fervent reactions. In the ante-chamber were the usual guardians of the four directions, and the Wheel of Life, which was being completed. On one of the wings was a large Wheel of Poetry, which is so written as to say the same things no matter which way it is read. It was done in the royal Buddhist colors, which are pure in contrast to the delicate shades and nuances used by peoples in other parts of the world.

From the main temple we went to the upper shrine, according to the custom. This was one of the shrines of the Thousand Buddhas, revealing costly splendor in the form of exquisite decorations by expert artists, past masters in the formulas of religious murals. There is a set for every design which a master craftsman comes to learn, and from which he never deviates. All the accomplished Tibetan artist needs to know are the formulæ and the technique, which comes from years of practice. What we call a creative artist is practically non-existent, though they have some highly trained individuals who have specialized in the execution of their formal art.

Next we were permitted to visit the private shrine of the late Geshe Rimpoche. It was only a small shrine with various private deities from which he obtained his spiritual strength.

It was our good fortune to arrive at the monastery when their oracle was about to go into one of his trances. We witnessed the entire performance from the time he entered the separate shrine, where the spirit is supposed to dwell, amid the chants and clashing of cymbals which are said to prepare him for his trance. The spirit in him then started talking at a frantic speed and writers tried to take down every word as he floated about the room. When he collapsed from exhaustion several of the attendants caught him in their arms, lowering him to the throne without bodily injury.

Before leaving we made the usual devotional tour of the monastery. From the cliff we could see the devotees carrying heavy loads of rocks from the quarry below to the *chorten,* their burdens lightened by their great faith. After a cheerful salaam to the workers we returned to the Lingmo Plain and continued toward Gautsa.

That night we were lulled to sleep to the rhythm of torrents of rain. The morning, however, was crystal-clear, with a fresh layer of snow on all the ridges of the side-walls of barren rock which towered on every side of our bungalow. The trail that morning was treacherous. For the first eight miles it was strewn with boulders, and the mules had to slip between them to get their footing. Once we reached the Tibetan Plain at 14,000 feet, everywhere were rolling hills covered with a brownish gray carpet hemmed in by distant snow-covered peaks; the highest, Chumolhari ("The Mountain of the Goddess Lady"), stood out like a star sapphire on the hand of a Hindu Goddess. The sky was much like our Western ones, with everything crystal-clear. The hillsides were dotted, here and there, with roving herds of yaks. These plains remain ever fresh, and all along the way we could see typhoons in the distance, being carried away into the heavens, where they were lost among the gathering dark clouds. The dust, the soil, the clarity of the atmosphere, the mellow brown hills, the very colors of the landscape, were like our West with its power to awaken human awe.

7

As soon as we had settled for the day at the Phari bungalow, Tharchin made arrangements for a couple of calls that I had to make in order to pay my respects to the two officials here, the Tibetan Trade Agent and the *Jongpen* (Commander of the Fort). I was eager to stroll through the village, which is reputed to be the filthiest place on earth. I had seen places, both in Mexico and China, which I thought must hold the record, but had it not been for the high, dry, cold air, Phari would have held first place. The people were by far the dirtiest, greasiest specimens that I have ever seen. They were all draped in rags, worn threadbare with dirt and grease accumulated by their grandparents.

The village itself is nothing but a huge *Jong* (Fort), which looks like some mediæval castle of Europe. It is on high ground and with its turrets must rise some 150 feet from the plain. The stone walls are enormously thick and slant slightly inwards. There are few windows, but many slit-like openings. The whole impression is one of impregnability. The *Jong* is surrounded by narrow lanes of plastered dung, along which the villager lives in contentment. It is more or less a last stronghold between the Chumbi valley and the Tibetan Plain, and as such is a centre for the crossroads of all the trails leading to India. It was from India, by the pass from Bhutan, that nearly two centuries ago, Bogle, Turner and Manning came to Phari.

The only way to convey the impressiveness of Chumolhari is by comparison with our West. Imagine, then, Mt. Rainier rising 24,000 feet out of Arizona's desert, and you get the feeling one has sitting on Chumolhari's lap at Phari, which seems about five miles from the base, from which it shoots up like a rocket. Before retiring I went out to have a peek at the sky. I was overcome with its brilliance, one could count the stars, and their light cast a luminosity upon the earth.

It is little wonder that the Tibetan never leaves his country, but that he aches inwardly for his return, and is not happy until he does. There is a spiritual stimulus in these rarefied atmospheres that awakens the dormant self. The mind of the nomad is far too undeveloped to rationalize the processes which go on within, in that part of us we call the soul, but he traverses his three score and ten with that inner awareness that he is right with his God. It is only when man is robbed of his consciousness by the intricacies of materialistic society that he tries to compensate for the deficiency by the embankment of material complexi-

ties, rarely realizing what it is that is driving him, and what he should be seeking.

We finally broke the day's march at a four-walled dung enclosure. It was a midway station provided by the Government. We went in to get some water so that we might have a cup of "George Washington coffee" and thereby relieve the strain of the piercing wind that had just worked its way to the marrow. For the first five minutes it was impossible to see anything, because everything was black with the soot of yak dung, this being the only fuel obtainable for the first hundred miles north of Phari. Soon the eyes accommodated themselves to the gloom. What a place we had chosen for *tiffin* (lunch)! It was a room whose ceiling consisted of carcasses of dried animals, the only food they had. While we occupied this shelter a heavy snowstorm had worked its way over us. With a ten-mile trek ahead of us, we took our departure in a blinding gale of snow. We could not see a single peak in any direction, though the Chumolhari range was only a few miles to our right. It was an exhilarating experience, if a chilling one, to make our way through the storm. We covered the ten miles in less than two hours and got under cover expeditiously.

By the late afternoon the storm had cleared. The brightness in the room drew me to the window. I could see the dazzling sun-lit peaks. So out we went, equipped with every possible photographic gadget, in order to do justice to Tibet's glacial grandeur. At five the next morning there wasn't a cloud in sight, and all was brilliant and crisp, indeed a little too crisp, for the small lake beside which we rested for the night had completely frozen over.

The donkeys which were carrying the transport had left before midnight. Tharchin and I now followed. Our transport was becoming more difficult each day. One difficulty was in obtaining fresh relays of animals, even though we always sent on word ahead stating our requirements. The head man of the village is supposed to appoint the family which is next entitled to supply the beasts, so that every one might have an opportunity to earn a little. Usually no one family had enough animals, so that we often had to resort to a medley of donkeys, mules, old horses and yaks.

Around seven our party of five set off at a fast pace, and we did not pause until we reached a large camping ground alongside a small spring. It was all too much to resist, for the spot was hemmed in by the glacial peaks of the Chumolhari range which separated Tibet from Bhutan.

Before long the horizon became a solid bank of rising thunder-clouds, which made me feel very much at home in Arizona. The morning was spent in crossing the Lingmo tang (the Plain of the Weeping Elephant). With nothing but a flat tableland, covered with pebbles of sandstone from the barren cliffs to our left and ahead of us, and the turbulent heavens above, it is little wonder that my thought went on constantly reverting to my many experiences in crossing Arizona deserts.

The quiet Dochen Lake, along which we were to ride all afternoon, was just coming into view; it seemed more like a mirage than real water on top of the world. We pulled up at Dochen for *tiffin*, but with such a superb emotional stimulus I could scarcely think of eating. I found it difficult to tear myself away from the view, but Tharchin had a friend in the neighborhood whom he had not seen for several years; there was no alternative but to accept his invitation.

Upon our arrival, the yaks were on the point of starting for Kala, so I made haste to take pictures. The yak being one of the few domestic beasts of burden we do not raise in America, I felt it well worth making a record, and especially against such a background as offered itself at this moment, an imperial crown of crystals bathed in heavy clouds. It was fortunate that I took the pictures when I did, for when the time came to set off again, the sky was black with approaching storm, just as it was yesterday. We resumed our journey amidst a fall of snow, but this time there was less wind. Almost immediately we were on the edge of the lake, which we followed for the next couple of hours. Every minute provided its own inspiration. Hundreds of large birds rested on the lake's shore. Shortly we overtook the transport, for the yaks appeared to do more grazing than travelling.

8

Lhare, one of our boys, hoped to see his mother on the following day at Kangmar. It would be their first meeting in several years and I felt the trip meant as much to him as it did to me. Just as we were leaving Dochen, the *chowkidar* (caretaker of the bungalow), called Tharchin back and told him a message just came in saying Lhare's mother had died. Tharchin delayed telling him until evening rather than to let him ride all the afternoon on a jolting pony trying to nurse his grief.

Finally we left the ice-bordered lake and turned off into a narrow valley, dotted with small patches under cultivation. The wind was blowing violently from the opposite direction, laden, it seemed, with all the dust of Tibet. The next six or seven miles were intensely uncomfortable. Daylight was almost extinguished by the rising bank of dust which filled the valley for miles ahead. It was a great relief to reach Kala.

After about two hours the yaks arrived, but one horse was still missing. He had not reached Dochen by the time we left there, so it was hard to tell when he would reach Kala—and he was bringing all the bedding!

Tharchin was now on the sick list, so I had to carry on as best I could. I was a bit overcome when I realized that I had been talking for several hours and had no difficulty in understanding or making myself understood. We'd all kept pretty healthy except a couple of the boys who started to break out with fever when crossing the Nathu-La. This seems to be frequently the case when one has had malaria.

Pacing all day on these small Bhotiya ponies over the stony paths is a memorable experience. They have the same gait as a cow pony and they are able to keep it up steadily for an entire day. If the transport problem could be handled, one could cover this country rapidly. There are only 250 miles or so in the whole distance. But yaks will not run and donkeys cannot. Consequently, there's nothing to do but be satisfied with about thirty miles a day.

By early the next morning the sky was clear and the fresh snow from the night before was gleaming in the rising sun. It was very still. The toilers of the soil left for their distant fields with their yak teams, going to break the ground for their spring planting. Barley and wheat are the chief staples planted in these parts. There are, also, a few small fields of rice, peas, and mustard.

As soon as the transport was off, we made our way over the plains toward the canyon which leads to the famous Red Idol Gorge, reputed to be the hangout for robbers who attack lonely travellers. At one point along the way the distant hillside was dotted with large herds of *kyangs* (wild asses). These are plentiful in Tibet.

The transport which was to carry our provisions to the next station was waiting. The women were spinning away their time making woolen yarn. Each one of these black, greasy Tsang women had one arm run through the raw wool which she was patiently spinning out into yarn on a spindle which she kept constantly revolving in the other hand. Men, too, were spinning. Indeed, it is not an uncommon sight to see a trader coming along with his train of donkeys, with a bag over his shoulder, slowly spinning, as he walks the rocky trails.

By now Lhare had been told of his mother's death. He accepted the news in the complete silence of deep sorrow. Tharchin told him he need not wait, so he took the next pony and rode on ahead.

Our ride that afternoon was through a narrow barren valley banked on both sides with reefs of garnet, shelves of shale and crumbling mounds of conglomerate. The entire floor of the canyon had been covered centuries ago by a hail storm of rocks which had not worn away. All along the trail were the disintegrating ruins of the monuments of the previous cults. With the rise of every new religious administration the old was destroyed, so that when the Gelupa sect came into power its leaders did everything to banish all evidence of its predecessor, the Nyingmapas (old sect or Red Caps). In consequence, today we have nothing but stone ruins of the habitations of the first Tibetan teachers. The plain brown hills are still under the protection of the few remaining *chortens*, which had been erected to subdue the evil spirits which dwelled within. This was their method of preventing landslides and soil erosions. From the evidence available it is difficult to determine as to which have been the more effective—the Tibetans or the leaders of the New Deal.

At the upper end of the valley, beneath a wasting red sandstone cliff, rests the small village of Kangmar, which held the sadness of our friend Lhare, but for all that he was at the bungalow to greet us with a cup of warm tea. How they contain their feelings of grief and think of your comfort is something to marvel at. It is a trait to be admired among any group of people.

Lhare did not see his mother's face. According to the Tibetan custom at death, one is tied up in a ball with the head between the knees as it is at birth. When one dies a Lama is called to take care of the spirit. A high Lama is called in who plucks a hair on the top of the head and thereby releases the spirit. It is considered bad to let the spirit escape through any other opening of the body. This ceremony is known as *Phowa* in Tibetan. When these customary ceremonies have been performed, the body is taken at daybreak to the butchering grounds of the carriers of the dead where it is cut into strips and fed to the vultures.

This is followed by the sale of all the ornaments and other belongings of the dead, and the performance of a ceremony in accordance with the amount of their wealth. All this is not very different from the same customs in other countries.

After the *Phowa* the spirit is in the *Bardo* (the place it goes to after death), where it remains forty-nine days. At the end of this time it is freed from this world. Sometime during these forty-nine days the bereaved family or individual goes to a monastery, makes a gift in return for which the monks offer a prayer. Often a *maund* (eighty pounds) of butter is also bought and a thousand lights offered. At the end of the period, the Lama who first officiated will perform another short ceremony to release the spirit. Until the end of the first year the family remains in mourning.

This period is broken by a feast of sorrow, given for all the villagers, after which the death is forgotten and ordinary life is resumed. In many instances the villagers contribute a small amount as an offering to the dead and to assist in providing for the feast of sorrow.

This *Phowa* is said to have commenced with Marpa who went to India and gained power so that he could transfer his spirit into the body of another, even while living. He handed this power on to his son, who misused it and thereby lost it. Consequently this power no longer exists, and the ceremony is but a relic.

After a long discussion it was decided we should go on to Gyantsé in the morning. On what day they would dispose of Lhare's mother's body was not decided and we wanted to reach Gyantsé in time for the various ceremonies of the period, which is called *Sa-kar-dawa*, or the fifteenth day of the fourth month of the Tibetan calendar. This is a very special ceremony, for it is then that the Lord Buddha is supposed to have ascended. Lhare would remain behind in Kangmar and join us later. Since he was the oldest brother he was compelled by custom to see that everything was properly attended to.

9

The next day was spent going through a narrow barren canyon of sliding rocks. To make this trip is about the same as it would be to start from Tucson or Phœnix, Arizona, and walk across those barren deserts and climb the dense mountain barriers that separate the deserts from California, the vacation land of America. We passed through the kaleidoscope of transitional beauty, given a kind of unity by the tinkling bells of the little donkeys that carry most of the wool out of Tibet. All through the early morning the narrow corridor between the canyon walls was vibrating with the echoes of the sound of the passing ass on the rocky trail. The tinkling of the bells is to warn the pack trains coming from the opposite direction around the narrow ledges of the cliffs.

The Tibetan takes great pride in his beasts, and the leader is usually dolled up in a necklace of large bells and yak tails. These are commonly dyed red, and add considerable color to the animal. Often he has a piece of brocade or embroidery flap down over his forehead. The animals are very picturesque, forming a contrast to the dilapidated human animal strolling along behind—the trader.

It is not easy to describe the scenery, in a sense non-existent, unless one considers the rocks! Yet I, having been raised on the side of an Arizona rockpile, have an overwhelming urge to go into perhaps unaccountable raptures at the sight of such barrenness. It is not so much what is outside that counts, but it is what that little does to one on the inside, and a few tumbling rocks can just about make the old heart jump to one's throat. Our trail was a crooked one, winding its way along the Nyang River through the valley of desolation, which was marked by infrequent tiny patches of cultivated land upon the narrow banks of the shallow stream, where the Tibetan is trying to nurse along a modest crop of wheat. I am told that this region is colorful in the fall, for then the grass is high and changes the entire aspect of the country. I rather thought that the unbroken soil of the furrowed fields with their little stone-pile scarecrow for rabbit defence was in keeping with the tone of the landscape. We constantly passed the old ruins of the former holdings of the Nyngmapas, who frequented the valley generations ago. It was at the time of these destructions that the habit of putting out the tongue as a sign of respect developed. It was no easy matter for the Gelupas to overcome the power of their religious competitors. The Nyngmapas held the power of the *mantras* and were able to do great damage with this mystical endowment of misunderstanding, but ultimately the new order overcame them. The dread of the mystical *mantra* was still deeply imbedded, so they forced every one they met to put out his tongue to see if he possessed the power of the *mantra*, which manifested itself by a black coloration on the tongue. Consequently today you cannot look at one of them unless he drops his tongue to his chin and sucks back everything that started to pour out on the next breath, as a salutation of the very highest regard.

No sooner were the animals on their way than we took off through the valley of the Red Idol Gorge where we had been heading for the last day and a half. The only difference between this country and our own sterile valleys of rock is that our thermometer goes up to 125 degrees to 150 degress while in Tibet it is rather cool, due, in part, to the elevation of 13,000 feet. The Red Idol Gorge is an unending gorge of red sandstone. A huge Idol of Buddha, carved in the massive face of a boulder the size of a house, rises sheer from the river bank, among the tumbled rocks of the floor of the canyon.

Shortly thereafter, we came out onto the Gyantsé Plain, where the Nyang joins another river. Having come some 250 miles into Central Tibet over one of the oldest and longest trade routes in the world, the through route to Peking, we were at last coming within sight of our destination.

The last lap was the most interesting. We rode down a typical agricultural lane, with fields of wheat just breaking through the earth spreading for miles on every side. Neat farm houses and little houses in groves of trees came into view. But the unrepaired irrigation ditches overflowed in every direction. Just outside the village a barefoot girl was hurrying across our path, slopping water all over her threadbare apron, while she gave us a fleeting glance through the dust we kicked up about her. According to Tibetan custom this meant very good luck: water crossing your path as you entered a village.

The most interesting person from our country who has travelled this way is Mr. C. Suydam Cutting, who made his first visit about 1930, at which time he was refused permission to visit Lhasa even after sending many presents, including some fine dogs to the late Dalai Lama. In 1935, he returned with Mr. Varney and was again refused permission. On their return to Calcutta a wire reached them, giving the desired permission, so in good old American fashion they hiked straight back. This was the first time in history an invitation had been extended, and then only after years of friendship with the Tibetans and a continual stream of gifts. So what could I expect after a couple of months and no gifts? At the time it certainly looked hopeless. It was only another great adventure into the unknown. Coming to what is known as a forbidden spot on earth, people seem to think it enough if they walk the ground and make no effort to find the treasures beneath the surface. Not until and not since Waddell's book on Tibetan Lamaism have we had anything of real value, and every attempt since then has been more or less a rehash of what he recorded from his twenty-year-or-more contact with the Tibetans and his trip with the Younghusband Mission of 1904.

As we turned out of the canyon of boulders onto the alluvial plains that join with the vast Gyantsé Valley great was the contrast to the desert waste over which we had been travelling for days. At the mouth of the canyon rests a small Nanying monastery ("Monastery of the Ancient Ear"), which is one of the oldest structures in these parts of Tibet. It is a little fortified cloister, tucked away against the high canyon wall, on top of which a fort, with walls of great thickness, with its ribbon-like alternating vertical stripes of red, white and blue, is silhouetted against the deep blue. What is it that leads people to build such sanctuaries in such remote corners of the world and spend a lifetime working up intrigue within their walls? This is the habit in such places, just as it is in our small towns. One of the virtues of the large society of modern civilization stands out in bold relief when the two are compared. That is, we are in some measure forced to get away from personal jealousies and assume a more universal attitude for the growth of man as a silent sentient being. People in our time are much like the bull who has lost his way. He cleans up his system by plunging straight ahead through thick and thin, stopping for nothing and destroying all that comes in his path. So we found a monastery, far from being a place where one could find solace, was a place where this intrigue exists.

The entire valley floor, before the sanctuary, was under cultivation. A small village was formed of those who worked for the monks, under the domineering hand of those who are self-endowed with the power to dispense salvation in this world. Two large *chortens* are at either end of the agricultural area, erected to bring good fortune and to ward the district against evil. As another means of protection the villager clothes, houses and feeds the one who is supposed to hold the secrets of the elements. His business is to see that hailstorms do not come to these parts and destroy the crops. From the appearance of his majestic castle, he seems to have given complete satisfaction.

About a mile from the main monastery, built like an eagle's nest among the crags, is a small retreat which is used as a private place of meditation.

A few miles farther the Gyantsé *Jong* came into view, through the distant haze. The fort is built directly into the rock, with a magnificent superstructure looming above. The village and monastery, clustered at its feet for protection, were too much on our own level to be seen. The ride now became uncertain; the sky was darkening rapidly. A storm loomed, and we hastened, hoping to gain the city before it broke. Fortunately the wind carried it over to the small range of hills and we arrived in nothing worse than a dust storm. We followed a protected lane of willows to the bungalow. At last I might be able to have a little milk without the taste of yak dung.

CHAPTER III

GYANTSÉ

I

AFTER settling in Gyantsé my first trip was to interview the Tibet Trade Agent, who is also the head of the monastery. At the beginning only the courtesies of a visit were exchanged, but gradually the conversation drifted to the subject of my desire, just where I wanted to go, how far I should go, how best I could lay the foundation of future work. It was a rather uncertain venture into Tibetan psychology. On the whole, we considered our first two-hour visit our first victory. I had stressed the fact that I desired to learn everything possible about their monastery and the teachings of their particular sect.

The following day was the *Dawa Shinyma Chu Naga*, or the 15th day of the fourth month, according to the Tibetan calendar. This is the most auspicious day of the year, as it marks the enlightenment and the ascension of the Lord Buddha into Nirvana, and it is a belief among Tibetans that any good or evil that is done on this day is increased a millionfold. Indeed, the result of our visit to the monastery on the day before was that they were planning to honor me on this celebrated day, and I was almost afraid to believe that it would ever come true. But it came to pass, and the experience has become one of the richest of my life.

The Abbot of the monastery expressed a deep gratification that a foreigner should take such an interest in their teachings, and he felt that it was the working of the great God that I had come to Tibet at this particular time. He was going to honor me on this day by the burning of a thousand candles, which is the highest tribute that can ever be paid to one by ceremonial worship. All the monks of his institution would turn out and pray for my long life and happiness. It is a relatively small monastery, providing for only about 1500 monks. Drepung, the largest monastery in the world, holds about 10,000. Nevertheless, this smaller monastery is impressive.

When we arrived in the early morning, all the monks were seated on long hand-woven carpets in the large courtyard in front of the main building. It stirred me deep within to see such militant humility of ignorance. The higher Lamas formed two parallel lines in the centre of the great gathering, while the head Lama sat on a high chair at the end farthest removed from the entrance, through which we were led to the private room of the Abbot.

I have already spoken of the graceful way in which Tibetans mix the externals with the cherished feelings of reverence. Here, as later in Lhasa, we were conducted through a dark and spooky kitchen, where the great kettles of tea could be seen steaming and the workers were stirring the large vats of rice, which would presently be served to all the monks at this gathering of good will. These kitchens make a different picture from that advertised by the General Electric for the newly-wed wife, who will be able to hold her husband only by keeping the skin of her hands soft and velvety for his caresses. Here one finds nothing but a black chamber with small earthen ovens built on the floor in which the wood is stoked, while smoke fills the room when the draft is not working efficiently.

Ascending a flight of stairs, we entered a long balcony chamber overlooking the religious files through which we had just passed. Here the friendly Abbot greeted us in his woolen robe of yellowish brown topped with a gorgeous yellow waistcoat of silk brocade. We were promptly seated on the large Tibetan cushions adorned with their favorite carpets, which are used in all ceremonies, and as promptly served with a bountiful plate of sweets, cookies and nuts.

We remained here while the monks were being fed. Their chants drifted in, wafted by the wind; these faintly could be heard, as if from a distance, in the remote hills. In this marvellous setting I had the feeling that it was all happening in ancient forgotten days. The monastery is perched high, in a hollow, and is surrounded by a large wall, which skirts the buildings on the slope of the hill like a broad ribbon; and the whole of it might have been carried here by the wind. With our backs to the hills, we could peer for miles over the peasantry, which maintain this enormous population of religious dependents. To our left, towering into the lofty clouds, was the *Jong*, this rugged work of man merging with Nature's firm handiwork. The faithful hosts of humility camping below this magnificent fortress of uncertainty left an indelible impression on my mind. Here were the pillars of their society to which all must submit. You begin to wonder how such simple people could ever raise such walls of glory. Their beauty was erected centuries ago by the call of faith, evolving the hope of escape in the next reincarnation. The whole thing is a crime against nature. The insurmountable ego of the human animal must find a way to rise to power, and in Tibet the easiest avenue which leads to the greatest power is that of religion. It is about the only avenue where those on their glorified thrones do not have to offer something to the suffering downtrodden people who have been their means to power. All that is given here is a chance to pray, while in America there must be some more realistic compensation. Are these the conceptions and teachings of Buddha? NO.

It is all due to Asoka, whose insatiable ego came into power in

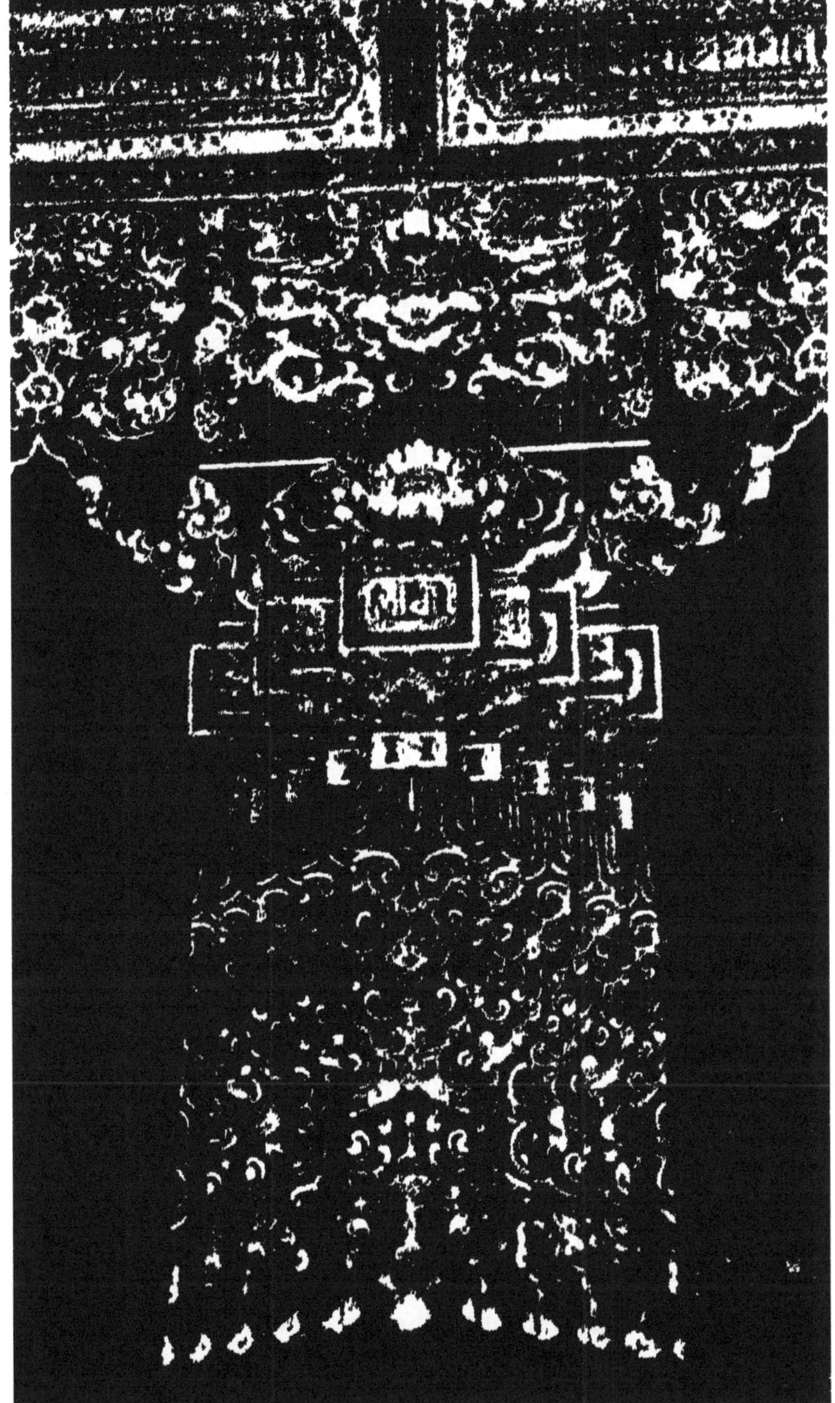

India. In the effort to unite his people, while lacking the power to control the religion of the period, he took up the teachings of Buddha, and established an organized religion. He built monasteries and offered rewards to all who would pursue the given line of thought, so we have the beginnings of the Buddhist religion dating back to the time of Asoka and not to the era of Buddha himself. Nothing holds a people together so much as a common faith; Asoka knew this. In the seventh century there came to Tibet a king, Srong-tsan-Gampo, who likewise possessed some understanding of psychology. This king sent an army of scholars to India who brought back in toto the teachings of the Lord Buddha; these today make up the Tibetan *Kangyur* and *Tengyur*. It did not happen in a single year, but was the result of the gradual process that was working between the seventh and eleventh centuries. Srong-tsan-Gampo had a great intellectual capacity; actually, his work was the inspiration of his Chinese and Nepalese wives, both devout Buddhists. The intellectual stream in this culture is derived from the Chinese; for the true Tibetan aboriginal of the country has a fairly thick skull. The will to power among the religious leaders is unquestionable. They will go to any extreme to maintain their position. A bodyguard is maintained to prevent intrigue within the walls of the court. Such a foundation will never lead to the development of humanity. Will a change ever come to Tibet? Transfer these people to a more enlightened environment, and the rulers would have their work cut out for them.

All these reflections came upon me because my eyes happened to shift from the lanes of the faithful to the power of the throne.

It was now time for me to be taken on my tour of religious devotion. I started down the stairs and finished in the pinnacle of the great *chorten* within the monastery walls. It would take books to describe all that I experienced on this pilgrimage of devotion which led us through the dimly candle-lighted shrines to dark passages, across thresholds where no foreigner had ever before set foot. I beheld the magnificence of the jewelled altars of gold protected by the glittering deities of the faith, representing the suppression of the intelligence over centuries. On each side of the images of religion I left a scarf that I might be further blest.

The pilgrimage commenced at the front of the monastery, where I devotedly knelt to the chair dedicated to the Most Reverent One, the late Dalai Lama. I went with the Abbot into the main monastery, always starting from the left as I entered and going around the temple to my right in a clockwise manner. There were 3000 candles in the lighted sanctuary. The wildest imagination could never picture the impressiveness of these thousands of twinkling lights in a double row completely around the room. The walls were decorated with paintings of the deities displaying master craftsmanship on the part of the Lama artists. The Buddha was of enormous size, all studded with precious stones. The sixteen disciples of Buddha, which are usually painted on the walls, were represented by giant figures, adding immensely to the impressiveness, which would instill religious devotion into any soul. Even the most hardened heathen would want to bow to such images. You feel you must do something, but you know not what, and you know not why. Something deep within is stirred—something that you never realized existed before. It is little wonder that they are able to wield such power over the masses.

This was just the beginning. Now we started at the private shrines erected for different deities. In most instances they far surpassed the grandeur of any Buddhistic spectacle that I had ever visited. Our next shrine of devotion was another of the Lord Buddha; it was protected by immense doors under the constant guard of its keeper. The entire image was gold-plated, and lavishly covered with jewels. The minor images were

equally valuable. Still the people die of starvation, that yet another precious gem may adorn this material representation of the Law of Life.

We went through dozens and dozens of gloomy hidden sanctuaries of this sort. Imagine the wealth that is stored behind these stuffy walls! This was only a small monastery, so what can be the wealth of Lhasa, where the Lamas have been damming up religious sweat for centuries? I had heard for many years of the fabulous wealth hidden away in these impenetrable dungeons of faith, but being sceptical I always fancied that the authors drew considerably on their imaginations. Now that I had come to see them with my own eyes, it was my impression that no one had even begun to describe the untold riches which had been amassed by this church during the centuries of its domination.

Never before, I was told, had a foreigner been permitted to set foot across these sacred thresholds. The enormous deities are at all times guarded with locks of iron. Even Waddell, Sir Charles Bell, and David Macdonald, who, of all Europeans, enjoyed the most intimate relationship with the Tibetans, fail to record any such opportunity. It is difficult to predict how long this will last, as throughout the rest of the world the church is losing its hold on the people. People are no longer willing to submit to such blind rule. They demand a place in this life as well as in the next. The church does not offer this to them, so today they are out to get it for themselves.

The late Dalai Lama has been dead now for over five years and they still have not been able to find a small child who is supposed to be his reincarnation. This is the first time in the history of the country that there has been such a lapse of time between the death of a Dalai Lama and the finding of his reincarnation. There is a prediction that the thirteenth Dalai Lama will be the last one, and the late Dalai Lama was the thirteenth.

Among the chambers which we visited was one in which all their weapons and implements of discipline are kept. It was a dark, dusty, dingy cell. As you entered you became aware of an enormous form overhead which could not be made out in the dim light. Once the candles were turned toward the ceiling you could see cobwebbed figures of yaks hanging from the rafters. They had been there for centuries and were almost as sacred as the deities themselves. They are the beasts which were used in building this enormous monastery. You cringed as you circled the room to examine its weapons of hostility.

After visiting all the shrines on the lower floors we went above where we found the usual chambers of the Thousand Buddhas and one erected to the late Dalai Lama, of which I tried to take a picture. The whole tour turned out to be a photographic escapade for me. I missed no chance to snap a picture. Besides the endless idols of pure gold in the sealed room containing the *Kangyur*, completely written in gold, there were endless representations of the deities in various sexual embraces, portraying the way of all flesh.

It was late in the afternoon when we finally got away from the monastery. We were let out by a monk who swung a long strap to beat away the crowd, so that we might pass through undefiled by them.

There is no question that this was the greatest experience I had ever had in my life up to this time.

2

The British officer in command at Gyantsé was to arrive early in the morning to accompany us to the monastery to witness the dance which is considered the biggest one they hold in this section. The head Abbot was engaged with a service when we arrived, so we strolled about the main nave of the principal temple. There are eighteen of them altogether within the walls which make up the Gyantsé monastery proper, but everything revolves around this one. The others are more or less private chapels. I was delighted to have the opportunity to observe these works of art more carefully and at my leisure. One of the most interesting things was an enormous altar of carved and painted butter before which the eternal light was burning. The designs were very intricate and the entire discs were painted in rich, raw colors.

It was not long before we were called to a very tasteful Tibetan lunch of about fifteen courses, every one of which I enjoyed to the utmost. It is most fortunate that I have been able to master the art of eating with chopsticks. Here nothing else is to be had. It is incredible how much food one can eat there and still be hungry soon. In the beginning I thought I took too much tea, but it had no ill effect.

It was a very gay party. We listened and watched the dance progress as we ate. There was no need to hurry as the dance would go on for hours. After lunch, the Tibetan barley beer, called *chang*, was brought. Enormous quantities are drunk. It is said to remove the evil effects of gorging. When dining with the Tibetans it is impossible ever to finish, as they never stop refilling your plate or cup. As soon as it was possible to call a halt, we sat down among the dancers after forging our way through the dense barrier of spectators lined up twenty deep.

The performance began with a long procession led by a torch-bearer and followed by several persons carrying beautiful silver teapots. As soon as the head Lama was seated with the orchestra, which consisted of cymbals, large drums, and a pair of long Tibetan horns, the dancers started to come on to the stage to the rhythm of the music which begins the devotional steps of the dance. First came a couple of dozen persons wearing huge weird masks, clothed in glamorous silk brocades, jewelled with strings of human bones, holding a skull in one hand and a large sword in the other.

The action might be better described as a religious chant than a dance, for it was slow and deliberate and accomplished at a snail's pace. By the end of the first hour the dancers all entered a pavillion and, performing a circle there, they slowly departed, while the next set of dancers came on, consisting of a pair of devils who went through a series of variations describing frantic gestures of mirth. They were followed by a couple representing skeletons, who caused much excitement among the crowd with their gyrations. Their final performance was to drag away the entrails which had been taken out of the Lama seated at the center of the scene by two little devils who had announced the appearance of the skeletons by means of gestures. The entrails, I should add, were actually lengths of rope. The ends of these innards appear to reach the hands of the skeletons, who by this means are dragged off the stage.

The music ceased for a brief interval, while the next set of dancers arranged their costumes. As they were ready to come on, and the accompaniment began, the Officer of the Day used long leather thongs to beat the crowd back and permit the performers to enter. A couple of slashes could scarcely be felt through the layers of heavy garments worn by the monks, but the psychological effect must be very deep. When these wielders of the lash were not so engaged, they circled among the dancers and saw to it that their costumes were at all times in order. The pride which they take in everything they do is astonishing. There are no extremes to which they will not go that all may be properly cared for.

The final act was performed by the same large group which had come on in the beginning. This time the procession continued until they circled the entire stage. They remained there for an hour or so, leaping from one leg to the other in time with the crashing cymbals and droning horns.

While the dance was still in progress, long carpets were unrolled in the pavillion, and tea was served. After another hour all action suddenly stopped, and the orchestra stepped out of the box, slowly filing off the stage, followed by the dancers in well-spaced procession. Thus ended one of the unforgettable pageants of the Tibetan Lamas.

The great crowd formed a deep wall of human flesh. They covered all available space on the housetops and in the windows. There were many faces worn with toil, finding the excuse to be merry for a moment, and I found them as interesting as the dancers.

I imagine I provided more amusement than the dancers. Regardless of where I went, friendly laughter greeted me. I do not know if it was just I, a stranger, or envy of my beard. A beard is something the best of them cannot grow or buy. They preserve their one or two hairs as if they were pure gold.

Throughout the masses could be seen waving heads of the *Tsang* headdresses worn by the women. When lavishly covered with pearls, it is a decorative ornament. On poor peasants, who are never without it even in the fields, it looks more like a check-rein to hold the head up rather than a thing of beauty.

The time had come to pay our respects to our host. The sun was already setting and a heavy storm coming up. After a last sip of *chang* we rode off through the fighting mob.

3

On returning to the bungalow I learned that Mary and Jigme had just arrived. I had been planning to meet them at Kalimpong before my departure, but something prevented them from starting on their proposed journey to India at the time. He is a general of the Confederate army and holds considerable influence in the Government, so a letter was sent immediately to make arrangements for a meeting. Tomorrow would tell the result of our effort. The head of the fort seemed to favor me, so much would depend on the friendship with Mary and Jigme, the son of Tering Raja, the rightful Raja of Sikkim, who, owing to some little trouble years before, had relinquished his place to his brother, the present Maharajah.

Jigme wore a peculiar hat with red silk tassels falling below the bottom rim. It was a conical shape, studded in front with turquoises and pearls. The peaked crown was of gold. When he removed it from his head, his hair revealed similar adornments of jewels. Mary was arrayed in the usual Tibetan splendor. Both having been educated at Darjeeling, they could speak perfect English, and we had an interesting talk about Tibetan matters. He was a young man of my own age and was the head of the military forces, but you could never guess this by looking at him. He possessed both a shrewd mind and a keen imagination, and he was eager to expand the outlook of his country. I had a feeling that he would go far in counteracting the influence of the older generation of Tibet with its hampering deviations into the past. As elsewhere, the younger people of Tibet are anxious to take on the newer customs of another civilization. One thing is certain: any change to be effected in Tibet can be accomplished only by the enthusiasm of youth determined to bring about a measure of happiness for the greatest number.

The following morning we were up at the usual early hour of four. For one thing, we were anxious to be at the monastery in time to witness the hanging of their sacred *thangka* of Buddha. Over 150 feet high, it is made up of three parts, one of which is missing today, having been taken by the British Mission in 1904. I understand that it now hangs in one of the museums in England. What remains, however, holds more interest than one is able to absorb during the one hour that it

hangs on this single occasion each year. I had heard of this masterpiece of ancient craftsmanship before, but little did I dream that I should be able to witness its single annual display; for not only do you have to be here on the right day, but also at the right hour. The *thangka* was raised on to a high wall of rocks which formed a part of the ridge of the surrounding wall of the monastery. It reminded me of the great wall of China.

The Abbot received us graciously. He had seats arranged so that we should have the best view. All through the morning there was a constant flow of tea and Tibetan cakes to which I generously helped myself, as I had missed breakfast. With his permission and a monk's assistance, I climbed from one housetop to another, taking and retaking pictures in the hope that I should be able to get at least one worth saving. The Abbot showed uncommon enthusiasm over my photography, and he brought out his favorite *thangka* for me to try to reproduce for him. It was by far the finest piece of workmanship that I had yet seen, but as luck would have it I had run out of my colored film.

The same day we rode out seven miles to visit Tering Raja, the father of Mary and Jigme. We crossed newly sown fields and passed pack trains of donkeys winding their ways over the dusty trails from Lhasa *en route* to India. Life for these traders is nothing but packing and unpacking, broken by intervals of prolonged tramping. They are, however, a cheerful lot, ever ready to exchange a jest with one another. Their jokes are closer to the type to be found around the campfire of cowboys than to the more sophisticated specimens of the *New Yorker*.

The servants received us in typical Tibetan fashion. When calling, we do not go to the door and knock, but we send our servant around to their servants' quarters; and our servant and their servant between them decide if the host is in and if it is time for us to enter. They always know when you are coming.

The custom is to send a servant around on the day before to announce that you intend paying a visit on the morrow. The message, "Come by all means," is usually sent back.

There were three different families in this one family, so there was some special etiquette to be complied with. We consulted the servants on the proper procedure. They informed us which cards were to be given, and in what order. I followed directions explicitly, and all came out well. Along with the proper *katas* very small gifts were given. It is improper to go anywhere in this land empty-handed. The Tibetan usually has a couple of dozen eggs on hand, which he passes on at such an occasion, and by the time these eggs have changed hands a couple of hundred times during the several years of friendly intercourse—well, you can imagine what state they are in. Nevertheless, the gesture has been made, and that is all that is necessary. It is not the worth but the gesture that matters. Being a mere foreigner, I could hardly get away with that!

I wish you could have seen the dried carcasses of yak and sheep which Tharchin had received since our arrival, along with a wonderful Easter egg collection. He is not in the least concerned about it. When he goes calling he merely passes the eggs on to the next group. If you have a few eggs to start with you are set up for life, as far as visiting is concerned. All who come to you must bring, too. And you never fail to return a visit. In the case of Tharchin, who had come with me, he fared luckier than most; as soon as his friends heard of his arrival in Gyantsé after his long absence, they sent around to him gifts of meat, and grain for the pony, gifts of some value. If you like *jerkey* (dried meat), you are delighted. I must confess I had been keeping a crate of it around me to nibble at whenever I felt that craving for raw meat which developed from this primitive existence of mine. Being of a literary turn of mind, Tharchin rarely visited anywhere without taking an armful of books along, which served as return gifts. More than once he saved my face by having them in readiness. Being a foreigner, to be sure, I was given considerable latitude in the matter, and every one made things as pleasant as possible for me.

Upon our arrival, Mary and Jigme offered us the regular Jacob biscuit and tea; after this we had some sweets, then dinner. It is the custom to start with appetizers, to be nibbled with chopsticks, from about ten, fifteen, or thirty small dishes. Then you are served with a bowl of Tibetan noodles, resembling vermicelli in well-seasoned soup. Scarcely have you finished this, when another helping is forced on you, then another and another, until you have had about six or seven bowls. They will not take No for an answer. There is no alternative but to keep at it, and the astonishing thing is that you are never stuffed. As usual, we finished off with *Chang* (beer), and for the rest of the afternoon I had a constant stream of this liquid trickling down my throat; Tibetan hosts insist on refilling your cup, and if you are not drinking the servant picks up your still full cup, a sort of delicate hint that he cannot refill it as long as it is full—so what is one to do?

As it happened, Jigme's hobby was photography. He brought out endless pictures of Lhasa, and of the monasteries which he had visited with the Regent. I need scarcely say how intensely they interested me. Jigme made a very god job of it, too. When he was in Lhasa he had his equipment, and did all his own developing and printing. An official of the Government, he could afford this hobby, which is rather expensive in Tibet.

We returned to our bungalow to watch the setting sun over the *Jong* after my first real Tibetan party.

4

At three-thirty in the morning I was awakened and told that the shots had been fired to start the wild horse race, or rather,

I should say, the riderless horse race. We hastened to dress and go out, but it was not until above five that they came rushing through the cheering crowds, driven on by several men on horseback. The crowd shouted at the top of its lungs trying to frighten the horses away from its path. It was a queer sort of race between the horses of the two biggest landlords of the neighborhood; and this riderless Marathon took place every year.

On the night before the race, the *Jongpen* goes to the stable where the horses are stalled and attaches his official seal. This is to prevent substitution. Then in the middle of the night the horses are taken up the road about seven miles. At a signal they are turned loose and chased the entire distance by riders on little ponies. The object is to get your horse there by hook or by crook before one of your rival's horses. Everything is fair; you can misdirect, hinder, or do anything which occurs to you. It is a mad rush from start to finish.

The most interesting aspect of the occasion was the way the people turned out at this early hour. As Tharchin says: "The Tibetan has so much joy in his heart that even the beggar feels it is his duty to make merry on such festive occasions."

I had thought few people lived in Gyantsé, but when I saw the multitudes that swarmed the hills, as thick as summer flies, I realized that it was true that this is the third town in Tibet in size. The night before Tharchin had arranged with a friend that we witness everything from the roof of his house. Like most of the houses in these parts, it only had one room that was kept clean. We were finally escorted into the beautiful private chapel.

No sooner had we arrived than tea was served. As I have often said, all the time is tea time in Tibet. As soon as word reached us that the ponies were coming, we dashed to the roof, from where we saw them running furiously through the divided crowd, all of whom were shouting, throwing stones, doing anything and everything to encourage greater speed on the part of their favorite.

The passing excitement was most revealing of the Tibetan character. Women stopped with water jugs on their backs and gave three cheers. Others made mad dashes to gather the dung before the next pony flew by, while others stopped mumbling their sacred *mantras* and only continued spinning their prayer-wheels. These they never put down. One of the most usual sights in Tibet is a woman with a revolving prayer-wheel in one hand, a baby in the other, and a large water jug on the bent back, cheerfully trotting along some lonely path.

The officials of the occasion were beautifully clad in royal silks which would make any woman cry out in envy. They sat like knights in saddles of gold on their small Bhotiya ponies. One rarely sees in any other country so much gold in everyday use. The Tibetan will do anything for gold or turquoise, or pearls or coral. Why these things should be such favorites I do not know, but you never find a Tibetan without his turquoise. Even the most humble trader has his earrings of plated gold set with turquoise.

Jigme was particularly anxious to find a way to import turquoise directly into Tibet, and also gold and silver. The color of gold is a royal sign and only those of official rank are permitted to wear silks of that color. Along with this color there is one other distinguishing feature of an official. He has the privilege of doing up his long braids, so that in most instances you will see a crown of black hair interwoven with red braid and adorned with a turquoise ornament.

5

We visited the *Jongpen*, a man of wealth, and with considerable influence with the Government. He was a very close friend of Tharchin, so it was possible to lay our case before him. I had already received warm expressions of his feelings toward me, owing to the great event at the monastery; he was a very devout Buddhist. When I first met him in Calcutta he was on a pilgrimage to Buddha Gaya; on his return he had telephoned to me; so something of a relationship already existed. We outlined our plan, and he told us exactly what to do, adding a prediction that we should encounter no difficulty in receiving permission. He himself strongly favored my so much desired visit, and he volunteered a personal letter to the Regent to go along with mine. My hopes rose to a high peak.

Before I took leave of the *Jongpen* he insisted that I visit his private temple. It was an immaculately clean room, beautifully adorned, and not a spot in it but was touched with color and reverence. There can be no doubt that these shrines instil a mood of peace and meditation in all those who enter them. And how fortunate is he who can retire to such a place of solitude and devotion in his own home! Can one have a better opportunity than here of beginning the day with an hour of communing with that inner self which is the source of spiritual growth? But this is incompatible with the speed of present-day life. The consciousness will not be forced. Relaxation and infinite patience are necessary; these must become a habit, if the consciousness is to have an opportunity of expressing itself, of satisfying its pangs of hunger after a long enforced fast. Here is where Yoga is helpful. Its greatest gifts can neither be measured nor seen. It permits us to understand the hidden purpose behind all the endless designs to be found in Buddhist art, such as the *thangkas* and the drawings of the numberless deities, whose nature has been influenced through the various aspects of these teachings. If one is trained in Yoga, all that is needed is a place where one may be silent, where the body is made restful by liberation from the numerous external needs.

Even so, I am forced to take leave of my contemplative mood, and to return to the realities of the day.

We made a hurried departure for the sporting ground. Countless hundreds were trying to force their way through the narrow streets. For over a mile the way was a solid reddish brown of slowly moving humanity. The women stood out by their enormous *tsang* headdress; there were many of them, and they formed a picturesque motionful design. I tried to take pictures of the great procession, in spite of the rain and almost blinding wind-storm. It was gorgeous beyond compare, this mile-long dense chain of golden silk brocade.

I hurried off to keep an appointment for lunch with an important British official, whose aid I needed if I was to secure permission to go to Lhasa. He showed a very friendly interest in my plan. By this time the British officer at Gyantsé had overwhelmed me with invitations to tea, lunch, dinner, and games. So far I had not been able to avail myself of his kindness. On that afternoon, however, my insistent host came forward and invited me to play a practice game of polo. He had to keep in form, as he was to play against the Political department as soon as Mr. H. E. Richardson, I. C. S., returned from Lhasa where he headed the Political Mission. To play this game at an altitude of over 13,000 feet is no small strain even for the rider. Nevertheless, I warmly consented. Living with the Tibetans twenty-four hours a day has its compensations, yet I found that a short breathing spell lent charm to the adventure. My problem finally resolved itself into the dilemma of reconciling study at the monastery and the indulgence in polo. The only way out was to begin the day at four, which would give me a long interval of work before any one should stir. This would necessitate my taking on a dual personality, which in any case seems to be my favorite pastime; I change so rapidly at times that I can scarcely tell what I really am.

6

Day after day the great whirl of teas and parties continued. I cannot forbear mentioning the extraordinary party at the home of Choktey *Jongpen*. Tharchin and I entered a small courtyard, which has a stable large enough to hold his twenty horses. I had been here only yesterday, but today I was conducted by a different entrance into yet another courtyard, at one end of which was the *Jongpen's* tent, which in itself was something of a palace; its grandeur impressed me. The women and girls present were attired in their best, and the men were in their enviable silk brocades. The latter were congregated for conversation on the customary floor-mats round two large, low Tibetan tables in the two far corners of the tent; while the women sat over a European table in the left-hand corner as you entered. I must confess that it would be hard to find a more charming face than that of the *Jongpen's* wife, with its sparkling bright black eyes so full of life and spirit when they smiled. We often think of the beauty of Japanese women as capturing the prize of the East. But we have cause here to revise this judgment. The astonishing thing is that the Tibetan woman's skin is as fair as our own, but imagine this fair skin against a frame of glistening jet-black hair, which has been done up in two long braids tied together at the bottom by a pink tassel woven into the hair. This coiffure makes it rather difficult to distinguish between a man and a woman, for the hair of both is arranged to hang alike in braids, with the same red tassel worked into the design. As for Jigme's jewelled crown of black hair, it could be counted upon always to hold your attention in much the same manner as would the top of a zebra woodpecker in these parts. But to return to the women: there is no more graceful sight than to watch their delicate white hands manipulate the ivory chopsticks, with which they daintily pick

Upper left The jewelled headdress worn by the noblewomen from Tsang province *Upper*
[illegible] from Tsang province *Lower left* Mr

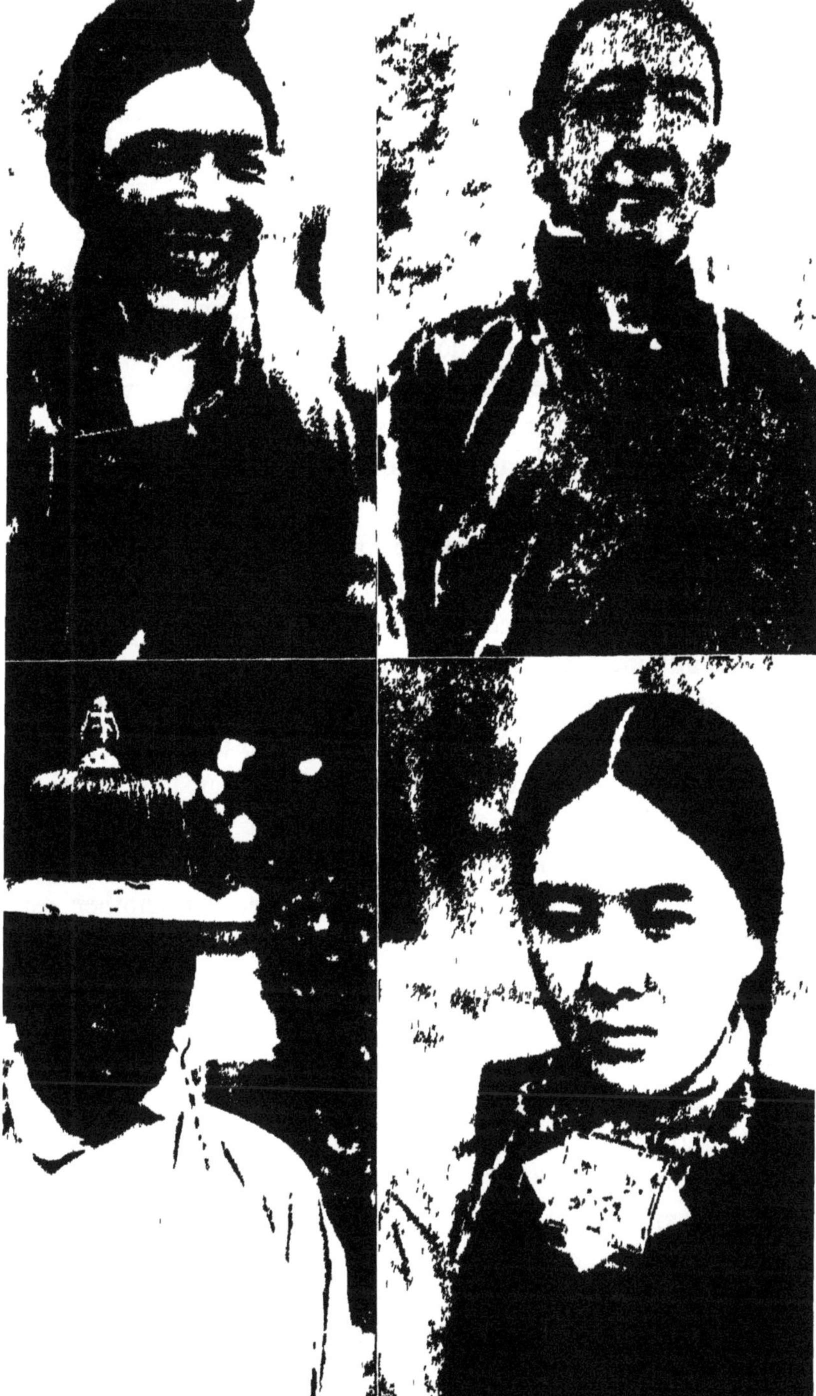

up the nuts or other tidbits from the table, and I warrant that even the poet Byron, who did not like to see a woman eat, would have succumbed to the grace with which an aristocratic Tibetan woman performs this unpoetic function.

And now, that we are on the subject of eating, perhaps you would like to know what a Tibetan banquet is like, and, luckily, I need not linger over it here as long as the actual meal lingers—and that is, literally, for hours and hours.

We scarcely entered the tent when we were served with sweets and tea, constantly replenished until the dinner proper itself. We had arrived early in the morning, and the main meal came on at twelve noon. At no time were there less than fifteen dishes on the table. I did not keep strict count, but from a rough check-up, there must have been fifty or more courses. I remember that when, after a couple of hours of feasting, pineapple was brought in, I felt inward relief, imagining that this must be the end. But no! There were eighteen other courses after this, and it must have taken another hour and more to consume them. Then—the dessert. I helped myself to that, too. But that wasn't enough. The hostess would insist that you took another helping. And then when you have seen the dishes removed, and are congratulating yourself in consequence, yet another set comes on, and these must be generously sampled. If they think you are being bashful, they will fill up a silver Chinese scoop, used as a rule as a spoon for liquids but often as a substitute for a plate, and hand it to you for you to nibble at. These tidbits may be trifles in themselves, but when you go on eating all day it amounts in the end to gorging. They would regard a nice thick steak with horror.

Having an interest in some of the dishes unfamiliar to me, I promptly made inquiries. To my astonishment, the ladies did not have the slightest idea as to how they were prepared, for a woman of their class had nothing to do with cooking or, for that matter, with anything that might be thought of as work. We in the West think that women should at least know how such things are done, whether they have anything to do with it or not; not so with these women. There are hundreds of servants around, so why should they even think of such a thing?

For the benefit of the curious, it might be well to go into some particulars of the dishes usually served at these festive Tibetan affairs. As I have already mentioned, upon arrival one is offered India tea with Jacob's biscuits and hard dried apricots. Later a bowl containing three sweet rolls, a flavored dumpling and some sweet milk are brought. At brief intervals many small dishes put in an appearance on the tables; they contain: stewed mutton in gravy, with onions, herrings; half green peaches, stewed peaches; tinned pineapple slices; dried dates; Chinese sweets; peanuts; Mongolian ham, yak tongue; pressed beef; plain beef; small dishes of sauce, etc.; and the Chinese spoon is brought in with a saucer. There is usually a continuous supply of *chang* (barley beer).

All these are a mere preliminary to the main meal, which is brought on in numerous small dishes. These are placed around the center of the table, whereupon there is a great diving of chopsticks from all directions. The only individual course is a bowl of dumplings or of vermicelli soup, which is a very frequent dish in this country. Every one has the opportunity of expressing his appreciation by eating the dumplings or the soup as loudly as possible, in order to demonstrate to the host how much he is enjoying his dinner. The customary courses are the following:

1. Minced mutton and gravy.

2. Fine minced meat rolled in butter with vermicelli, celery and cabbage.

3. Minced meat in pastry.

4. Slices of very firm fish with onions, carrots and boiled bacon.

5. Sea slugs in soup, with boiled pork.
6. Round meat dumplings.
7. Green peas and wine.
8. Hard-boiled eggs quartered in a sauce.
9. Pastry dumplings.
10. Bamboo roots and boiled pork.
11. Eels in soup with pork and onions.
12. Rice with raisins and cherries.
13. Small squares of sweet fried bread.
14. Jam dumplings and sponge cake.
15. Shark's stomach, boiled pork and carrots, minced yak, pieces of mutton, steamed rice; four varieties of white bread pastries, and also soup.

A meal such as this, of course, is to be had only in the homes of the very wealthy; for most of these ingredients have to be imported from India and China, and some of them come in sealed tins. But these importations are no more extraordinary than our own from Europe or from the Orient.

On the whole, I held up very well under this elaborate menu, though I was not anxious to repeat the performance for a few days at least. Altogether it lasted seven hours, with brief intervals of talk and picture-taking. I must confess I was not bored. Several important personages were there, including the British official whose support I needed for the realization of my dream of going to Lhasa.

7

I was leaving no stone unturned. There were constant conferences with the Choktey *Jongpen*, who seemed greatly encouraged with my prospects. There was nothing to do, however, but wait another two or three weeks for the outcome of our effort.

In the meanwhile I was making every effort to pick up a

Tibetan *Tengyur*, and, contrary to reports, I did not find this at all easy, though I had been more than a week at it. The fact is, the Tibetan is very reluctant to sell anything that has any connection with his religion. It is his belief that it is wrong to do so. Even a declaration of my desire to familiarize the Western world with Tibetan teachings did not seem to be a sufficient inducement to make them part with the books. There were a set of blocks near Shigatsé, but they had been used for so many hundreds of years without being cleaned that it was next to impossible to read the print any longer. I had feelers out in various directions in the hope of securing a good copy. It is odd that, in spite of the deep feeling the Tibetan shows for his sacred books, he rarely reads them, although the very scholarly pore over the time-worn lines, but these are so few that they might almost be numbered on the fingers of your hands. The chief purpose of a copy of the *Tengyur*, it would seem, is to throw it into the mortar that goes into the building of a *chorten* or a large image of Buddha, or put it on the shelves of a new monastery in the course of construction. Indeed, it has become a thing of no great value in itself, but a religious ornament of antiquity.

Yet in the matter of living the average Tibetan exhibits great gifts. The "joy of living" is, indeed, no idle phrase, when applied to him. It was while still waiting for permission to go on to Lhasa that one morning a large group of Tibetan folk gathered in the courtyard of my bungalow to gamble and to drink *chang*. They collected in a great circle, with their main source of supply in the center. Throughout the entire day they drank and sang and danced. When we returned in the evening after a day's activity we found them still there, old and young prancing to the rhythm of the choir and the clapping of the audience. Their singing went on for hours and tea was served them; I imagined that at the end of the day we should see the last of them, but in this I was mistaken. They explained that it was time for them to have their picnic, and that very likely they would remain for an entire week. They were out for a good time, and neither love nor money could make them move along.

On the following afternoon, while I was writing, a group of Lamas boldly made themselves comfortable in the rear part of my yard, on the grass, beneath the willow hedge. They spent a happy hour engaged in conversation. I had almost forgotten about them, when suddenly a tune carried on gusts of wind broke upon my ear. I looked out to see whence it came, only to discover that I now had a party of Tibetan women at the other end of the grounds, being inspired apparently by generous helpings of *chang*. For the rest of the afternoon their happy voices filled the air. They reminded me of the first time that I rode into a party of Navajos singing; their melody was much the same, and sung in the same key.

I think I have made it clear that it is hard to keep lonesome in these parts; there is always a party going on, and this seems to be the favorite picnic ground of the neighborhood. It is not at all unusual to return from a visit to find a long row of head ornaments stirring above the tops of the low mud walls in front of the grounds; when you come nearer and peer over the wall you will see three or four sheep grazing at the end of a rope, while their caretakers are discussing the gossip of the village, personal intrigue concerns them as does those of our own race, whose imagination is no greater than their petty jealousies. Having some kind of mind, they have to yield to its natural tendency to be active. And, their imagination being scant, they spend their waking hours on these trifling externals.

Every morning at four a Lama from the monastery came over to give me instruction. One morning about eight another visitor arrived; he had an overwhelming interest in American skyscrapers, about which he had heard a great deal, so a copy of the rotogravure section of *The New York Times* came into its own. He pored over its pages like a child, and when he was done with that he plied me with questions about the American flag. In the absence of Old Glory, I did my best to give him some idea of what it looked like. Another thing that always amazed these people is how I have managed to learn to speak English. They appeared to think that we of America had a language all our own. They were utterly flabbergasted when they were told that England and America had the same language. After this they would ask what other matters the two peoples had in common, and everything intensely interested them.

I know of no other people so easy to entertain. They reveal awe on learning of the most common details of our everyday life. The simpler the thing seems, the more they appear to enjoy it. Perhaps this is natural, as their own life is different in so many respects. Yet America is a fabulous place to them, and when they learn that you are from this country they are sure to overwhelm you with questions.

8

A wire from Lhasa, sent me by the wife of one of Tibet's most powerful individuals, encouraged me no end.

The time had now come to begin our calls at the homes of several of the large landlords of the neighborhood. I recall one of these visits with particular interest. The house was a large three-story structure surrounded by the customary mud wall fifteen feet high. On entering we were greeted by the usual loud growl of a Tibetan mastiff that was housed in a small enclosure to the left of the gate as you stepped into the courtyard. Through a hole about a foot and a half square he could see every one who came in. Fortunately, he was chained. Just to see him and hear him put the fear of God into one. He was the size of a large St. Bernard, but he resembled an African lion, decorated with a big woolly red collar round his neck. The Tibetan likes dressing up his animals. The finest horse to the lowest little donkey is always provided with some sort of adornment to enhance his appearance. Bright red is the predominant color. The traders will often attach a couple of large yak tails, resembling grandma's dusters and dyed a scarlet red, to the necks of their favorite animals.

The courtyard we entered had the usual stable fitted up to accommodate twenty-five horses. In a small patio within the compound of the house, similar to that of a Mexican dwelling, there was another large stable, so that on calling you conducted your horse into the house with you and left him at the foot of the stairs, which led into a dark, dingy, smoky, gloomy and filthy attic veranda, connected with the servants' quarters.

With the interior walls of the courtyard covered with cow dung and the stables near, you can imagine what the dining room would be like when it is within spitting distance. Moreover, the only sanitary arrangement consists in vacating one of the lower rooms of the house and cutting a small hole through the ceiling, thus enabling the use of the room above as a toilet. Fortunately, it is a cold dry climate here, so that everything freezes up quickly, and the lower room is entered only once a year for the purpose of cleaning it—that is, among the more high-minded. The door, however, is usually left open, and the dogs manage to keep the place fairly clean, so that when you are visiting in Tibet and that moment of embarrassment comes over you, just search for a room with a hole in the floor. It can usually be found next to one of the stairways.

After getting through the dung smoke, we were led to the next flight of stairs, which consists of a pair of large beams extending up and beyond the next floor, much like the long sticks coming out of an American Indian's Kiva. The cross-pieces which formed these steps were at convenient distances—that is, if you happened to be a tall person. As for coming down, I suppose they always figured you could fall down. At all events, we presently found ourselves in the so-called parlor, which is the one immaculate, polished room in the house, for which thanks are due to Buddha. Here is the small private shrine, with Tibetan cushions and the customary small carpets arranged on the floor around a very low table about a foot from the ground. Directly beneath the table the cushion is invariably a little higher than elsewhere, and whether you sit higher or lower depends on your rank. In all my visits I was always accorded the honor of the highest seat, with my host either on the level or just below me. They are very hospitable in this matter, and a protest on your part leads nowhere. After much obsequiousness on both sides, you finally settle to a friendly conversation, which begins by your host asking what sort of life you have had, if you have had a pleasant journey, if you are tired; he hopes that everything has gone well with you, that no injury has befallen you, that no misfortune has overtaken you on your journey, and now that you have arrived everything is comfortable and your animals are well taken care of. Actually, all this is merely the equivalent of our own custom of opening the conversation by talking about the weather.

A person of inferior rank will always address his betters in a whisper, and at no time will he permit his own vile breath to contaminate the other. He will hold his hands down and look upon the floor, or put his hand over his mouth and speak in very subdued tones. To the stranger from the West his humility must seem sickening. Among persons of equal rank, however, conversation is carried on in the same direct fashion as among us.

Another little gesture that is entertaining to watch is the way in which a slightly inferior person will accept a piece of cake, a sweet or a tidbit that is offered him. He will bend forward on his feet, arise, and then, with his head hung low, break off a small crumb with his hands in the customary "lay me down to sleep" fashion of praying, murmuring all the while obsequious thanks in the usual undertone. And, of course, he would not think of sipping his tea so that it could not be heard by the servants at the other end of the house.

Among these people there is virtually no privacy, whatever their rank. You are sure to be served by some greasy servant, or even a half dozen of them, if the host happens to be one of the higher rank. The latter have learned some acquaintance with cleanliness, and you naturally expect their servants to be clean in their dress and appearance; yet such is not the case. They are as greasy and as dirty as if they were servants of the lower classes, and regardless of how immaculate a room may be and the richness of the clothing the wealthy may wear, it is something of a shock to see the servants trailing in with their five-year-old gowns, their sleeves rolled up to the elbows, giving the impression that they have just been interrupted in some other piece of menial work to attend to the wants of their master's visitors. The host might be clad in the finest of royal silks, but his servants will be like all the rest of the unfortunates in the land. The contrast is surely impressive.

I must admit, however, to having enjoyed my morning. We began by imbibing India tea, then China tea, and finally, just before leaving, the tea of Tibet. My host was one of the intellectuals in these parts. There was never a more homely face attached to the shoulders of an individual, but never did a face pour forth greater radiance than his. It was one of the most irreconcilable combinations that I have ever encountered; for behind that repugnant exterior was one of the finest minds that I have ever met. Our exciting conversation lasted for several hours, and I left when I did leave only because I felt I had no right to remain any longer.

That evening I dined at the bungalow. Every meal is a mystery, but this evening I was served with a typical piece of uncuttable yak meat. There can be nothing in the world tougher than yak, when it comes to the eating of it. Even a buzzard would be tender compared to it. Once I did have a special treat, and a surprise—the finest looking roast chicken that I have ever seen on a plate. Alas, appearances are deceptive. This chicken was older than the hills and tougher than a Goodyear casing. So I made a wry face, and philosophically turned to the old stand-by, a bread-pudding, which I enjoyed. After all, the boys had me at heart, and took a heap of trouble to please me, and that was something. Life is easy-going here. Laundry is sent out, and is returned with the handkerchiefs nicely folded, and you are asked if they do not look well enough without being ironed, and if you say nothing, nothing is done, and you let it go at that. The same holds true of your other clothing. Once you have learned to overlook such trifles, life becomes a continuous picnic, but beware of having a desire for something different. The important thing is to have other interests, perpetually to keep busy. Then the burnt eggs one gets for breakfast, and which make hardly more than a swallow, do not seem to matter. As to that, the only palatable dish that I can be sure of is oatmeal, which I brought with me. It is served to me in the form of a paste, but I find that it goes down with little effort if drunk down with a little yak milk, well flavored with yak dung.

CHAPTER IV

TOO GOOD TO BE TRUE

I

IT WAS in Tibet that I played my first game of cricket. It seemed odd to come to such a remote place to play the national game of England. This game is the slimmest excuse that I have yet encountered for doing nothing when one is supposed to be doing something. That is about all the game amounts to. Outside the two fellows who bowl, every one else stands around and waits for the game to be finished. If your side is up to bat, there is absolutely nothing to do. As a game for a week-end house party, it would be little short of perfect. It would provide the excuse for coming, and act as a silent theme song of activity. In this particular instance it enabled me to be social without having to strain myself.

My dream of Lhasa was very much on my mind. After going through my share of the motions of cricket I sent word to find out how things were going. Together with the letters, gifts had been sent to the officials of Lhasa and should have arrived before we reached Gyantsé. On our arrival at Gyantsé Tharchin and I wrote to a friend in Lhasa asking about it. The answer came back to the effect that nothing had been received. After several consultations with the *Jongpen* it was decided to send a personal message. Then the question arose as to the gifts to be sent with it. Not to send such gifts was about the worst breach of etiquette that might be committed in Tibet. We had to make a proper choice for the various officials, then wire our order for the gifts to Calcutta. The plan was to send Tharchin on to Lhasa with my application, while I return to India alone and live in the hope all along the way that a wire would overtake me, or that I could get an extension of time in Gyantsê. With Tharchin taking things in hand and journeying to deliver my messages in person to the Regent and to the members of the *Kashag*, I felt my chances were good. The Choktey *Jongpen* himself helped us no little in composing these letters, taking a few ideas and spreading them out in the "King's English of Tibet." The letters were, in their own fashion, masterpieces; ornate and calculated to win the hearts of Tibetans.

If luck should be with me, I would be the first white person to be allowed to penetrate behind the mysterious walls of the sanctuary of Lhasa. Others have seen the barren streets of Lhasa, and taken excellent photographs of these and of the buildings; I myself had seen the marvellous photographic collection of the Political Mission; but what do they tell us of the sacred mystery behind the walls which has maintained the social structure together century after century? And because of my intense desire to know something of this, and this precisely, I laid emphasis on the religious aspect of my studies. Perhaps I should be permitted to go only to Shigatsê, and that would be just as revealing; but Lhasa being the Sacred City carries with it the prestige.

Having arranged with Tharchin the details of his journey to Lhasa, the *Jongpen* and his wife and I settled down to a stimulating talk on religion. His wife was as intelligent a little woman as one was likely ever to meet; not only was she well-read, but she was as beautiful a woman as I had seen in these parts. It was indeed a pleasure to watch her read the manuscripts which they had on their shelves, to see her race over the lines faster than I could go if they were in English. When I thought how difficult it was for me, I could not help but feel envy. She was thoroughly familiar with the teachings of Buddhism as well as with Tibetan literature. You are forced to admire the Tibetan who, in contrast to the Indian, makes his wife his constant companion in everything he does. The Tibetan wife is always with her husband, and if you get the notion into your head for a little private conversation with him, you will run into a snag; for she is always there. Not that you would have her away, for you soon discover that she has many valuable ideas and suggestions to offer. She has the perfect knack—or shall we say charm—of giving the impression that her husband is running everything, yet of accomplishing anything she wants unobtrusively. This holds good in all circles, regardless of station in life. In the case of the nomadic trader you find the woman paddling along, doing just as much of the packing and unpacking as the men; you also find her doing her share in the fields, not merely something else, but actually the same task as her male companion in toil. The same thing prevails on a higher level in the upper strata.

Choktey *Jongpen* and his wife having discovered that my favorite teacher was Guru Rimpoche, who was also theirs, the bond between us was promptly sealed. He favored the old sect, *Kargyupa*, rather than the present school of religious thought, which is in the majority. It espouses all the esoteric teachings of Buddhism as preached by Guru Rimpoche, known as Padma Sambhava, the great Tibetan *tantrik.* Today it is almost impossible to find any of the old books revealing the teachings of Guru Rimpoche, and those who know these teachings will not reveal them to any one except of their faith. Once I demonstrated my faith to their satisfaction, Choktey brought out his set of seven volumes which embodies the fundamentals of this sect, so rare nowadays, and began to narrate their contents. Although it took him years of searching to find his set, he promised to let me have it if I failed to find another during my Tibetan journey. Naturally I felt myself to be very fortunate to have the opportunity of procuring so rare a treasure, never seen outside the chosen circles.

2

On the next day I was supposed to go hunting gazelle with Captain Gordon Cable. Hunting, however, is forbidden to a Buddhist. I could, nevertheless, go along for a ride, and try to get some photographs of the animals. The day was perfect, and the horses were in fine mettle.

From Gyantsé we rode direct toward the hills bordering on the polo field, then followed the extensive flats up to their edge about six or seven miles beyond the field in which the troops were preparing for tomorrow's game. It was a fine ride, but a bit trying at times; it is no easy task, while travelling at a fast canter over gopher-hole flats, across rocky river bottoms and over deep ditches, to hold down a bouncing Leica camera from the neck and field-glasses at your waist and telephoto lenses shifting at a great rate; but once we settled these details all went well and I had about as good a ride as though I were on a cow pony dashing across the wide open prairies. I do not know how the horses can stand it, but I do know that after you've ridden at this pace for several hours you feel you've done a good day's work.

The valley of dahlias which we traversed was something to remember for its beauty. It reminded me of the sweltering hills bordering on the desert of Phœnix, Arizona, or the Mojave Desert of California. I had my traditional hunting experience: the gazelles must have gone on one of their temporary migrations. At all events, we did not encounter a single one. My companion, however, insisted that such a thing now happened to him for the first time. Never before had he failed to see one, though he admitted it did not mean that he always got his prey.

The countless herds of grazing sheep might have been the cause of the failure of their appearance. I fully enjoyed my outing, and secretly was even pleased at the absence of gazelles, for I did not wish the embarrassment of having one killed.

On our return we rode in the canyon around the opposite side of the hill which we had passed on the way up. This took us over freshly plowed fields and new crops of wheat and through small valleys solidly carpeted with iris, all in full bloom. Thus, a perfect morning had been provided; and there was tomorrow to look forward to with its game of polo, of which I had grown inordinately fond.

3

At this time a piece of unanticipated good fortune came my way. The *Jongpen*, on hearing of my efforts to obtain the seven-volume set of the teaching of the Guru Rimpoche, came forward and offered me his own set which he had procured with difficulty some years before at Kham. He gave the books to me after submitting me to considerable scrutiny in order to assure himself that I was worthy of his trust and that I should use these books to spread their teachings to all worthy of them in America who should happen to desire them. Only with such a purpose in view was he willing, and even eager, to part with the books. I do not remember anything more touching than the manner in which he brought me the gift of a famous *thangka*, which had been blessed by one of the head Lamas generations ago and had remained in his family ever since. I had been told by others even before it came into my hands that the possession of it made success sure in the propagation of the teachings. It seemed absurd to think that I could ever possess so revered an object. Yet there I was, to my own surprise inspiring this almost fabulous trust, and being offered this extraordinary gift, after the fitting ceremony at his temple by the head Lama, this event appears to have coincided with another event, which they considered a particularly auspicious augury, inviting other ceremonies. In any case, the full import of the gift and all the deep meaning attached to it were conveyed to me through the proper ceremony peculiar to the occasion. I fear I revealed greater emotion than I should have done. Yet it was a strangely solemn, strangely impressive situation; it overwhelmed me and left me a prey to my feelings. The presentation was made in my tiny shrine at the bungalow. Here the *thangka* was hung on the wall, and below it was placed a small butter lamp, which was lighted by the light which had been glowing for years and years in the *Jongpen's* own home. His head Lama also came, and there in front of it the three of us sat in the customary Buddha posture while the Lama recited the secret chant and we remained in silence meditating on the symbolism which expressed their teachings. After this, the blessings of the sacred painting were passed on to me.

It was impossible to go through this ceremony and then discard it as merely another experience. After my visitors were gone, I sat for hours before the *thangka*. It was not possible to go to sleep with all the feeling that had been imbedded deep in my heart by these fresh happenings.

That evening indeed was to be one of the memorable spiritual milestones on the way to the ultimate experience in the solitary cell after my final initiation, and in that cell I was to linger long over this particular episode culminating in a sleepless night filled with quiet ecstasy. The fates were surely propitious, and the realization of my dream of Lhasa seemed a step nearer.

4

The assistant British Trade Agent, Rai Sahib Wangdi, and I had a very friendly chat. He was a Tibetan who had learned to speak perfect English and had been working for the British Government a good many years. In the absence of Tharchin he offered his services as an interpreter, as my knowledge of the Tibetan tongue was not yet all that it should be. Before taking his departure Wangdi told me that Rai Bahadur Norbhu Dhondup, Dzasa, British Trade Agent at Yatung, was expected to arrive on the coming Saturday and asked me if I would take over the single rooms of the bungalow, as Norbhu was travelling heavy with his outfit on the way to Lhasa and would need to use the entire suite.

Regardless of what the day held for me I never began a day without my regular assignment of meditation and study, in consequence of which I found that I could handle my tasks more readily when they came around. On this day even an interpreter was unnecessary. I was able to explain everything that came up, and I felt that I was making definite progress with the language, which was getting into my system and becoming an integral part of it.

My mornings of meditation led me to give some thought on its absence in our Western world. There is the case of the successful business man who, on retirement, experiences a great deal of unhappiness after shutting himself off from that universal flow of life, which is the very thing that has brought him his success. Naturally, it is his invariable plan that as soon as he retires he will do as he pleases, only to discover that as soon as he cuts off this flow of life it becomes an impossibility ever to get it flowing again; he seems utterly unaware that it is that which has given him his greatest joy in his work. On the other hand, the Tibetan is taught the nature of this conscious flow of life, so that he is able to awaken it and make it flow through any channel he might choose; and if the particular channel of his choice experiences a stoppage, he still has the alternative of diverting the same flow to yet another channel. This knowledge has its obvious advantages for the individual in that it enables him to carry on with perfect consciousness of what is taking place, thus putting him in a position to extract so much more out of worldly activity and also to contribute more to human endeavor with much less suffering. On retirement from such a life, he is still able to continue his inner growth. In other words, he is taught by this ancient method to see the likely outcome of all external activities, and by this knowledge to choose and direct. He approaches all life with understanding, knows the sources of stimuli, and is able to penetrate beyond the fiction of worldly forms. Thus also he finds solace, and adjustment to misfortune, pain, discomfort, and grief; for there are precise laws which govern all of these phenomena.

On the day of Rai Sahib Wangdi's visit there was a parade at the fort, and I went around to get a few pictures as well as discharge a social duty, Captain Cable having invited Jigme and Mary. Jigme happened to be a Tibetan military leader, though the Tibetans as a rule do not take the military profession seriously. It is true that little by little they are learning something about it from their outside contacts. Jigme, of course, had the advantage of a European training, rare enough among Tibetans, who are a race of stay-at-homes. The late Dalai Lama, however, sent four boys to England, and one of them, after finishing preparatory school, stayed on for several years for further study; he was at the time of my pilgrimage in charge of the electric light plant of Lhasa. It is surprising how proud they are of their electric city, as they call it. From what I heard they had small electric irons and similar minor gadgets, which held a peculiar fascination for them, as they did in our own country when electricity was first introduced.

After the military parade, which took place under a clear sky, providing ideal conditions for mine and Jigme's photographic efforts, we took part in the polo game; then accepted our host's invitation to tiffin. The repast was only an interlude between games. It is odd to reflect that strangers from the corners of the earth meeting in the heart of Tibet cannot keep the conversation going, but must resort to games. This, too, was not without its lesson.

Back in my bungalow, I gazed out of the window across those vast plateaus and watched the dance of the late evening shadows, and all inner restlessness was promptly settled. If I could have been left alone with the Tibetans, all would have been perfect. Although their imaginations do not extend beyond their own physical surroundings, they at least live their limited existence to its fullest and are eager to talk about things of interest concerning their teachings and literature. There is but little doubt that theirs is the way of attaining a greater spiritual development at the end of life and in this life. The circumstances of my own existence at this moment, however, left me no alternative but to yield to such activities as were in store for me. Indeed, I was awaiting the arrival of Colonel —— ——* on the morrow, and that my next five days would be very much at his disposal. He would then return to India, while at the same time Captain Cable would be going down to Yatung for ten days. As for myself, my fate would surely be settled by then, and I should either turn my footsteps toward Lhasa or in the reverse direction to India. In the meantime there would be more polo on Saturday and some races on Monday, and on the morrow Tharchin should be arriving at Lhasa, and I should soon know the best, or the worst. My heart counselled patience.

Next morning, with the help of my boys, I moved over to the other side of the bungalow, in preparation for the arrival of Norbhu.

*I cannot now recall his name.

5

I spent a large part of the day in going over the ritual used by the reformed Tibetan church (*Gelupa*). It should be remarked here that at the time of the introduction of Buddhism into Tibet from India there were several strongholds of the Christian faith on the Chinese border of Tibet. The Tibetans had some contact with these, which accounts for all sorts of survivals of Christian ritual in Tibet. In the year 1300, we are told, there were several Catholic priests living in the Holy City, and though they remained for some years they made scarcely a convert during their entire stay. A great deal of their ritual, however, was taken over and incorporated in the Tibetan faith, with modifications, by the ruling caste of the country. In the course of time, however, various disagreements crept up, with the result that some of the ritual was dispensed with, leaving only their external forms.

Some scholars of India assert that their ancient sages, aware of the limitations of the human mind, had built up an elaborate system of ritual for the benefit of the great masses which lack the capacity for comprehension. The entire ritual of Hinduism has been developed upon this. The original teachings, however, which came from the *Tantras* have been lost; and today the scholars call the prevailing practices degenerate and attribute all the other undermining influences to be found in the religion of India to this source. With the coming, however, to Tibet of Padma Sambhava (whose reincarnation I am believed to be), there developed this elaborate body of Catholic ritual which makes up all the exoteric worship of the unreformed churches, the Kar-gyu-pa and Nying-ma-pa, along with much of that which is to be found in the regular practice of the established order. The happy mixture only helps to complicate matters. The real problem is not so much to separate the components as to try to trace the resulting product to the ritual of Catholicism, for how did it all arise, and how did it grow? It is true that the Greeks had a well-developed system as had all the other communal groups before the birth of Christianity. But whence came it? What was its beginning? Was there a common single source, or did it arise in several places simultaneously? Once in being, what processes furthered its development? What has been its purpose?

As for the ritualism of Hinduism, there are many written records available to tell us of its historical development, the *Tantras* providing the greatest encyclopedia of ancient wisdom inscribed by the sages. There are volumes and volumes on ritual alone, which answer some of our questions. Unfortunately, only a small part of these writings have been translated. For the most part they have been lost in India. Records of their existence, however, have been made by the Indian pundits (Sanskrit scholars). It is believed that they will eventually be discovered in Tibet. In the life of Padma Sambhava, which I have been lately translating, it is recorded that he left eighteen volumes, embracing all the *Tantras*, for which I have also been searching. If it is my good fortune to dig up these books, between them I should be able to fill in many gaps in the picture. The theory of life as taught by the *Tantras* is the reverse of our evolutionary theory. It is, indeed, a devolutionary theory of mankind, with some evidence in its favor. For the moment, however, we must pass this over and keep our eyes on the development of the ritual.

Above all, we should like to know how it came to pass that all these complicated ritualistic systems should have developed throughout the world, more or less isolated from one another. Beside this, the question of the beginnings of the major religions is a relatively simple one. For one thing, it is interesting to observe the many similarities to be found among such peoples as our American Indians and the Tibetans. How has it happened that there exists a tribe called the Hemis Indians in the United States and that at the same time there is the great Hemis monastery in Tibet? Both have their devil dances. In Tibet there is the *Garuda* bird, while the Indians have their thunder bird, which is its equivalent. Indeed, such similarities between the tribes of the world—as well as differences, of course—are infinite; but if I mention the American Indian it is because he is so remote from Tibet.

It is taught by the *Tantras* that life first began around the North Pole, and not in Egypt, as is the theory of Elliott Smith. All their earliest lore expresses the notion that humanity in those days consisted of supermen; but ultimately the process of disintegration set in, and the continuing story is very much like that of Adam and Eve. Climatic changes followed, humanity broke up into small bands, migrating southward. Those who wrote down the *Tantras* for the benefit of men to come had settled in India, while others fled to various parts of the world; nevertheless, the great stronghold remained here.

It is pertinent to note that the myths of so many races indicate their origin as in some place in the North. One thing seems clear: all the ritual of the Western world has been influenced by the *Tantras*. And, if this is true, it makes little difference whether the Tibetans borrowed it from Hinduism or Christianity; we do know that in either instance it had been devised for the same purpose as it was borrowed. I am putting this down as a matter of record, as something that has come up in the course of my studies and throws some light at the issues discussed. I did not come to Tibet to prove anything or to teach any one anything, but only to learn. It was clear, however, that I must accept the Tibetan teachings with a free and open mind and not have formed any preconceptions at this moment, allowing any judgment to come only after many, many years of concentrated study on such manuscripts as are available to me, which might enable me to see into some of the problems here suggested. It seems to me that nothing is so difficult in life as the beginning: the search for the problem. Once the problem has been established and well formulated, it is relatively easy to examine and tabulate the records. My chief effort at this time was to organize the available literature.

6

While sitting in the cave of solitary confinement and reviewing the details of the great experience I found no small difficulty in trying to separate those early experiences from the names and forms of Tibetan culture and to recall to mind the various reflections that came with them, and at the same time to recapture the original attitude and mood forever gone because of the various initiations that I had been able to pass through.

The mind's inherent potentiality is activity, which is no respecter of forms but will attach itself to any available external manifestation, and if this be lacking it will turn upon itself, and consciously learn to know itself in the universal energy of life. It is in this that is to be found the purpose underlying the teachings of "mindlessness" in Buddhism, for which Yoga is the tool. The reason for my being in the isolated cave was that I might be sure of all the external names and forms, and, once they could be eliminated, the mind might be enabled to turn upon itself. Yet it was precisely at this point that I found my greatest difficulty in maintaining the thread of my external experiences, as the more of them I removed by bringing them before my mind's consciousness the easier I made the task of the subconscious to break through and express itself. What the mind accomplishes is of little consequence; what is important is that the inner self should experience an accession of power, that universal energy called *Chit*, which is the life source of the individual. It is felt that we have laid stress on the consequence of life and made it our goal, instead of putting our emphasis on life itself, that is why we suffer if we fail to attain the desired end. If we could reverse the direction of our efforts, all such consequences would be ours without the asking. According to Tibetan teachings, the direction of life in the Western world is all wrong, this explains why we look upon all our effort as a confused, chaotic mass of an infinite variety of irreconcilable forms.

7

The message which I had been anxiously awaiting came; it told of Tharchin's arrival in Lhasa. And now I even more ardently awaited another telegraphic message, telling me that I had an invitation to visit the Sacred City. Knowing how slowly things were done, I did not expect any kind of a message for at least a week. Only one thing might make them act quickly, and this was the announcement of the discovery of the new Dalai Lama, and since I could hardly fill that rôle, I had no alternative but to exercise patience.

The same day I received a message from Spencer Chapman, telling me of his successful ascent of Chumolhari, a beautiful peak of which I have already spoken in this narrative. This meant that he had climbed the highest peak yet reached by man, a feat which required courage and endurance, to be remembered thereafter and to serve as an inspiration to others who will follow after him. I could not help feeling a personal interest and pleasure, for I had lent a modest hand in his final arrangements. Now he was off to London after a very successful year's stay in India, having accomplished this ascent as well as having spent six months in Lhasa as private secretary to Mr.

Gould and as official photographer to the English Mission. A man to envy.

All that morning and late that night mules went on arriving, bringing the personal effects of Norbhu, who would be with us tomorrow, *en route* to Lhasa to relieve Mr. Richardson, who would return to Gantok via Shigatsé. From here on, into Lhasa, there are no accommodations, so one must provide one's own. The advance transport consists mainly of tents, and a vast amount of other travelling paraphernalia. A caravan, such as the high officials and wealthy landlords of Tibet take when they make a move, presents a sight of great interest. It is almost a small city in itself. In keeping with the custom of the country, there will be multitudes to meet Norbhu on the morrow at the fourth mile. It is the practice to meet the incoming traveller, so the welcomers might accompany him on the final lap of his journey; likewise, when he takes his departure a farewell party accompanies him for some miles. When one has travelled for days over the dark plains, one can understand the meaning of this revelation of esteem. The traveller being a native Tibetan elevated to his position by the foreign British political office, his own countrymen conceive an admiration for him; in consequence of which he is honored by both sides wherever he goes. This, of course, is what the English want, and explains why he has been chosen for the job. He has risen to his rank because of his great capacity and many qualifications, to say nothing of his vital personality.

My evident anxiety to go to Lhasa prompted Captain Cable to have some fun with me, and he was forever at his leg-pulling. Thus, in an apparently earnest manner he mentioned the man from America who was looking for a 1700-year-old Yogi near Gyantsé, and asked me if I had ever met this mysterious sage who made herculean but fruitless efforts to enter the forbidden land. Then, to rub it in, he spoke of a Swede who had similar ambitions and made a successful crossing of the border, only to be rounded up and returned to India. And these were by no means isolated cases. Therefore, it seemed all the more astonishing that here was I "carrying on," with every one lending a helping hand. And now if fate should deal me the winning card and send me to Lhasa, it would merely emphasize the mystery of why the bars have been so unaccountably let down in my case, and it would instil deeper than ever before into my heart the already growing desire to gain a real understanding of the Tibetan teachings, so that others who have striven or are still striving to reach this forbidden corner might learn through me all that which they are seeking to know. An immodest ambition on my part? Perhaps. Yet, considering the matter realistically, they have nothing to lose and something to gain; for if those who have come and, after catching a glimpse of the streets, were promptly despatched under escort to India, with no prospect of return, might I not compensate them a little by reporting what I have seen?

Yet, for all my good fortune so far, I was not without misgivings, and hoped with all my heart that if I were denied Lhasa I might at least be permitted to remain a while here in Gyantsé and continue my studies. The opportunity for this seemed auspicious, as the Europeans were leaving and I should have no alternative but to devote my entire time to work.

8

Once the Colonel and his wife and Captain Cable arrived, the day was spent at cricket and eating. At four we had a large tea party and we wound up the day with a fine dinner at the officers' mess. The party was given in celebration of Norbhu's arrival, for which Jigme and Mary had come into town at dawn in their lovely silk brocades. To see Jigme with his graceful figure attired in silks would drive any society woman wild with envy; and if the silks weren't enough, his long hair was done up with the official crown of turquoise, set off with a red ribbon skilfully woven into the long braids; this is an added touch hard to surpass. It must be confessed that a personality has something to do with the appearance of distinction; Jigme has all the polish and finesse of a salon favorite. You wonder how he could have achieved it in this part of the world, but my experience so far has been that all the refinement of traditional culture to be found among this class of Tibetans has had its roots in China. The Colonel proved a stimulating figure in the interesting and enlightening conversation.

For the Colonel's further entertainment a series of races was planned for the following day; sweepstake tickets were put on sale, with 50 rupees as the first prize, and a saddle as the second. We hit upon the brilliant idea of playing roulette, and we used the money to buy tickets, with the first three winners dividing up the tickets on the agreed ratio. We got an entertaining evening out of this, and it kept us up until one. Now and then the incongruity of it struck me—I mean the idea of a pilgrim like myself indulging in such ultra-Western pastimes; yet who knows, may there not be something in detaching one self from the other, and have one examine the other with that penetration which comes at such odd moments?

There was life to see, social duties to accomplish; I thought the following day would never come to an end. In any case, I managed my routine schedule up to nine o'clock, when it was time to leave for the big event. The whole countryside turned out for the occasion. Indeed, I scarcely recognized the place; the entire parade ground had been converted into an extensive race course with large tents and a grandstand, under which were easy chairs for honored guests; there were flowering potted plants, and a carpet under your feet, which made you feel as if you were the guest of some powerful potentate or sheik. The grandstand bordered on another large enclosure, which held the ticket office; it was doing a rushing business all day. The track itself had been with miraculous expedition fenced off, and there were several corrals for the animals: dogs, regimental ponies, country ponies, amblers, mules, and yaks, all of them participating in the various races, each race according to its own class.

The first heat of the day was a first-class dog race of Tibetan mongrels. Their owners were even more interesting than the dogs, for they were the raggedest bunch of urchins that I have ever seen come together in the hope of winning something. The fact is, the winning boy proved to be the littlest, filthiest, and uncomeliest youngster of all. His dog won both races, and, as a result, he got a nice handful of rupees, probably more money than he had seen since the previous year, when his mongrel won a similar race. The excitement caused by this race was almost incredible; and even such high personages as the Raja Tering, Norbhu, Mary, and Jigme, the Colonel and his wife, Siddique (head of the Commissary department), were all fervent bettors. The odd part of it is, none of them would disclose to the other on which animal he or she placed bets. Anyhow, the fun indulged in by all in this remote spot at 13,000 feet altitude was scarcely different from the fun to be had at our Western races, and the animals fought just as hard for place as they do with us at sea-level. It is astounding how much excitement can be worked up for a little play, and the Tibetan hardly needs any excuse to drop everything and go forth to have some fun out of doors; and he loves his out-of-doors mightily.

The dog race was more exciting for what you heard than for what you saw. Owing to the wind from which this country is rarely free, all you saw was an onrushing cloud of dust, and out of this cloud of dust you heard an ungodly yelping, ever

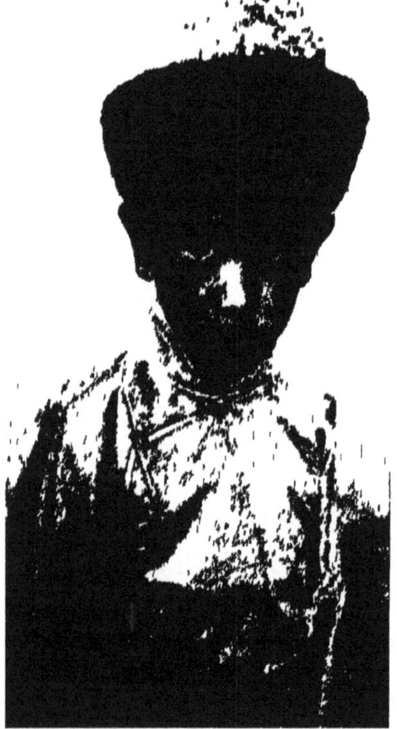

Tibetan children

approaching nearer. The dust pervades everything, you eat dirt all day long, until your lips are parched, tongue thick, and lungs outraged. The Tibetan seems to be accustomed to this, and accepts it as a matter of course.

Once the regimental horse race was over, the real fun began; for it was never possible to tell what would happen in the races of the remaining motley assortment of animals. I placed a bet on one of the mules. He took off down the track, as though it was a sure thing, but just as he was about to make the last curve he decided that it would be more fun to go straight on ahead, and by the time he was convinced that this was a mistake he was hopelessly far behind. And so the race went on, until the last beast had crossed the finish line. It was very entertaining to watch those who had entries beating their animals in the effort to make them do something—anything—it mattered not what. Nothing on earth is more stubborn than a mule, and these were superb examples of the beast with a will to balk.

Another entertaining event was the yak race. Half-way one yak had the race all to himself, so far ahead was he of the rest; then, for no accountable reason, his yak intelligence decided that walking was easier, and far more restful. Thus, with its ups and downs, the race went on. I went up to the finish line to make a few shots with my camera at the end, and just as I changed my position to take close-ups of the winner I was forced quickly to swerve, for the yaks were unceremoniously making a stampede for me. The race ended in confusion.

Some of the sidelights were as interesting as the races themselves. All along the wall, behind the pens, were large mobs of people in a state of almost continual excitement. On investigating it, I discovered that Tibetan gamblers had brought their games to the gathering; between events the onlookers tried their luck. The chief game is one with dice. Behind it sits a man with a large outspread cloth covered with various designs, resembling somewhat those used on our cards. The dice are the same as our dice. They are placed in a small box which is shaken, after which they are flung out on to the cloth, and if your choice is exactly as the dice turn out to be, you win; otherwise, the house takes all. As often as not a member of the mob puts his last coin on the game, with the enthusiasm of a small child. Such gambling is the common pastime of the petty traders and beggars.

By the time every one was so exhausted that he or she could not look even friendly, let alone speak a kind word to any one, the big event of the day came on, and since we had stayed up half the night before in order to win tickets, the big drawing was held, and if you had the number you got the horse corresponding to it. The horses were lined up, and made the start. Everything looked hopeful for the first few hundred yards, but the leaders began to wrangle, while the horses which had failed to start suddenly made a wild dash for it, throwing everything into confusion. At the next curve matters were more or less straightened, and all horses were in order, except the few which were running about in circles and raising the dust, whole clouds of dust. A single horse emerged out of the dust cloud, to take the first prize, until some one discovered the fact that he had made but a single lap, which caused a great hullabaloo; for there was a prize of 50 rupees at stake. Two servants of Raja Tering, who had chipped in 4 annas each to purchase a single ticket, won the race; and well that it was so. Nothing could have been more embarrassing than to have one of us win, seeing that we held half of the tickets.

Then came the final events, the drawing of the saddle, for which we had also bought no end of tickets. As it happened, Captain Cable won. Not that the fellow could help it. He had only five tickets on the saddle out of the several hundreds that were sold. Each time he drew his luck held, and in all fairness he had to take it. This climaxed one of the dustiest days I ever hope to survive.

The day came to an end with tiffin at the officers' mess, after which we took the usual round of photographs. The Terings had a long drive to their place, and Norbhu was scheduled to leave the following morning for Shigatsé; so the party broke up rather abruptly.

9

This was by no means the end of the social activities. The following morning held a polo game for me, after which I went to the Terings' to join in a Tibetan dinner. Reluctant as I was to give up another precious day, there was no way out of the situation. On the other hand, I had a fairly reassuring talk with Mary and Jigme, who were doing all in their power to procure for me the much-desired invitation to Lhasa. Mary told me that her sister, Mrs. Tsarong, whom I had met at Kalimpong during the winter, was actively interested in my plans and was doing everything to help me, putting in a good word for me on every possible occasion where it might do some good. The Terings had a great feeling of friendship for everything American, and as they were among the most powerful families in all Tibet, Mary thought my chances of going to Lhasa were exceedingly good. Mary herself had written to one of her relatives, an influential Government official, urging that permission be given me. Yet it is all a slow process of the greatest uncertainty, and, for all the assurances, I realized the folly of taking things for granted.

The tinkling of the bells of toil that hang on the necks of all the pack animals of Tibet reminded me that it was time for Norbhu to start for Shigatsé; so I hustled to bid him farewell. Preoccupied as I was with my heart's desire, I found myself wishing that he were at that moment at Lhasa pleading my case for me; for he was a good friend and a word from him would have gone a long way. Just now you would have thought that he was going to a fancy-dress ball, for he was clad in a new costume of the finest silk brocade. The incongruity of it was that he had thirty miles of the dustiest trail in the world ahead of him. And there would be the further contrast of the hosts of petty traders and beggars in rags from the seven frontiers of Tibet he would encounter en route. To seek a contrast further afield, just place beside Norbhu's costume one of our own dinner jackets with its unalterably monotonous pattern of black and white, the product of a shamefully limited imagination. Let us not waste our time, however, on futile reflections. There are important things ahead.

Tharchin had now been in Lhasa for several days, and as yet there was no news from him. I was not one to sit still with folded hands while my fate was being settled, and so I wired him to find out how things were developing. When the answering wire arrived, it was full of hope, but not an iota of precise evidence on which to build up my faith. They were all like that. "You're going to be invited" was the customary response; but of any material indication—none. Thus I continued in suspense, hatching momentary schemes for stirring things up in this matter of Lhasa.

Then a telegram came. I shall never forget it as long as I live. It was from the King Regent of Tibet. Here it is:

> BERNARD OF AMERICA, GYANTSÉ. RECEIVED YOUR LETTER. HOPE YOU RECEIVED WIRE FROM KASHAG THAT YOUR MUCH RELIGIONSHIP MAY VISIT LHASA AS YOUR DESIRE. WIRE IF YOU NEED DWELLING HERE.
>
> (SIGNED) REGENT.

Too Good to Be True

10

It seemed too good to be true. Now that the permission I had been so ardently seeking had come, now that I had gained my heart's desire, I experienced the temporary mood, a reaction perhaps of the long suspense under which I had been living, that it made little or no difference whether I went or not. This was quickly followed by a mood of exhilaration, of the prescience of the thrill of realization yet to come. There had come to me the knowledge that what had been a dream was on the verge of being translated into reality. This knowledge energized me, set me feverishly to work to make the final preparations for the final lap of my journey. Little did I realize that, in a sense, my real work would begin only upon my arrival in the Sacred City.

It is a human trait to feel unbounded satisfaction in achieving something which others, in spite of tremendous effort, have not been able to achieve. So many interested in Tibetan Buddhism had tried for years, to no avail, to make a religious pilgrimage to the Sacred City, the Mecca of all Meccas. It seemed incomprehensible even to myself why I of all persons should have been so richly favored. Certainly, my reception by the religious orders gave me the confident feeling that I would be granted the opportunity to enter every shrine in Lhasa as well as have the tutorship of all their learned ones. To look at this from the other side of the world, it would seem as a victory over insurmountable obstacles. When one is so close to it, it seems commonplace—until you learn of the impossibility of getting there. Indeed, it had all to be done under cover, so to speak; for if it had even gotten out that I was trying to get there, there would have been short shrift for me; such news had to leak out slowly, and only in the right places. The greatest thrill of all this had been the task of trying to bring it about.

Actually, the idea had never entered my mind until I finally settled at Kalimpong in order to study the language; and in order to gain what I had gained, it was essential to learn not only the language, but the religion, as well as the manners and customs of a people. With it all, came the inevitable knowledge of their psychology, the attitude to be assumed towards them, the art of dealing with them and being friendly with them.

This was no time, however, for a complacent resting on one's oars. There were so many things to be done preliminary to the journey: photographic equipment to be attended to, arrangements to be made for provisions, a rush order to be sent to Calcutta for gifts which I should have to present on my arrival at Lhasa. Not having any too much faith, I had brought with me only what was absolutely essential. I had heard of too many disappointments to drag along with me a superfluity of chattels. Perhaps I had too much pride to run the risk of seeming foolish. Had I failed it would have been too much like the elephant walking up the hill and down again.

I set to work to review everything I had already done. I had a fairly complete library of externals which I had read and which I now re-read, in order to formulate for myself the problems which would help to reveal the source of the life of Tibet. The purpose was to penetrate to the bottom of its religious teaching, for therein lies the secret of the driving power in the past and the waning framework of today. Why has it been able to survive these hundreds of years? What is the cause of its breakdown? No race of men in the whole world remains as untouched as the race of Tibetans. Why is this the case? Why, indeed, with four world potentates trying their best to conquer them? On the other hand, a breakdown is surely coming. Through what avenues will it proceed, and why must it come? Is the entire past to be discarded, or will something be salvaged? What is it that has made these people collect the writings of the ancients and worship them as sacred truth in spite of almost complete ignorance of their meanings? How much of it all is truth, and how much the usual empty ritualistic forms which are to be found throughout the world?

It was important to find the answers to all these questions. It was essential to peer beyond, in order to sound bottom. As it is with the hidden mineral rock of the world, one does not see the precious metal, but for one provided with knowledge it is possible to predict 999 times out of a 1000 what minerals will be found there. So it is with the hidden elements of life. One begins learning to understand a character, then one examines the facts in the light of this knowledge, after which it becomes fairly predictable what is in store for this or that person, even though the persons themselves are unaware of their own futures, and are equally lacking in a comprehension of the probable outcome of the events we and the world are constantly experiencing.

Looking forward to the journey, it came upon me, and by no means unpleasantly, that I should have to make it wholly on my own, with no companion who could speak English. That, I thought, should be an excellent thing, as it would make me feel really at one with the country and with the mood of my adventure.

II

I also used the interval of waiting in taking stock of myself, of my advantages and limitations, weighed in the light of my own experience.

At various times in my past I had been taken to task for neglecting so many things in Western culture. Why should I have neglected these in favor of almost incomprehensible volumes on an esoteric culture? And, indeed, at times I had been made to feel in the wrong, and again and again I wavered, forced as

I was to wonder to what end it could all be leading. And now, as I was being swept up toward the crest of my adventure, it dawned upon me perhaps for the first time with astonishing clairvoyance that this was what I had been preparing for my entire life, and that some inner urge had been driving me and directing me toward some mysterious yet definite goal, from which I could not deviate without violating my best inner self, at any rate, that self, which was in every sense *I*, the whole *I*, liberated however from all petty personal preoccupations. To be sure, for fifteen years I had been building up the consciousness for the absorption of all that was about to be offered me. I saw that it took more than a mere grasp of all factual material to understand the meaning of the highly complicated system of ritual. The essential truth was in itself simple enough. This could be grasped only by means of the feeling.

What seems wrong with the world today is that human beings have emphasized the development of the mind and that so-called "brilliancy" has been accorded the highest place, the one thing to gain the rewards of society. Unhappily, our own country furnishes a classic example of this. The conversation of almost any group is about what this brilliant mind has or has not got. On a first acquaintance with any one, even with a small child, the first comment is, "What a brilliant mind!" But one never stops to consider: What sort of imagination does he have? What capacity does he have for feeling? Does he possess a rich consciousness? Does he have an understanding which comes from contact with the flow of life rather than an understanding from a familiarity with the external facts of life? Does he grasp the significance of one and the other? Our school system singularly neglects the problem of the development of the imagination; it makes no designed effort to awaken the poet, the musician, the philosopher. No, it is concerned with teaching one the technical laws of versification, of music, of philosophy, and of the history of these things; then condemns the individual for taking no spontaneous interest in the arts it has taught him. Technique is taught, but not the secret of tapping the flow for which technique should merely serve as the craft for making the molds to receive it. This is where Yoga comes in, for Yoga provides a control over this fountain of life, and gives the individual a chance to use it constantly and at will.

12

There was excitement in the air, and wires flew back and forth between Gyantsé and Lhasa as fast as the line would permit. Arrangements were being made for a place for me to stay during my visit. At the same time Mr. Richardson was getting an extension of time on my Tibetan pass. One by one, everything was being taken care of. Here in Gyantsé things were being rushed to get my transport together, so that everything could leave on scheduled time. The bungalow was in a state of confusion, with endless boxes stacked about the place, while we separated the things we had to take from those which we were to leave behind, to be picked up on our return. At times I could hardly believe that I was actually making preparations for a journey to Lhasa. Indeed, I constantly lived in fear of something arising to prevent it.

To one thing I had made up my mind. I should endeavor to cling to my chosen subject, that of the monasteries of Tibet, which had never been dealt with to any extent by other explorers. Considering the opportunities I should have of visiting all the sacred shrines, I felt it to be my duty to give details to the outside world which held an interest in this aspect of things. Originally, while still at Kalimpong, I had intended to collect what material I could about the monasteries I had already seen, and to crown the record with the monastic gem at Gyantsé. Now, however, with Lhasa within sight, the horizon widened, and it was all the more incumbent upon me to carry on. Yet, I realized, too, the length of my stay at Lhasa was still an uncertainty, and I might be forced to crowd the work of years into the brief period of a few weeks.

Returned travellers tell us little of the treasured faith which keeps the Tibetan race in poverty while they erect a tomb of solid gold, covered with precious stones, for the late Dalai Lama. You will not meet a Tibetan from Lhasa who does not go into ecstasies about this famous treasure. What is it that has inspired the imagination to design such a building as the great palace? Waddell, indeed, speaks of the "unartistic Tibetan," then goes on for pages to provide a detailed account of the beauty of this divine structure.

The bulk of the literature attendant on the Younghusband expedition into Lhasa was written from the military point of view. The English, as respecters of the rights of others, made no attempt to intrude in any way upon the religious predilections of the Tibetans. They presented the terms of their mission, which was to negotiate a peaceful treaty establishing trade relations; in no sense did they wish to influence their religious thought or custom. At all times they stuck strictly to business. It is true, they did make a record of the external facts of the forms of the Tibetan religion. It was very much as if a Tibetan had come to America and visited St. John's the Divine and one or two of our other great cathedrals, then returned to his native land and offered detailed descriptions of the buildings and of the people as they came to worship in the morning, the choir, the prayers, and the sermons, without telling what the prayers and the sermons were about. Again, the record the English made, while offering brief descriptions of the physical stature of the people, and of their attire, say little or nothing of the function of the individual, nothing of the inner soul of the Tibetan.

Here I saw a country wholly isolated from the rest of the world; its aim has been to keep out all the effects of the spinning Western civilization; and the only records available to the Western world comprised descriptions of external forms. And at once I realized my rare opportunity, all the more as I had now the promise of becoming the guest of one of the most powerful and wealthy individuals of Tibet, and he one who had risen to his exalted and influential position from the lowest strata of society. Now, what is the avenue by which an individual may ascend from rags to silks? How does the society function in which this can happen? How does the individual function? What is the relation of the rest of society towards the individual who has made such a material—and spiritual—victory? Is he a solitary example, or do other bundles of rags bear the potentiality and the choice of rising to silks? If these questions are answered, other questions will be answered with them, directly or by implication. It had been my desire, and now it had become my intention, of learning to look at life through the eyes and consciousness of a Tibetan.

These thoughts were rudely interrupted by a hammering, a sawing by the *mystery* (the Indian name for carpenter) who had come to make the necessary boxes for the extra things it was necessary to take along on my journey.

13

About nine-thirty I heard the tinkling of bells, the usual prelude to the arrival of the animals of some traveller. Upon investigation by one of my boys, it turned out to be Mary and Jigme, who, on their way to Shigatsé, were stopping to say good-bye to me.

Over tea we talked with joyous fervor of my good fortune. Plans were made for a celebration on my return, when I would meet them either at Kalimpong or Calcutta; for in July they would be making pilgrimage to India. They seemed even more happy than I over my coming journey; and, indeed, Mary and her sister had played considerable rôles in my obtaining the invitation. They gave me some parting directions, and told of sights not to miss on the way, all the more as this was the most beautiful time of the year for a journey to Lhasa.

I have already spoken of Norbhu's manner of travelling, which made me think of a fancy dress ball. And now I had another opportunity of seeing how a high Tibetan travels. Along with his regular official headdress of turquoise mounted on a conical hat draped with red tassels hanging down from the point, dropping around the edge, he wore a beautiful silk brocade gown with its brilliant yellow waistcoat of the same material. He gave the appearance of being scarcely two minutes from a tailor's shop, and here he had come seven miles and had yet another thirty ahead of him. Mary likewise was adorned in all her jewels.

Scarcely had Mary and Jigme taken their departure, when the telegraph boy came bringing a message from the *Kashag*. I reproduce it here, without comment:

> BERNARD OF AMERICA, GYANTSÉ: RECEIVED YOUR LETTER WHICH WE SENT UP TO THE REGENT PRIME MINISTER STOP AS YOU PROBABLY KNOW TIBET BEING A PURELY RELIGIOUS COUNTRY THERE IS A GREAT RESTRICTION ON FOREIGNERS ENTERING THE COUNTRY BUT UNDERSTANDING THAT YOU HAVE A GREAT RESPECT FOR OUR RELIGION AND HAVE HOPES OF SPREADING THE RELIGION IN AMERICA ON YOUR RETURN, WE HAVE DECIDED AS A SPECIAL CASE TO ALLOW YOU TO COME TO LHASA BY THE MAIN ROAD FOR A THREE WEEKS VISIT.
>
> (SIGNED) KASHAG.

At the same time a message came from the political officer, giving me a six-weeks' extension of my pass from the date of its termination; this meant that I need not leave Tibet until August. I already began to wonder what would happen by then. Anything was possible, I was beginning to believe.

Though the Regent rules over everything through the administration of his cabinet known as the *Kashag*, whose signature to the telegram should have been good enough to secure me in all respects, I had still a number of minor difficulties to overcome. Petty officialdom is perhaps the same the world over, and here I had my *Jongpens* to deal with. A *Jongpen*, I must explain, is the head of a district corresponding to one of our states. Each district has its own *Jongpen*, who rules over a *Jong* —a fort, which serves as the county seat. Actually, the whole thing is more or less the old feudal system under the guidance of Heaven, the system which we left behind in the Middle Ages. Now in order to make a move it is necessary to procure a passport from the *Jongpen* in charge; otherwise the head men of the villages *en route* will not render the traveller any assistance. Gyantsé was in one district, Lhasa was in another.

The fact is, the prevailing red tape associated with officialdom gave rise to a series of irritations, all the more irksome because it involved delays, and I was anxious to set off. I saw the prospect of good days slipping away. Worse luck, transport in Tibet might be secured only on two days' notice; and, indeed, I am ashamed to admit that as a last resort I was forced to utilize the power of the almighty rupee, and happy to say that it worked.

14

On returning to the bungalow, I presently had a call from Siddique, the Mohammedan in charge of the Commissary department at the British fort. Little did I dream of coming to Tibet for instruction in the teachings of Mohammed, but such turned out to be the case. Siddique and I spent the next three hours in a heated discussion of the principles of Mohammedanism, comparing its teachings with those taught by the other great religious leaders of the world. Oddly enough, we reached perfect agreement, with the sole difference that he will remain a Mohammedan and I shall go on to Lhasa, and not to Mecca. There is, indeed, no question about all religious teaching heading for the same goal, with a different teacher for each group and every leader working on the same principle of human nature, the principle that the only way to develop the spirit is by first gaining control over the mind; this is to be achieved by means of concentration. For this purpose endless ritual has been devised in order to help the ignorant masses who lack the will power to do it otherwise. But for those of greater capacity, all such inventions are as unnecessary as is the Chinese adding machine when we have the more efficient modern ones. For this reason there is but little need of going into the pros and cons of this time-old discussion. We might as well at the start accept the fact that all the religions are headed in the same direction, and that they have an important rôle to play in the life of the individual. In many instances we may be able to modify old forms or substitute new ones, but never can we get away from the fundamental principles, or smother the spiritual aspiration that burns in the heart of every man and gives the basis for the existence of every religion on earth.

For the time being there was the morrow to look forward to, the morrow, when I should start for the City of the Gods, averaging about thirty-two miles a day, and by no means easy miles, for I had yet to cross the Khambu La, ranging almost 17,000 feet, and nearly always covered with ice, so that regardless of what time of year one moves in this part of the world it is certain that he will encounter snow. Restless and impatient as I am by nature, matters always move too slowly for me, and there is a decided disadvantage in the Tibetan slowness when not able to cuss in the language which I must henceforth use. If I had to live this adventure over again, I should certainly learn this aspect of things before I undertook to study the legitimate literature of the country.

CHAPTER V

FROM GYANTSÉ TO LHASA

I

THE day of days is here. I can scarcely believe it. There must be a mistake that this privilege is being offered to me. If one could read my heart, this feeling of incredulousness would be easy to understand.

The day started bright and sleepy about three-thirty. The reason for this early rising was that I anticipated trouble with getting the transport started, and I knew that I could do something to urge matters along. As a result of my strenuous efforts, the entire transport was off by seven, and with it on the way I could sit down to enjoy my bowl of oatmeal, until it was time to be off to the telegraph office to despatch some cables and wires. I had the little fellow in charge on the jump.

At nine-thirty I was off to find the road to Lhasa across fields of wheat and up large gulches, until I had the feeling that I was on the wrong track; whereupon we retraced our footsteps and took another direction. We found our trail. It gets mighty thin at times, so that one has to look sharply. The problem is to find again and again the telegraph line, and follow in its direction. Regardless of where the road is, as long as it does not go up over some inaccessible cliff it will be possible for us to find our way.

The road is exactly like any barren strip across the mining section of Arizona and New Mexico, canyons of rock and soil rising up sharply on either side of you for several hundred feet, with a small river rushing through at the bottom. The only difference is that such places in the West provide no water, while here there is water everywhere because of the perpetual snows that feed these streams.

It gave me an unaccountable sensation and thrill to be heading towards Lhasa in the company of a chap who could speak nothing but Tibetan, and I was feeling highly pleased with myself because in so short a time I had mastered it sufficiently to be able to make a real use of it.

In any event, I was appreciative of my good fortune, as mentally I made a note of my predecessors. Since the time of Manning in 1811, the only persons who reached the Mecca of Buddhism were Kawoguchi, a Nipponese; Sarat Chandra Das, an Indian; Madame David-Neale, a Frenchwoman, and Wm. McGovern; and every one of these had had to steal his or her way in one disguise or another. The only person ever to receive an invitation to visit Lhasa was Mr. Cutting. Other persons to enter the Holy City were Europeans connected with the British Mission; but these entered by force of arms. And, of course, going farther back into history, there were the Catholic priests, the first being Friar Odoric in 1330; then no one else until the Austrian Jesuit, Grueber, came in 1662, accompanied by the Belgian, Count Dorville. The next group followed in 1706, when the Capuchin Fathers, Joseph E. Asculi and Francesco de Tour, came, and soon after them, in 1716, two Jesuits, Desideri and Freyer, made the journey for the purpose of converting the heathen. Yes, and there was Nain Sing who reached the Forbidden City in 1866 and again in 1874, to be followed by A. Krishna (AK) on his second trip in 1878. The two last-named personages were connected with the Indian secret survey work, and by disguising themselves as natives they travelled the length and breadth of Tibet, revolving their prayer-wheels, which contained papers for geographical notations, and dropping off their beads at every hundred paces. These articles being of a religious nature, the customs officials never thought to examine them; consequently, their owners were able to bring their records back without any difficulty.

From this it could be seen that, considering the centuries, the number of outsiders who managed to get in was exceedingly small. In any event, never before had the Government permitted a foreigner to enter with the purpose of making a religious pilgrimage to the Holy City. The British, to be sure, now enter quite regularly for political reasons only, because they can always use the threat of force; but even they pay their visits usually accompanied by an armed guard, for the passes are still very dangerous. Indeed, it is not so long ago that a Nepalese was killed and robbed on his way over this very trail; so the journey is not wholly free of adventure and excitement. Mr. Cutting alone, accompanied by Varney, an Englishman, was allowed to enter on other than political grounds, but even in their case, as I learned later, their strong political connection, together with a plenitude of gifts sent many years ahead, was largely instrumental in securing the permission to enter.

2

The trail was interesting, in spite of its lack of vegetation; for I am used to the beauty to be found in nature in the nude. The entire valley was adorned with small monasteries hidden away in high ravines, each monastery marked on the road by a *mani*, a small wall built up on which there are paintings of the deity and the inscription of the sacred words:

"*Om! ma-ni pad-me Hum!*" ("Hail! The Jewel [Grand Lama] in the lotus-flower!"*

*The syllables of the sacred formula have been interpreted as follows: OM=of the Heavenly word, MA=of the World of Spirits; NI=of the Human World; PAD=World of the Animals, ME=of the World of Ghosts; HUM=of the Spaces of Hell. These are the six divisions in the Tibetan Wheel of Life.

If you are a believer in the faith, it is your custom to pass on the left side of this, and now I must be careful with every act. Along the river's edge are the homes of the more powerful landlords whose outside walls are decorated with the usual rows of red, white and blue stripes, and "prayer-flags," utilized as good-luck charms, posted along the corners of the roofs. Called "dragon-horses," these talismans reveal as the centre of the design a horse, which displays the mystic "Jewel" on its back, encircled by symbols of Indian-Chinese myths and mystical Buddhist incantations, to say nothing of divine invocations. To see one of these houses, one of these monasteries, or a single mile of this canyon, is to see all of the houses, all of the monasteries, the whole of the canyon. They are all so many slight variations on a single theme.

Here, for the first time, you do get the feeling that you are in a wholly new world as yet untouched by contact with Europeans. This is clearly evident even in such trifling things as the head-dresses of the men and passing travellers of the upper class, which you never see below Gyantsé. The novelty of it intensifies the excitement. Indeed, even the character of the people seems to be different. They do not show that sense of inferiority, of submission, which the English knock into every race with which they come into contact. It is a matter of speculation, however, as to how long this state of affairs will last. I fear not long, for the British are entrenching themselves nearer and nearer Lhasa, and it cannot be many years before one will see a railway coming up the Chumbi Valley, and the English will have a permanent post at Lhasa, as they have now at Gyantsé.

As for me, my delight increased with every step that I was receding from the Europeans. It was the feeling of Tibetan culture that I wanted to ingrain into my system; for a brief space at least I wanted wholly to eradicate every mood of my past, that I might with better grace don the new cloak of consciousness. The English could be neighbors to this culture for the next ten thousand years and still be stewing in their ignorance, without once thinking to ask a question and forever making damn sure that every one passes them by with the proper greeting. At moments I become so infuriated with this attitude that I wish I could wring every drop of English blood out of my veins, for I feel that they are absolutely lacking in imagination.

I wish that some of my finicky and delicate friends could be led through the same dark stables to their dinner table as I was to my would-be-lunch, which was consumed to the rhythm of the barking dogs chained at the entrance of every Tibetan house. The first thing you see on entering a Tibetan home is the stable, and out of the stable you climb up to where the native lives, and by the time you get into as low a stratum of society as I did on this particular day, you learn that the top floor is no better than the bottom. As I climbed up their ladder and raised my head above the floor, all that I could see was a big cloud of dust. Then I ascertained that they were cleaning a spot for me to sit. After finding my way through this screen of yak-dung dust, I discovered a chap spitting on the table which I was to use, in order to brighten it up a bit. My attention was distracted, however, by the appearance of the next character, a woman who had no more upper lip than I have a tail, which did not prevent her from greeting me. I've seen hare-lips before, but this one would have won the highest award anywhere. They stared at me, fascinated by my cup of tea and cracker with a piece of sardine hanging over the edge of it. They all had to sit and watch me, just as at breakfast, before leaving that morning, I had to watch the muleteers sit around their pot of *chang* and see them consume their handful of barley flour.

What gave me a real jolt was when I had to urinate. After ducking around all the corners that could be found, and thinking I was perfectly safe from observers, the old girl of the house had to come around to have a chat with me about nothing while I was in the middle of the performance. Then and there I sensibly decided that I was now in Tibet and must act accordingly. I promptly discarded my embarrassment in tune with her nonchalance, and I am sure she minded me no more than if I had been one of the mules, which should have been there.

3

With fifteen miles still before me, I was presently on my way, arriving at the next stopping-place around four-thirty in the afternoon and waiting until nine for the transport. It was then that my regular meal of yak and potatoes was brought in. It reminded me of my childhood days when I used to visit my friends on the cattle ranches during the summer months, when they were rounding up the cattle. We got ready to leave on the drive about four in the morning, and did not return for our last meal until around ten at night, only to repeat the same process on the following day. This is the daily rhythm of Tibet. The place in which I spent the night was in no wise different from the one where I had my lunch; so now I slept in filth as well as ate in it. I now found myself wishing I had brought my own tent. I hoped I should come out alive, let alone learn something. Not that I should fail to make an effort to do both.

About eleven o'clock that night, while writing out my notes, I looked up through the smoke that filled the room lighted by a small Buddha lamp and discerned a strange-looking individual, who loomed up from nowhere. He had heard that I was on my way to Lhasa, and as he was going there also, he had come to ask if he might join with my party for the rest of the journey, especially as many dangers lurked in the narrow canyon trails for solitary travellers. On scrutiny, his face appeared trustworthy, so after conversing with him a while I gave my assent, although I had previously refused one party in Gyantsé. But as this traveller was on the spot, and, indeed, on the move, there was little reason to say No. At the end of the first day I was glad that I had shown him favor, for he had already made himself worth his weight in gold by managing to get the transport in at a reasonable time. The fact is, thanks to the new man, the transport got off a little after five, having caught up with us when we stopped to have a snack at an altitude of 16,400 feet.

As soon as they were off and breakfast was out of the way, we set out again, not catching up with the transport for some little time. It was a beautiful start; the sun was just rising, and the valley was lighted up with its reflection from the ice cap of Mt. Nöjin, which loomed at an altitude of 24,000 feet; our side trail wound its way along the foot of the glacier for the entire morning, until we crossed the Karo Pass, and began our descent to the *Ta-t'ang*, or "The Horses' Plain," a not too extensive meadow formed by the valley broadening at this point; this plain is but a couple of thousand feet below the pass, but at no time is there any impression of being at sea level.

Innumerable tiny gopher-like animals kept on darting across the path, while diminutive gray sparrows went on flitting to one side until we went by; these were the only manifestations of life on this day; there was no human company along the road as had been the case the day before. Doubtless, this was due to our extremely early start. Later we encountered countless small herds of sheep and goats nosing among the rocks in the effort to find a blade of green. The entire day was spent in tripping and stumbling over the rocky ribbon of the heavens.

Shortly after crossing the pass we spotted a party coming up the trail, and as we approached each other nearer I recognized Norphel's hat. He was the boy that Tharchin had chosen to take with him, and he was now sent back to assist in bringing me to Lhasa. I was very grateful to Tharchin, as I was ignorant of the trail. Nevertheless, it had been an interesting and valuable experience to have travelled so far to all intents and purposes alone. Lhare, the boy who was left with me, was as loquacious as an Arkansas farmer or a New York taxicab driver. He couldn't understand even "Yes" in English, which forced me to speak Tibetan at all times. At the moment of our meeting, Norphel broke into a storm of enthusiasm, to reveal his own joy over all that had taken place in Lhasa.

Now, with Norphel to look after me, I could proceed where few had trodden before, living next to the earth, for that is about all a house amounts to in this country: the heaping up of a lot of mud. In the larger centers, however, the houses are made of rock. I must admit that we had a more respectable place for lunch, for we sat at the edge of a corral, and I was able to see the sky and have birds for company. It is really astonishing how starved the creatures of this country are. A familiar sight is that of dying dogs bracing themselves with outstretched legs before the door of a dark bungalow, in the hope that you will throw them something to eat. On occasions I have done so, and watched them swallow bone and all after only two bites. When you see these starvelings it makes you ashamed to eat. On the other hand, if you tried to feed them first, you would have to bring in a railway in order to import sufficient food for all of them; as every household has dozens of these beasts. Apparently, the only ones fed are the mastiffs chained at the gate, and the tiny native terriers; again and again I was almost tempted to buy one to take back with me. As for the rest of the mongrels, they are so weak that they will not even run after a piece of food. The one nearest is the one who gets it. They cannot run for lack of energy.

A sight that fascinated me one morning before leaving my stable was a train of animals, half yaks half cows, which came in with their loads, and those belonging to the household were within the walls waiting to get the few drops of milk promised by the appearance of these cattle, while those attending upon the animals made a dash for them as soon as they came to a stop. Upon reaching them, they began licking off the eyes of their travelling friends. It was one of the strangest things I had ever encountered in all my barnyard experience. The only way I could account for it was their thirst for salt, for none was available in this particular section of the country. As soon as they had cleaned the eyes they began to lick the bodies which had been sweating under their loads. How on earth they are ever able to get a cup of milk out of these sacks of protruding bones is more than I can understand; yet after applying all the energy they have they manage somehow to get enough for their needs, after letting me have the most of it. I should not want to risk living on it, for I felt that there could be no more food value in it than there is in a rock.

That night I rested in some dark little hole sitting cross-legged on a Tibetan mat in an effort to jot down a few details of the day before they have been obscured by the details of the morrow. My abode at the moment was somewhat cleaner than those I had so far encountered, as I was living in the home of a villager who had his house in the city, making it impossible for him to have his stock sleep with him; so we stepped out of a dusty lane shadowed by waving prayer-flags into a small patio which lies within the outer walls of the house, flush with the street. In this tiny square everything happens: work, visiting, cooking, indeed everything that goes into the task of living. Just off it is a small dark dungeon with a hole in the roof, a hole just large enough to let the smoke out when it is too cold to allow the door to remain open. An effort is made to hide some of the blackened walls by hanging a few drapes behind the cushions which line them; on these cushions you sit or sleep. You

Crossing those mountainous plateaus of solitude

A small Tibetan village where I spent the night while travelling through the country

simply squat on a mat, which is covered with small rugs, and you carry on, eating, writing, drinking off a small stool or Tibetan table, a mere few inches above the mat. Then, when you are exhausted, you simply roll over on your side and go to sleep, with every one waiting on you. Having done all of my work during last winter in this position, I found it most comfortable; indeed, I was not particularly looking forward to the nervous desk, at which your feet do more work than your head. My falling in with Tibetan ways did more than astonish the native; it convinced him that I was one of them.

4

It had been my plan to go as far as Chu-shu on the morrow, but on ascertaining that it was over fifty miles from there to Lhasa, I decided to push on more quickly and do forty miles a day. This was another of those easy runs at 15,000 feet, and we covered a little over thirty miles in four hours. There was no loafing about this. Padee was our scheduled stop for lunch, but as we arrived earlier than we anticipated, we went on, covering the entire distance without a rest. I should have liked to go on to the next village, but we had already overstepped our transport limits by one stage. In any event, we should have to pause to recruit the necessary animals for the morning. So here I sat a few thousand feet beneath our highest pass, the Kambu La, almost 17,000 feet, feeling as fit as a native bird, and wishing that I could be on the move. I realized, however, that if I pushed the horses any farther at the pace at which I had kept them going I should have to walk the rest of the way.

The hovel, in which I took shelter, was nothing to brag about. I was comfortable, however, and what more could one ask for? The effort every villager puts forth to make you enjoy your surroundings was so touching that if you had to hang yourself by your feet in the corner for the night, you were bound to find some compensation for it. On our arrival there was a great commotion, for they had not been previously appraised of our approach, so all the folks of the village, mostly women, started running from all directions, with babes on their backs, bringing their mats to furnish my room. These women seem to carry their infants on their backs as comfortably as I wear my hat, it was as though the baby were a part of them, its sleeping head jolting in this direction and that, as the mother got around corners and over rough spots. One of them stepped forward and arranged a comfortable place to sit on the ground, while the others swept out the retreat with handfuls of bundled straw. This was not a bad place, until a cloud of dust started rolling out of the doorway; in the end I was forced to yield, and move. Shortly they beckoned to me to come in, and I forced my way through the smoke screen set up by the dung fire arranged to make me comfortable. They were so confoundedly thoughtful that there was no alternative but to suffer in silence. Still, it's all a part of the game.

Not having had a bite to eat since about five-thirty, I was ravenously hungry. I contented myself, however, with a couple of crackers with fish and a cup of coffee. It has been my experience that the less one eats on such journeys the more successful the journey usually is; and at all times this abstemiousness is stimulating to the imagination. Yet I must confess that the appetite is always there with me, and it seems insatiable.

Each house, as I have already said, is nothing but a corral with a few adjacent rooms into which children, goats, sheep and cows pass freely, and equally freely out again. In all the corrals the women were standing about with their wool spindles making their thread. It is fortunate that their needs do not exceed their mentalities, or there would be a woman problem on Tibetan hands. As it is, they are content to bask within the protective enclosure, spinning their yarn, playing with the children, and gossiping. With such expanses of natural beauty about them, it is interesting to reflect upon the fact that they always choose to congregate in some filthy little hole, piled up on top of one another. I suppose this is what is called the social instinct.

5

The day had been a glorious one, starting with the tinkling of bells as my horse drove his nose deeper into his nosebag around three-thirty. There was no question about the men trying to make an early start, but it is the eternal talk that eats up the day. As it was, we did not get off until about five-thirty, when it should have been at least an hour earlier. You watched men sit down on the ground around their keg of butter tea, which they poured into their small Chinese bowls; then they snatched a handful of ground-up barley from their homespun bags, and made it into a thick paste, which they rolled into small dough-like balls and ate in small bits. After consuming two bowlfuls of tea, they would begin to wag their tongues over the business in hand. First they would collect all the boxes, after deciding who was going to carry the heavy ones. Once all these details were arranged, the real wrangle would begin. Whose pony was going to carry which boxes? Etc., etc. In the course of a few hours such problems were settled, and they would make a start, not stopping except for a brief break to consume a few more balls of barley dough.

And so we were ready to leave Nargatsé, a stronghold on the banks of the Yam-dok-tso (Scorpion Lake because of its slope), just a few miles from the famous Sam-ding ("Restful Meditation") monastery, situated a few hundred feet above the beautiful lake of the Yam-dok-tso, resting at over 15,000 feet. The head of this religious retreat is a woman known as Dorje P'agmo, and she is supposed to be a reincarnation of a deity of that name, whose translation is "The Thunderbolt Sow," with sources in ancient Eastern mythology relating to the principle of productivity. She is the only nun in Tibet allowed the privilege of keeping her hair and of riding in a sedan chair when she is travelling, sharing this exclusive right with the Dalai Lama, the Tashi Lama, the King Regent and, formerly, the two *Ambans* (Chinese officials). She receives divine honors from all the Lamas. The Sam-ding monastery is one of the most important nunneries in the country.

Shortly after six we cantered off along the western shore of the great Yamdok Lake, whose border is reputed to encompass 150 miles. This lake is also known by the name of "The Turqoise Lake" because of its color, while the Capuchin monks who first travelled along its winding shores called it Palte Lake after the name of the chief village fronting its waters.

The trail wound its way twenty or thirty feet above the shores of the lake for most of the way, except where the slopes were precipitous, when the trail rose somewhat higher. The lake's water is said to be very saline, as is to be expected of a lake without an outlet, and from the ring of salt that hemmed in its borders, I presume such is the case. All along the way we passed through small stone villages of typical Tibetan sanitariness, and adding color to our stony course. Throughout the morning the lake constantly changed color, as the sun rose higher into the heavens, until it ultimately reflected in its azure blue the rolling thunder-clouds that were stacking high into the skies above.

At Yarsi we crossed the projecting arm of the lake and joined the trail which follows from Shigatsé, the largest center in Western Tibet. This reminded me of Norbhu, who would be arriving at Lhasa on this very day, and would undoubtedly be surprised to hear that I was on my way. We first met at Calcutta last winter, and we had been crossing each other's path ever since. Our means for getting over the narrow end of the lake was by a perforated causeway, known as the "Blessed Bridge." Our chief companions of the road were the fish, which could be seen swimming about in the clear waters off shore. There were literally thousands of them, so thick in some places as to seem like a moving mass. From time to time we caught sight of geese, ducks and their new flocks of goslings and ducklings. The entire country is a huntsmen's and fishermen's paradise. Several foxes crossed our trail. Upon seeing us, they would comfortably relax and watch us pass. They did not reveal the slightest fear, a fact sufficiently unusual in my experience of this animal as to be worth while to make a note of.

All along the way Norphel went on to narrate concerning the various spirits which dwelt in the crags to our left.

At nine we reached Padee, a fort on the edge of the lake, and here I found a face that would be worth a small fortune for any museum, and I did my best to snap a picture of it while its owner, a grotesque gargoyle-like figure with knotted hair in filthy attire, was tending to the horses. The fort once belonged to a rich baron who controlled this part of the country. On looking back we saw the snow-covered peak of Mt. Nöjin reflecting its glory in the serene gleaming waters below.

Before beginning the 2000-foot climb going over the Kambu La we were perched for the night on the slope of the hill at the small village of Tamalung. There were more women than men about the place. These looked after the details, leaving the heavy work to the men. They tied up the boxes, and collected them in one place. Women in Tibet would make any athlete envious, for they have arms such as are the pride of the top-notch disciple of Bernarr McFadden. Indeed, they do just as much work as their male counterparts, and the same kind of work for the most part. The loads they can wield on their backs are really astonishing.

The next morning we were assured of a successful day, as the village Lama was present uttering his blessed omens as well as burning his incense, the smoke of which could be seen issuing from the top of every Tibetan home at the break of day. Almost anything can be used that will burn and throw out a good stream of smoke. Cedar boughs, however, are preferred. The principle of the use of incense here is very much like our own. Its burning is supposed to propitiate the good spirits.

It was about four-thirty now, and most of the arguments of the day had been settled. Until the mules, horses, donkeys, or whatever other beasts there may be, are actually on the move, there is always the chance of a last-minute dispute to hold up things for another hour or so, and such was the case of this day. I was fortunate in getting them started by five, and it was not long afterward that we followed them up the icy trail through the chill shade of the early morning. At an altitude of between 16,000 and 17,000 feet, it can be cold at any time of the day, regardless of the time of the year, if you happen to be in the shade. Here we were at the end of June, and the trickling streams had not yet broken through their nightcap of ice. At this time of day wind was but rarely encountered; this made the crossing of the pass very pleasant as we basked in the light of the rising sun, taking in the glory of the valley, divided by this great range which separated Western Tibet from Central Tibet, the land of the Sacred City, to which we were slowly winding our way.

The ridge was marked with the customary collection of streaming prayer-flags, as well as its pile of rocks, which grows with the passing of each party bringing another rock to add to the pile for good luck. This was the largest I had yet seen; it was many feet above the head of a man on horseback. As it happened, we arrived at the summit with the pack animals and watched the men one by one adding their gift of stored-up fortune in the great beyond. At this point we had the most encompassing view so far of the great Yam-dok-tso, even though it was only an arm of it; we could see it for miles in both directions, with the small village where we had spent the night still sleeping in the shade of the breaking day. Except for the vast expanse of the country, there is little to hold your attention; for the hills are as bare of vegetation as are the New York streets. It is not, however, what you see that enthralls you and stirs a desire in you to linger in order to fathom it all.

And now we turned toward Central Tibet, with the mighty Tsangpo-chu winding its way into the deep valley below, a matter of some 4000 feet, which meant a four-mile walk on our part; for at this point the trail is so steeep and rocky that it was not safe to entrust our footing to the small animals. There was little to be seen through the rising haze of the early morning. The mere fact that we were aware that from this point we would follow the hidden valley that led to the Sacred City was sufficient to compensate us for the absence of visibility. So few Westerners had gotten this far, and this, too, was a source of perhaps pardonable satisfaction. A mild word, for what I felt was exultation.

It was a long, arduous, dusty descent down hill. We passed several trains of wool on their long journey to India, from where the product would be sent on to America. It is truly astonishing to think of the high mountain passes which must be crossed to bring this wool to our country and to be sold for virtually nothing. How can it be done? On reaching the bottom of the hill, there was yet a tremendous canyon to drop into, cut by the torrents of heavy rain and melting snows. It was strangely reminiscent at times of our own great Western erosions. The floor was nothing but a stony way of uncertainty. Indeed, I felt very much at home again.

Our first greeting in Central Tibet came from a large herd of black pigs, taken out to graze for the day by the children of the owner's family. They were grunting along in typical pig fashion, even if they did live in such a remote corner of the world. At the bottom we had our first sight of trees, and of green patches, since we left Gyantsé. The small farms that dot the barren valley are all surrounded by large clusters of trees, in much the same manner as those isolated ranches in our great Southwest.

We were headed for Chu-shu, which meant a little over thirty miles for that day; so we lost no time in dashing through the small villages along the way; the roads and trails, as they used to be with us, all lead through the heart of each village. This lends a bit of color and variation to travel.

6

Behind us were to be seen the snow-capped ridges, but then the vision of a snow-ridge was unavoidable in a country like Tibet; but this particular valley was enclosed on all sides. Doubtless, one of the reasons for choosing this of all places for the centre of the faith and the capital of the land is that it offers an almost impenetrable barrier and obviates the need of maintaining a large and costly army. Judging from the accounts of the 1904 expedition and from my own travel experience, I should say that if the Tibetans had just a little fight in them, it would be impossible for any one to enter. But, apparently, there is too much religious superstition to encourage the development of an appropriate if limited armed force, such as is possessed by the tribe of the Afrides, who command the Khyber Pass. They were actually ready for the British at the time of the invasion; for there are spots between these narrow canyon walls where a handful of men could keep out an army, because it would be necessary for the advancing hordes to send their men all the way around to China in order to carry out a counter-attack. Such, however, did not in this instance prove the case;

for, after a few shots by their imperialistic cousins, their opponents took to their heels, except those who stood still and drew a ring around themselves and said a prayer to ensure their safety. Such things are really pathetic, but I suppose we must accept them as a part of the irrationality of life. Yet at one time they did entertain some idea of self-defensive military measures, and of this the ruins of the decaying fort we had passed by stood witness.

Here and there small monasteries can be seen tucked away in the rocky ravines that lead up the almost perpendicular walls of crumbling sandstone. When their inmates want to go out and meditate there is no question of any intrusion on their peace; would even a crow want to visit them? How they manage to exist is something of a mystery. I assume that there must be a hidden spring near by, and that the neighboring villages pile up virtues for the next life by supplying them with grain. Every now and then you see a nunnery, and from all accounts the nunnery population always holds its own.

Soon we traversed a few miles oddly reminiscent of the Yuma desert; or it might have been the Arabian desert rather than the high plateaus of Tibet. With all this sand, they are wind-swept. Such was our scenery for the remainder of the journey that day; the hills and the valley were almost obscured by these floating carpets raised by the winds. Many of the shallow nullahs were well-nigh covered over. Wherever there was a wall to help bank up the sand, there would be small mountains of these motionful sand dunes. It is easy to guess how bare the valleys must be, broken up as they are into small fingers of sand and gravel by the mighty Tsangpo-chu, which slowly rolls its way across the entire length of Tibet around the formidable Himalayan barriers into the plains of Assam and down to where it meets the sacred river of India, the Ganges. In India this river is known as the Brahmaputra.

There was a diversion for us from the sands in the Tibetan ferry which we had to take to cross this great river. The small boats used for the crossing are made of stretched yak hide and can be easily carried by one man. There is scarcely any limit, however, to what they will hold. When we parted from the ferry pier of rock down the stream to Chu-shu, where the Lhasa River joins the Tsangpo-chu, we carried beside the boatman and our party of three, four Tibetan muleteers, as well as a goat, a dog, and a large load of lumber. As for our horses, they were sent directly across by a long narrow wooden ferry, which we hired for taking over the transport. Each of these huge barges of walnut planks is capable of carrying twenty horses, a dozen men and a ton of miscellaneous articles.

After sending everything else over the barges, we took small *Kowas* (leather boats) and floated down on the Chu-shu past the famous Chaksam Chö-ri* monastery with its old iron suspension bridge which still hangs across the river, attached to a small island of sand. It has been out of use, however, for many years, owing to the fact that the river has changed its course and left the end opposite the monastery only a tiny island in the center. The bridge is said to have still been used in 1878, when visited by one of the survey spies, who made a map of it. The Holy Hill of the iron bridge is supposed to have been built in the fifteenth century by T'angtong-the-King. This monarch has now been canonized as a saint, who is represented by an image with a dark complexion and long white hair and beard. Seated holding a thunderbolt in his left hand and an iron chain in his right, he is reputed to have built eight such bridges at various times. All that remains today are the crumbling chorten-like pillars and the span chains of huge iron links about a foot long each. The span is about 150 yards, and fifteen feet above the floor level.

*"The Holy Hill of the Iron Bridge."

Chu-shu was reached about lunch time, so we had a cup of Tibetan tea and a cracker while we waited for the transport to catch up with us. Here we had to arrange for a fresh transport of animals. For the first time in ages I enjoyed resting in a clean room, decorated with colorful Tibetan *thangkas* and a small Buddha shrine. It formed a tremendous contrast to the barns in which I had been previously taking my repose. I do not know who the owner of it was, but from all indications he must have been one of the powerful landlords of this region. Indeed, there was every reason to think that henceforth life for me would be different. From this point the great way of toil to Lhasa was bordered on both sides by large willow trees, which provided a welcome change in the scenery. There were other radical differences in the landscape; from now on, below the bare mounds of disintegrating hills on either side, trees, flowers and fresh crops began to appear.

Chu-shu itself lies behind the powerful old fort built in the sharp ridge, that drops down in an almost perpendicular wall to the seething tides of the Tsangpo-chu below. The trail was chiselled into the side of this sheer wall, making it an almost impossible entrance to the Forbidden City. The rest of our trail varied from crossing sections of dried-up gummy bottoms of the river to picking our way cautiously across the loose rocks in the trail cut into the sides of the wall of the great cliffs. There was a distant view with extensive meadows of mustard in bloom. It made a fine sight for the eyes, and once we should get beyond it, Lhasa would be only fifty miles away.

This had been a hard day; we had covered nearly sixty miles, only to arrive at the filthiest, crummiest place for the night's lodging. For company we had a couple of whining old women, to whom however we paid not the least attention. We had already eaten up the little that we carried in the saddlebags for lunch, so there was nothing to be had but some Tibetan butter tea and a couple of old eggs that we begged off the chickens which made their abode in this corral. I had been eating so scantily during the journey that now for the first time I was beginning to feel fatigue. I realized that I had been living on my reserves, now at the vanishing point. I did not feel, however, like complaining.

7

All through the day I went on noting the evidences of being in another part of Tibet. The headdresses that now adorned the heads of the peasants working in the fields were different from those I encountered before. Even the earrings worn by the men were not the same. Indeed, I was able to detect differences in the language. Only in one respect were the people emphatically the same, regardless of the region in which they lived, and this was their belief in their faith. All whom we passed, trudging their way along the dusty road, were wrapt in a mood of the pilgrim on his eternal quest, and they went on audibly murmuring the sacred incantation: *"Om! Ma-ni pad-me Hūm!"*—at the same time dropping off the beads of their rosaries as fast as the thumb-like fingers could push them along. Many of these souls were so heavily engaged in this ritual that they seemed hardly aware of us as we passed them. Only now and then an old woman would condescend to give us a flitting glance, but her lips would not pause for an instant, preoccupied as they were with mumblings which had to do with eternity.

So this was Tibet, with the Penthouse of the Gods just around the corner. Only a few hours away. What was it going to be like? Were all the stories I heard of its beauty going to be true? What would be my feeling on the first glimpse? And with these last thoughts, I slipped from my seat for a brief nap.

The day brought what was to be the greatest event in my entire life, and I was so stoked up with emotion as to be almost afraid to remain alone, or to stop moving even for a moment.

Lhasa was our next stop, so there was no need to think of not being able to wake up in the morning. I would have just as lief ridden that night, for by the time you have covered 350 miles in this kind of country, a matter of a few additional miles to reach your destination does not amount to a great deal. After all, I was going to Lhasa, the city for whose sake I had devoted many years to study, a city of which I had been continuously dreaming.

We were off again through the glittering fields of gold richly aglow with the early morning sun. From this point on the country was one continuous area under cultivation; so our main company along the way consisted of the women who were directing the waters by banking up the broken spots in the ditches. It was not long before we came into the main Lhasa valley, a view of the city was prevented only by a small arm of the mountains, which help to break the winds coming up the valley.

All of a sudden I heard a loud whoop. You might have imagined that it was a band of wild Indians on the war-path. Actually, it came from none other than Norphel. He had rushed to tell us about the exact position of the city, and was overflowing with fervor to reach the first view, so that we could have an advance glimpse through the field glasses. Eagerly we rode on, so that we might see around a small ridge. Norphel pointed out a high pile of stones on the trail ahead, and said that from there one could get the first view of the Sacred City, adding that every passer-by always flung a stone on the growing hill as he gazed at the remote goal. So at a fast gallop we made for this mark, where it was possible to discern our destination through the passing mists of the morning.

At first we could see nothing. Then, suddenly, as the sun rose above the mountain range, a cluster of golden roofs gleamed forth a radiance and a splendor such as I scarcely ever dreamt of. We were now eight miles away, heading straight for this Mirror of the Gods.

The trails were marked with endless rock carvings of Tibetan saints. There was a tremendous image of Buddha carved in the rock facing the Holy City. The houses were rich in their broad stripes of red, white and blue. The sacred colors are *om* (white), *ma* (green), *ni* (yellow), *pad* (blue), *me* (red), *hung* (black or dark blue). There was also the tomb of Atisha, an Indian friar who came to India in the eleventh century and brought in the reform movement, from which has gradually developed the Gelupa sect of today, the Yellow Cap. The shrine in which he was buried is in a very ruinous condition, which is surprising, considering that the ruling sect is presumed to hold him in so great esteem.

About five miles beyond, we crossed over the pride of Tibet, their newly constructed all-steel bridge, which they had been building during the past three years. I should add that the actual construction had been a matter of some six months, and the rest of the time was consumed in bringing up the necessary materials from India over the Jelup La, a word which in itself tells the whole story, for this is a precipitous pass, almost 15,000 feet high. I must admit that they have done a good piece of work for Tibetans, who have no appreciation of engineering, with the possible exception of one chap who was sent to England with three others about twenty years ago to get a Western education by the late Dalai Lama. The idea was conceived and executed by Tsarong, Tibet's most up-and-coming personality, now more or less in the twilight of his life. He appears to have aided Western civilization in an invasion of his country at every opportunity, and, incidentally, to have accumulated a fortune in the process. He is, in fact, the only private millionaire in Tibet, I speak in terms of the American dollar, not the rupee. An interesting story is told in connection with

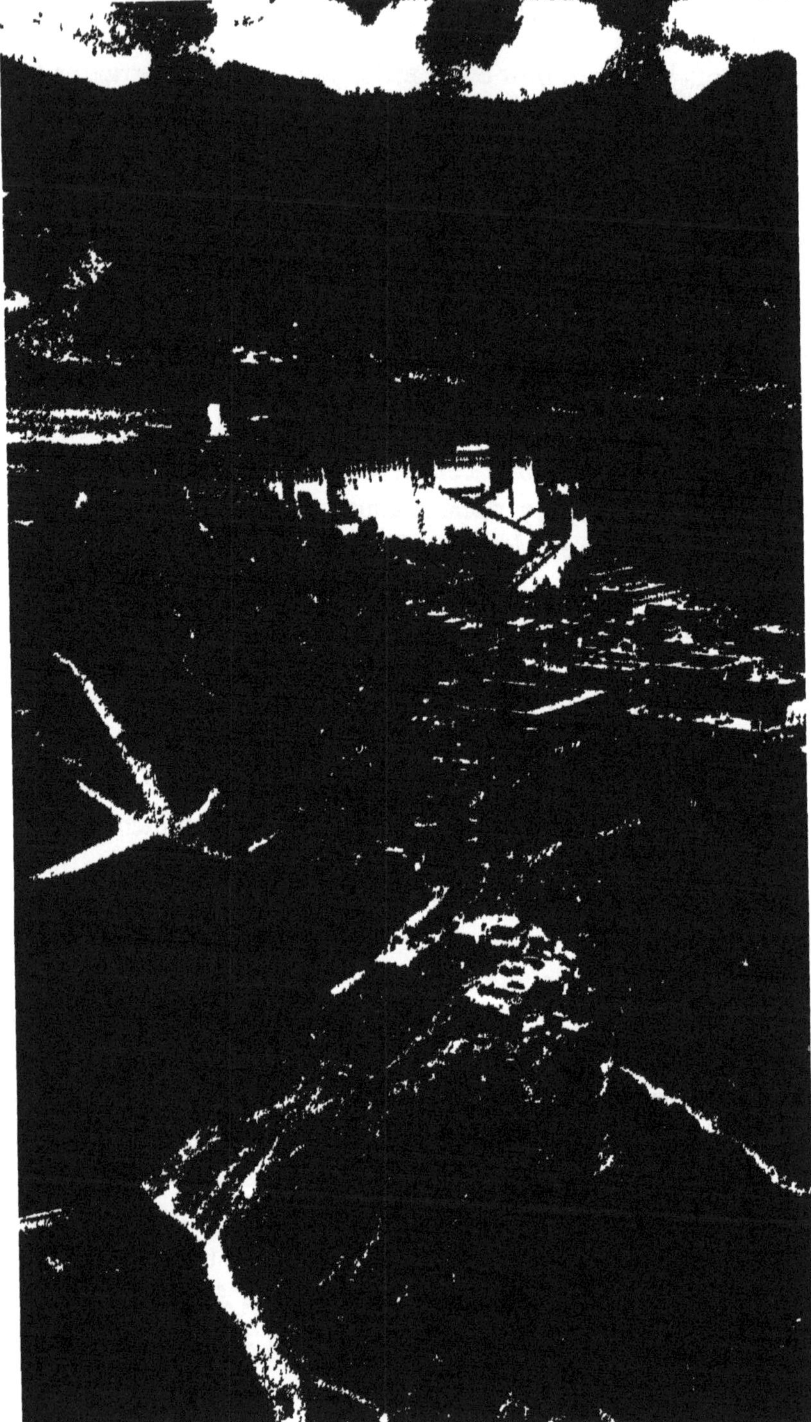

the building of this bridge. In order to have a knowledge of its construction, it was first planned and set up in India. Then, with the plans already sent on to Tibet, the bridge was dismantled, and each piece was carried upon a coolie's back into Lhasa. Tsarong followed the directions to the letter, yet when the bridge was finished there were six pieces left over!

A still more astonishing sight was that of an aerial radio. Had I known that this was the house built by Tsarong, to be used during the construction of the bridge, I might have expected it. As it was, I had no option but to make the only possible guess, and the right one.

I espied an old woman sitting beside a decaying shrine with a basketful of turnips in front of her, in the hope that a prospective buyer might show up. One did, for I am a lover of raw turnips. I bought a couple of bunches and broke the morning fast. I never ate a better vegetable anywhere; it was certainly better than anything that could be found in India.

After negotiating a rocky ridge, we entered upon a broad highway, which still further widened into a twelve-lane thoroughfare, overcrowded with yaks and donkeys, and us on our royal horses riding in between them. It was but a short distance before we came around the bend which sheltered the great monastery of Drepung, the largest in the world, holding in the neighborhood of 10,000 monks. It was a startling sight: white masonry studded over with the black spots, which indicated the endless series of chambers, gloomy cells of meditation. Innumerable questions ran pell-mell in my mind, but I restrained myself. After all, the time would presently come when I should pay a visit to the monastery, indeed to its every shrine before taking my final departure. I had seen endless pictures of this sanctuary, yet it was wholly unlike such preliminary impressions. The truth is, no film could possibly convey its majesty. There is a sense of immaculateness about it which eludes the camera, so faithful in capturing external forms.

Later we passed the slaughter-house, which provides the meat for those sacred souls who are not permitted to take life but must have something to eat. Through the open door great carcasses of butchered animals could be seen hanging from the ceiling, with the dry, cool weather of Tibet acting in lieu of a refrigerating system, the stomach in lieu of a government meat inspector. A small way beyond, tucked away in a beautiful grove on the sloping hill, could be seen the glittering roof of a sacred tomb and the shrine of the government Oracle. By now we could see the Potala as well as Chak-po-ri (the Medical College) at the opposite end of the hill, on which the Potala is built, crowning the pinnacle with shadows from the valley floor.

8

At no great distance, on the side of the road, I espied a small black area, which turned out to be the official meeting place; for it is the custom of the Tibetans, as I have already indicated, always to send some one to meet a newcomer on the way to pay them a visit. So the Government had sent me an escort and a guide. The most striking thing about the individual who greeted me was the strange little yellow hat he wore, so different from anything I had ever seen or heard that I can hardly describe it except to say that there was as little hat about it as about some of the more recent models tied on the heads of the women in our Easter-Day parade. The yellow, to be sure, was a token of officialdom; as no one not of the ruling group is permitted to wear this color. He was a man of average stature, draped in a heavy dark dress of hand-made *nambu*, or Tibetan cloth. He seemed extremely well fed, and his plump little face was never without a smile. He wore his hair in a long braid down the middle of his back, with large turquoise ornaments adorning it. From his left ear hung the long earring worn by the upper class of Tibet, as indeed I observed when I first met Jigme at Gyantsé. On the right ear was a small button of turquoise. On a previous occasion I asked why they wore only one long earring, and a small button on the other ear. The reply was that they thought it looked more smart that way than if both ears were adorned in a similar fashion, and there is little doubt that this is true.

We had scarcely exchanged greetings, when I spotted Tharchin racing through a cloud of dust. It was a cheering sight in a lost corner of the world to see a friendly, familiar face. I rushed towards him as fervently as he towards me, and as we met there was an infusion of deep emotion. Had it not been for his loyalty, which enabled us to work quickly in the brief time at our disposal, I should never have been able to manage to be here. When he left for Lhasa neither of us was by any means sure that we should meet again there. His animated face with the flowing moustache stretched out from ear to ear revealed how great the joy my arrival afforded him. I almost felt that he was getting a bigger kick out of it than I was. Perhaps I should not be using so blatant an Americanism in writing of a pilgrimage to Tibet; but the fact is, the sort of personal exuberance I experienced at the meeting is always conducive to a reaffirmation of the native idiom. After a few minutes he insisted upon taking a couple of hurried shots with the movie camera which he had brought along.

Tsarong Shapé had sent a fresh horse to bring me the rest of the way. I must admit to the pleasure I had in mounting it, for it was a real horse and not one of the small Bhotiya ponies such as I had been riding. Officials in Lhasa, and in neighboring China, have horses hard to beat anywhere. They are by no means the Arabian race horse nor a thoroughbred, but there is no question about their strength and capacity.

To our left was the great wall which surrounded the beautiful Jewel Park, the summer palace of the Dalai Lama. This is undoubtedly one of the finest parks in the city, which is often mentioned throughout the land as the city of the four parks. The Lhasans take much the same pride in their lovely parks as does Chicago in its green spots, and San Francisco in its Golden Gate Park, and New York in the efforts of Mr. Moses.

We approached the huge *chorten*, which forms the entrance arch to the Holy City. It was a great moment for me. Once I passed through this worship memorial I should be within the city walls, the first American to live in Lhasa itself, and not as the other white men, who must remain outside the city walls. The British, who are great respecters of other people's privacy, have never attempted to violate the rule of going only when they are invited. Police are stationed at the entrance to forbid the unwelcome from entering.

We had barely passed through the famous gate, when there loomed to our left, seeming to penetrate the clouds themselves, the palace of the Dalai Lama, majestically dominating the landscape. It was the home of Buddha's vice-regent on earth. How was such a structure engineered? It was here centuries before our country had even come into existence, and while Europe was still more or less in the dark ages. It seems to matter little what materials man has at hand with which to work; once he is able to conceive a thing of beauty, he is also able to reproduce it, even under the most difficult circumstances. The structure, however, had not all been conceived at once, nor erected in a day. It has come into being by a series of constant new starts and new additions. But with the accession of each new wing, its builders have always adhered to the flowing rhythm of nature, such as is found in this mountainous land. Its ma-

jestic sweep left me breathless, and I had to pause for a few moments, to take it in, to feel it, to let it sink into my soul. Yet I knew that I should be seeing it every day, should be rambling through its long corridors, should be praying before its shrines, perhaps meditating beneath its golden roof. And, strangely enough, I did not even think of taking a picture of it; for something different possessed me, and I had not the least inclination to bring the mechanical note into the mood of the moment. Indeed, I was aware of nothing but the sense of the life and feeling it had created in me.

Once I came to myself, we moved on again, toward the home of Tsarong, where I should be a guest during my stay in Lhasa. He had gotten the permission of the *Kashag* to invite me. Nothing could have been better than to be granted the privilege of living in Lhasa's most beautiful home. To be sure, I had not yet met Tsarong Shapé, but I had no doubt that there must be something to a man who had risen to his eminence. Then, too, I knew the experience of living in his home would give me an intimate insight into Tibetan life, which was what I wanted. He was to have returned to the bridge that morning, but on hearing that this was the day of my arrival, he called off the journey in order to be at home to greet me. Could one ask for more consideration in any part of the world? I was looking forward to meeting the Tsarongs.

We rode through the heart of the city, for the Tsarong house is just on the edge of the other end.

One of the first things to jolt me was the use of the streets for toilet facilities. It was not an uncommon experience to pass by a woman squatting for purposes to which we in the West avoid giving publicity. The first time I was just a bit embarrassed, but when I observed that the only expression on the woman's face was one of astonishment at seeing a strange face I gave the matter no further thought.

9

Through a clean and decorated courtyard made for the waiting horses we entered a lovely garden, from which the entrance to the enormous Tsarong dwelling was visible.

Tharchin had dug up a couple of *Kata* (silk scarves) for me to present to my hosts, so the two Tsarongs and I met in the doorway, both unrolling our geeting cards. It was a great pleasure to see the Lady Tsarong again, and in her own magnificent home, and he was as friendly and jolly as though he had been my lifelong friend. My first impression was that of a little chubby ball of glow and fervor, with a face slit from ear to ear with smiling hospitality. He could not speak a word of English, and I was too much embarrassed to attempt colloquial speech, which is not the speech they use, thus rendering all of my experience useless; what I stood in need of now was the elegance of the honorific. In any event, there was too much tacit understanding between us to be bothered about the difficulty of such external mechanics.

I was conducted to my suite, which was to be my home for a while to come. It revealed my hosts' thoughtfulness. Not only did it contain Tibetan chairs and tables, but also a desk had been fitted up for me in typical Western fashion, though, from the moment I laid my eyes on it, I knew that I should never use it. With this there was a large living room, arranged in regular Tibetan fashion, its supporting beams all hand-carved and painted in accord with the usual artistic arrangement of the royal colors; the design, however, is by far too intricate to attempt a description of it. But any one familiar with Chinese art can well imagine its magnificence.

The low cushions upon which I would do most of my work were covered with lovely Tibetan rugs of dragon design. The walls likewise continued the pattern of the room with a beautiful border painted in red, green, yellow, and blue.

In my living room there was a Buddhist shrine, with the Lama of the house to carry on the chants for me each morning and to bring fresh holy water daily, as well as to keep the Buddha lamp filled so that the eternal light should never go out.

So this was to be my home in Lhasa. Never could I have dreamt of such comfort. Not that I have listed everything. Indeed, I also had a separate bedroom, a toilet with our old-fashioned arrangements, towel racks, portable bathtub, etc., as well as a storeroom for my boxes.

10

By now tiffin time was here, and everything was prepared for me upstairs in the private living quarters, which presented a grand duplication of all that I had below.

At Kalimpong I had had a Tibetan dinner with Tsarong Lacham which had been prepared for us by Mrs. Perry, but now I was to be her guest. She was a gracious hostess, animated with a friendly enthusiasm.

Food was brought on, but as I have already amply described high-class Tibetan meals in the past it would be superfluous to recapitulate the catalogue of courses here. Tsarong, however, is just Western enough occasionally to call for a whiskey and soda, and since this was a gala affair he had to celebrate. It was a leisurely meal, and I nibbled at the endless dishes with the ease of one who felt thoroughly at home.

We discussed Tibet and the question of the country's being modernized. At the end my host expressed the opinion that it would be difficult to introduce new ideas into Tibet. Nor did he think that it would be desirable. He contended that the Tibetans were, on the whole, a happy people, and that changes might only serve to bring trouble to them by involving them in international commercial traffic. China and India, to be sure, could be used as markets for import and export. But it all meant an involved life and the banishment of peace; and so it was best, perhaps, that they should remain isolated from the rest of the world.

My hosts insisted that I take all my meals with them, a satisfactory arrangement, since it gave me the sort of contact I wanted; it would enable me to learn Tibetan ways during my stay. It also would give me the much-needed opportunity to hear more of their language and to perfect myself in cultural conversation. The Tsarongs suggested that Tharchin have his meals elsewhere, in order to preclude my speaking English. I had little difficulty in conversing with servants, traders, and the people of the lower class; it was only in speaking to the highest Tibetan officials that I encountered difficulty, and felt tremendously shy.

My constant association with the Tsarongs would fulfill another purpose, that of acquainting me more fully with Tibetan history and psychology; all the more as Tsarong was the closest friend of the late Dalai Lama since his early childhood. As a matter of fact, it was through his efforts that the Dalai Lama's life was saved during the Chinese trouble in Lhasa, when he had to flee to India for safety. During the Dalai Lama's stay in India the father of Tsarong Lacham and Mrs. Tsarong's brother were doing all they could to straighten out matters, when rumors began to spread to the effect that they were plotting to betray him. The feeling became so acute in the city that it culminated in the killing of both of them. In consequence of this, upon the return of the Dalai Lama to the holy city, he gave his favorite and most promising friend to the Tsarong family so that it might have a leader. This family is one of the largest and oldest in the country, and the person whom the late Dalai Lama had appointed to take charge of the family was none other than the present Tsarong Shapé, and it was this event that marked his marriage to Mrs. Tsarong. Having come from the poorer class in the country and entered the Drepong monastery, it was not long before he was noted for his keen mind and dominating personality. It soon brought him into the graces of the Dalai Lama. He was still a boy at the time, and the Dalai Lama, on observing his potentialities, asked for the opportunity of bringing him up. Taken into the Dalai Lama's household, the boy attended to his holiness until he became a Shapé—a member of the Cabinet. At the time of the 1904 expedition he accompanied the Dalai Lama on his flight to China, where he took care of his master for seven years. During this period he picked up many Western ideas, and he made hosts of friends everywhere he went.

The return to Lhasa, Tsarong told me, was only a year or two before the Chinese trouble broke out in the Holy City; this time they fled to India. He was then about twenty-four, and he demonstrated his ability at Chaksam, where he held back the enemy with only a few men at the top of a high cliff, until the Dalai Lama could get far enough ahead to avoid being overtaken. Had he been caught, death would have been meted out to the whole group. Because of this episode, Tsarong was appointed Commander-in-Chief of the Tibetan military forces, which was the beginning of the first army of Tibet, and it was he that organized it. Preoccupied with modern ideas, which he wished to instil into Tibet, he sent several men to India to receive the requisite military training. He also introduced the modern rifle and the revolver, in use everywhere today.

Fortunately, at the death of the late Dalai Lama he was with his family on their estate in Western Tibet, or he would have suffered the fate of the other members of the ruling group of the Government. They were all either killed or injured.

Some had their eyes gouged out, others their tongues cut out, still others were imprisoned in dungeons for life. When he finally returned to Lhasa, the conditions were safe. It was not long, however, before there were rumors that the military officers were planning to overturn the Government. This focussed attention on Tsarong, who was in charge of the army. Whether there was any truth in the accusations, there is no way to determine today. In any event, they resulted in the dismissal of all the officers from the service; the lower officials were exiled from Lhasa for the remainder of their lives. The person next in rank to Tsarong, who had the reputation of being one of the best scholars, had his eyes put out; he is now sitting in a dungeon at the Potala waiting for the end to come. Tsarong himself had to suffer demotion to a lower rank.

Among his duties today is that of the head of the mint, which manufactures all the coins used in the country, as well as prints paper money and postage stamps. He also takes charge of all Government engineering contracts, which cover such projects as the bridge so recently built. He has an ambition to build a road that will enable an automobile to travel from Chu-shu to Lhasa within a few hours; today the journey takes two days. To be sure, there are no automobiles in the country to travel over the proposed road, but it would serve as a beginning, and should the road ever be constructed, the wealthier people of the country would doubtless import automobiles; that would be the beginning of the end.

II

The conversation at the breakfast table turned to travel in Eastern Tibet, in which Tsarong had considerable experience. Little is known about the country, as no white man has ever travelled from here in that direction. This put an idea into my head, and I plied my host with questions, about what was worth while there, the trail, and what not. I was already aware that the present center af all the *Tantrik* teachings was to be found in that region, as also much of their learning; it being indeed the stronghold of the Kargyupa sect. Then, too, I knew that the best set of blocks of the *Tengyur* existed in Eastern Tibet about a thousand miles from Lhasa. I refer to those in Derge. Not only are the blocks in a fairly good state, but they are also more accurate than the set of scriptures to be found at Narthang, near Shigatsé; I have already mentioned the fact that the latter blocks have been used so often that it is well-nigh impossible to read their print. The Derge blocks are not nearly so old, and, hence, are more legible. It was a part of my mission to bring back a set of these books to America, and I should be loath to leave Tibet without one. Naturally, I was interested in any possibility to visit Eastern Tibet. Tsarong was confident that I could secure permission to leave Tibet through China instead of through India, and since I had his support I felt that half the battle was won.

The morning was slipping by, and Tsarong had to visit the bridge this day. He stopped long enough, however, to look over the gifts, which had arrived on a rush order. I needed his counsel as to which of them were suitable for different occasions and which should go to the various *Shapés*. So we went downstairs and opened up the packages, to find everything had come through in ship-shape order. I was amazed that nothing had been broken in transit, as there was no parcel that did not contain glass. As it happened, I bought only one gift for the Regent, and now I discovered that it was customary to bring him two, since he is the highest personage in the country. Tsarong came generously forward with an object he had in his house; he thought it would serve my purpose.

Just as Tsarong was about to take his departure, a representative of the *Kashag* arrived. It is the custom of the country for the Government to send a gift to a newly come guest, while each individual member of this body sends an additional personal gift. This always consists of a consignment of butter, flour, rice, eggs, and vegetables. My friendly visitor arrived with half a dozen sacks of flour, about fifteen dozen eggs, four large sacks of butter weighing about eighty pounds each, and a large tray of vegetables. After all these things had been stacked in the middle of the room by his servants, he presented me with a *Kata* (silk scarf used as a calling-card), which, however, he asked me to return after his speech had been made, so as to enable him to use the same *Kata* for a like purpose in the future. It never seemed to work that way whenever I happened to be the donor. Once I presented a *Kata* to any one, I bid it a fond farewell. What with such calling-cards running into about five rupees each, and a hundred calls or so to make, it was something to make one pause. I was driven to make arrangements to buy them wholesale.

He was a handsome-looking buck, standing over six feet, with a very intelligent face and a very soft and pleasing manner. After he had addressed me in flowing Tibetan in a tone of voice which rang from the heart, and with a sparkle in his eyes which helped to express the meaning of his words, as I looked, perhaps helplessly in Tharchin's direction, my visitor suddenly broke into perfect English, without the suspicion of an accent, and with a command of words that would have excited the admiration of an English or American purist. Who was he, and how had he learnt it? The explanation, soon forthcoming, was that he was one of a group of four sent to England some twenty years ago for training. Before taking up the study of mining engineering, he had taken the pains to perfect his English.

Presently we joined the Tsarongs upstairs, and had a long chat about his travels and experiences, and about his sojourn in England. He expressed a wish to see his former classmates, now scattered to the four corners of the globe. On his return from England he entered a monastery, and is now a government official, very happy in his work. Tsarong had to be on his way, so we adjourned. I hoped to see more of Mondrol before I left Lhasa, for he was a charming personality, none better to spend an hour with.

12

The same afteroon I was summoned to tea upstairs. I noted with no little astonishment a beautiful silver tea-set, a large cake with many cookies, and a large bowl with sweet-bits, all resting on the low Tibetan table. It seemed strange to see such a lovely-looking cake in Tibet. Mrs. Tsarong greeted me with an effusive smile. No sooner had I taken my seat than I asked where, in the name of heaven, had such a cake miraculously come from. Then she told me that they had sent their cook to India for four years in order to learn how to make various English dishes, because on their many travels to India they had grown to like some of them and considered it a treat to have them from time to time. The real surprise came when I took my first bite. It was one of the most delicious cakes that ever came my way. Indeed, everything about it was perfect, except for the fact that it had been made with yak butter, which was several years old. This detail in no way hindered the pleasure of tea-time, which became a daily custom with me all the time I stayed in Lhasa.

Mrs. Tsarong showed me their house temple and the private shrine. As a matter of fact, every room in the house contained a small Buddhist shrine. There was also a room devoted wholly to worship. It was a lovely chamber, impressive as to color and design. The wood carvings were done by especially invited craftsmen from Kham; the images were adorned with jewels, and in every instance gold was substituted for other metals.

It was an exciting afternoon. Dinner soon followed, and Mrs. Tsarong and I talked ourselves right into a midnight cup of tea.

CHAPTER VI

THE FORBIDDEN CITY

I

SHORTLY after my arrival in Lhasa, messages were sent to the Regent and Prime Minister and the various members of the *Kashag* announcing my desire to pay them visits. Prompt responses came, setting a time.

One morning after breakfast I made my preparations for visiting the King Regent of Tibet. There were other things to think of besides the gifts. Considerable formality had to be complied with, since I was determined to carry out such duties in accordance with the native custom. Soon Tharchin and I, accompanied by servants carrying the gifts, left for his Lhasa home, his real abode being at Re-ting Monastery four days' journey north from here. He was the head of this monastery, and I learned that he would be shortly going there. It was this knowledge that made me act quickly, all the more as his permission was necessary if I intended leaving Lhasa by way of China; and a Lama in a remote monastery was like a bird in the bush.

He had but lately built a new palace here, a beautiful structure, presenting a Tibetan interpretation of Chinese architecture, with a flowering garden surrounding it. This garden was rather formal, with its green lawn broken by abundant beds of flowers. His audience room is so arranged next to a small balcony that he can enjoy the full beauty of his garden.

There was a formal air to my arrival, with the servants running in all directions announcing it and making endless arrangements for the meeting, while I sat in the anteroom and drank Tibetan tea, waiting for the details to be settled. Along with the gifts I brought, it was customary to present three other gifts, which are provided at the place, the visitor being given the privilege of paying for them. It is just another means of religious revenue. Indeed, all gifts offered him are, to all intents and purposes, holy offerings; he is the most holy man on earth as far as the Tibetans are concerned. His palace is a modest small home decorated with the exquisite taste which would do credit to a king, and it must be said that it reveals nothing so pretentious as countless acres adorned with French chandeliers and the like. It was just clean, convenient, comfortable.

When the various articles were duly prepared, I entered the audience chamber, where they were given me one by one, as I presented them to him after having made my three devotionals down on my hands and knees upon entering his holy sanctuary. They consisted of a small butter offering, a small image of Lord Buddha, and a small manuscript. Then he in turn gave me a *kata* and his blessing, so that prosperity might always be with me. The small room was well lighted by windows which went the whole breadth of the room in lieu of a wall. There was quite a large Chinese screen, which permitted him to look out at his beautiful garden and at the same time provided him with complete privacy. Everything seemed very new, and I found excitement no matter which way I looked. And it was a joy to find a place in the world in which men did not fear to use color. It certainly has a cheerful effect on the soul. A small shrine close to him, and *thangka* decorations, were very modern. His "living box" was about as elegant a one as I had yet seen or was likely to see. It is as if we were to build a small framework around a davenport cut about three quarter's length with a back behind it; in it one cross-legged all day, instead of sprawling out in the typical Western fashion of slovenliness. This "living box" was all painted in gold, in keeping with his position, as was his robe, with the border and the inside done in red. The only dissonance I found in the room—that is, as far as my own feelings at the time were concerned—was an electric fan, attached to the ceiling. For aught I know, it might be a good idea, but quite unnecessary I thought, for at no time did I find it hot enough in Tibet to need a fan.

Never shall I forget the excitement as I stepped across the sacred threshold and looked into the sparkling eyes of this young man, who is not yet thirty years of age and head of the last theocracy on earth. A thrill passed through my entire body, as I put my hands together on my head, slowly folded them into my chest, bowed down on my knees to the floor before him in the customary way, paying respect to a divine soul. He was standing in his golden box, watching with those sparkling eyes of his every move I made and the rhythm of every muscle of my body, as I tried to merge with the vibrations of the room. It was a strange feeling that came over me as I then knelt before him and received his blessing, his long, delicate hands resting on my head.

I was seated just a foot or so in front of him, as we maintained a long conversation about the Buddhistic religion and my plans for spreading it in America. He offered to do all he could to help me and expressed a willingness to pass on to me the necessary sacred objects blessed with his own hands, and at the same time to bestow upon me the power to execute certain divine instructions.

If he had been an American, we would as likely as not find him a doctorate in literature, or confer upon him an honorary degree, and, in general, make a fuss about him. But this is neither here nor there.

He revealed a very frail physique, which harbors a delicate spiritual personality with a very sensitive nature. He was the sort of selfless, sympathetic character with whom you might spend hours without feeling a strain. And the radiance about him was such that no matter how you felt on coming to him you were sure to feel the stronger for having been in his company. A singularly spiritual individual, certainly, yet at the same time with a keen mind, full of wisdom and understanding, and alive with ideas. A reasonable sense of humor was here also; again and again the earnestness of the meeting was relieved by laughter. There is nothing so universally comprehended as a good laugh, and I find that a laugh is good medicine in any language.

He was eagerly attentive as to my aspirations and my plans, and he marvelled at my deep interest in Tibetan Buddhism. He attributed it to a past life in this part of the world as a spiritual teacher and leader. Such an explanation was within the scope of Tibetan understanding. He counselled me to make lists of all the things I was anxious to secure and promised me every assistance in procuring them. Now I had some confidence in that I should be able to obtain copies of the *Kangyur* and *Tengyur* from the available blocks. We also discussed my plans to return by way of China. He expressed himself very anxious to watch my work and help me, if necessary even to the extent of visiting America to bestow his personal blessing on my labors in this country. All this seems absurdly strange when I think that I am the first American who has had the opportunity of seeing him and the first white man to receive a personal blessing from his hand.

Several hours passed very quickly. Before I left him, he asked that I put in my requests promptly, as he should be going to his monastery in a short time. As I took my leave he put around my neck a small red silken scarf tied with a triple knot, indicating that I had received a personal blessing from the Regent. In all of Tibet only the Regent and the T'ri Rimpoche have the power and the right to bestow this blessing. At the moment I did not realize its full meaning. But scarcely had I mounted my horse and begun my ride through the village on the way to Tsarong's home, when all the people ran out of doors or peered out of the windows in order to see the strange person riding through the streets in Tibetan attire with this red scarf around the neck. This decoration told them that I had received the personal blessing of the King Regent himself. Did they not pray their life away for the privilege to receive this blessing? But this was something unheard of. Never before in the history of the country had such a thing happened. And the gossip travelled fast—and far. Who was this fortunate individual who had come from a strange world to be so generously welcomed by their great Divine Soul? From that instant, every one in Lhasa, from the highest to the lowest, was eager to do everything to help me.

2

That afternoon I made a call on the Prime Minister, who lived just around the corner from the Tsarong estate. You had to traverse acres and acres of grounds before you reached the massive three-story structure, which was his residence. Then you had to climb up the Tibetan ladder staircases through the gloom of the reflected light until you reached his penthouse, which was indeed very clean and comfortable, but nothing to be compared with the interior of the Regent's house, except for his shrine, which was done in gold and heavily jewelled, while the walls were decorated with colorful *thangkas* representing the life of the Lord Buddha.

He is thirty-four years old. This is quite accurate, because I asked him. In Tibet, indeed, it is proper to ask one's age. It is one of the first questions to ask, after you have made due inquiry about the state of his health, if he has had a safe and comfortable journey, etc. Not that the Tibetan will specify his number of years. He will rather indicate the number by stating that he was born in the bull year or the dog year, and leave it to you to figure it out. In this section of the world it is a great honor to be an old man rather than a young one; it is felt that no one has gained true understanding until he has passed the half-century mark.

The Prime Minister presented no small contrast to the character of the man I had met that morning; and the afternoon tea developed into a combat of glittering personalities. It is difficult to say how much ground I gained in the matter of friendship; as everything done in Tibet is so indirect. It is the custom in Asia always to be amiable and smiling and jovial, to talk about everything except what is uppermost in your mind, and for which indeed you have made the visit; yet when you leave you know the answer by implication.

The Prime Minister's duties are limited strictly to civil labors, having little relation to the religious life; and it does not take long to see that he is possessed of all the shrewdness of the Chinese, a circumstance that indicates the difficulty one may encounter in dealing with him. He is actually the son of a brother of the late Dalai Lama, who appointed him to his position before his death; while the King-Regent is a reincarnated Lama of the Re-ting Monastery. On the death of the Dalai Lama the Government is put in the hands of the Regent, who is chosen from the four of the high incarnate Lamas of Lhasa. Once he comes into power, he will hold his position until death or until the new Dalai Lama is found and becomes of age, at which time the Dalai Lama might appoint a new Prime Minister.

Throughout the day loads of barley and eggs were sent to me at the Tsarong home. All that remained now was for two

more officials to pay their respects, according to their custom. As soon as all the gifts were accumulated I intended to take a photograph of them, to show to the Western world the Tibetan way of welcoming a visitor to the Holy City.

3

There was little hope of continuing my studies until I had disposed of our official visits and social engagements.

The following morning at eight we went to the home of Nangchunnga Shape, who lived at no remote distance from us. I had been warned beforehand of his loquacious and argumentative nature. Indeed, Tharchin had had some difficulty with him when he delivered my application to visit Lhasa. He not only had to make several visits but he had to listen each time to a long lecture on the evils of allowing strangers to enter their precious Lhasa. After the servants had taken our horses to the stable, they announced our arrival. Then the head servant escorted us to the anteroom, where the *Shape* awaited us. On meeting we merely folded our hands and bowed our heads, postponing the formal introduction until after he had escorted us into his private living room, where he had laid his *kata* aside to present to me. I pulled mine out of my sleeve to place across his folded hands, as they were extended in front of me. I cannot say that there was anything warm about his personality; his greeting was barely more than a faint smile, and his eyes seemed to indicate a host of thoughts behind them, thoughts he intended keeping to himself until he arrived at some conclusion about me.

He was dressed in the typical golden robe worn by Tibetan officials, and it gave every evidence of years' service, for there were no cleaning and pressing establishments in the country. His head was adorned with the customary jewels of authority matted into his braid, which was done up in the usual manner on top of his head, which incidentally bore no indication of having been brushed out and redone for many a day. There was something drab and dingy about every aspect of him and his home. During the entire visit I found it difficult to be friendly, no matter what Tharchin or I said, he always said it was wrong. If we made haste to agree with him and admit that it was wrong then he would promptly plunge into a long tirade to show that that was wrong too. There was no pleasing him, no matter what we said. At the same time I realized that behind this extraordinary manner he was testing me, trying perhaps to confirm the suspicions he had about me and everything that persuaded others to allow me to come to the Holy City. I promptly realized the need of exercising caution, even while conforming to all the little finesses of Tibetan customs of respect. It is difficult to say what might have happened if he had been convinced that permission should not have been granted to me; Tibetans have no scruples about getting rid of an individual they do not want; in this respect their imaginations are not wanting as to means.

4

There was just enough time left to us to hurry back to the Tsarongs for a bite to eat before visiting Kalon Lama Shape, who had been very instrumental in my coming to Lhasa. I was anxious for this opportunity to express my appreciation of his faith in me. He lived at the Potala, which meant that after the visit we should have to make offerings before its sacred shrines.

Once more we entered the private living quarters through a corral, which is always the case in Tibet. I never ceased being astonished at the necessity of having to pass such filth in order to arrive at such beautiful living quarters and altar rooms. The only exceptions that I had so far found were the homes of the King Regent, of the Prime Minister, and of the Tsarongs.

Our host came to the stairway with open arms to greet me. Never have I felt such a flow of friendly warmth flooding me as I did on meeting this individual wrapped in his Lamaic blanket of golden silk; for he was the Lama official in the cabinet. He was an elderly man, and just a bit stooped, as are all of the *Shapes*, doubtless due to endless hours of study. He put his arm around me, and begged that I enter ahead of him. I looked forward to a conversation that it would take years to forget. But after he had taken his place in the usual painted box, there was very little said; yet I felt a great understanding rise on the waves of silence. I knocked at every possible door of entrance, and he always came back with the question as to how I had enjoyed my journey. Yet his personality did not change for an instant, and I enjoyed being with him; we stayed longer than we anticipated.

He plainly showed that he had been anxiously waiting for me to come to him. As soon as he heard that I was in Lhasa he had set up a small English tea-table in his sanctuary. He served us English tea, which had been the case in every instance except that of the King Regent, who clung to his customs and added the auspicious bowl of rice, sprinkled with sugar, from which one takes only two or three grains as a token of friendship on arrival. It is very interesting to watch them serve foreign tea. Invariably they will do it properly except for some one detail, never the same. It may be that a tablespoon will be missing from the sugar bowl, or it may be that the cup will be first half filled with milk. The spirit of friendliness wipes away such petty errors of custom. When Tibetan tea is served, the servant will lift your cup to your lips for you to drink, so you will not be troubled with the effort of lifting the cup yourself. A fresh supply is given at each serving, so the tea will always be hot.

There was an altar in the living room, beautifully decorated. A description of it would involve a complete inventory of all major and minor deities. It is enough to say that every person will have his own choice of deities, which is dependent on his inner feelings, each deity being symbolic of an aspect of truth. There are always to be found different sets of *thangkas*, in keeping with the nature of the shrine, hanging from the moulding all around the room; and from these the understanding individual will grasp the complete emotional story of the person whose shrine it is; for the shrine, the deities and the *thangkas* carry their own symbolic meanings to be picked up by one who knows.

My host asked me if the people on the other side of the world also had their shrines in their homes as had the Tibetans. When I gave him a description of our matter-of-fact Western ways, he was profoundly shocked. He thought religion was the most important thing in life, and that the sole justification for existence was spiritual development. Therefore, it was essential that religion should be carried into every phase of life. He added that it did not make so much difference what religion a person had, but he should have some religion that its power may guide him to the necessary growth and understanding which alone can transmute his hardships and griefs into wisdom and benediction.

5

On taking leave of him, our host offered us a guide to take us through the Potala and some of its shrines. His home was within the Potala walls at the very foot of the palace, and it was a long and slow climb up the stony stairways which led to the upper world of sanctity where the deities reposed. I do not know how tall the Potala is reputed to be, but looking up gave me the sense of a height greater than of any American skyscraper. By the time I climbed all the stairs I felt the way one should feel if he had taken the stairway instead of the elevator to reach the top of the Empire State Building. So immense are the stones which form the endless stairway that I was under necessity of taking several steps to reach the next upward stone. Obviously a structure which owes much to Chinese influence, it was built by Tibetans of rock, to endure for centuries.

On the stairway Tharchin and I reviewed our visit, and I was happy to learn that our host had a reputation for taciturnity, that indeed he had deigned to speak more to me than was his usual custom; this information cheered me no end.

So up and up we went, resting from time to time in order to take a few snapshots of the countryside. When we were about half way up the clatter of hooves struck upon our ears. Behind us came dashing a couple of saddle horses that had been left standing and gotten a bit frisky, having apparently decided to run along and entertain us with their mood of frolicsomeness.

From the time we stepped across the first threshold at the top until we came out we passed through corridor after corridor, each beautifully decorated with life-sized murals of Tibetan design, depicting the life stories of their saints and of Buddha, along with those of the various patrons of their religion and of their deities. All of the woodwork was carved and painted. There was scarcely an inch left untouched. The stairway leading into the anteroom was divided into three sections, the middle of which was roped off, being exclusively preserved for the footsteps of the Dalai Lama; the right and the left stairways were accessible to all. If, however, you adhere to their customs correctly, you will ascend by the left and descend by the right.

On the left wall of the anteroom was a large space covered with Tibetan writing. Below this writing was an impression of the hand of the late Dalai Lama. The inscription consisted of instructions as to the way a visitor should conduct himself in the palace. The impression of those sacred hands was enclosed in a glass case in order to protect it from the touch of profane hands. The other walls of the antechamber, to the right and left of the door leading into the main temple, revealed a variety of large figures of the deities of the four directions, also some murals and a number of astrological charts. The woodwork was hand-carved and painted, and over the spacious doors of the entrance was a hand-carved frieze of lions' heads which protected the temple against the intrusion of evil spirits.

At this point we started to climb up the dimly lighted stairways, until we finally emerged at the very top of the Potala in an open hallway, which led to the shrine of Chen-re-zi, who is one of the highest celestial Buddhas, who was represented in his earthly manifestation by the late Dalai Lama. I made my first offering before this shrine. There are several plastic versions of Chen-re-zi. This one showed seven heads and a thousand hands. Each hand had an eye in the palm, indicating infinite vision, which saw and encompassed the world and all that was in it. It was a relatively small shrine, with the deities all done in gold. The main image of Chen-re-zi was clothed in royal silk brocade, crowned with jewels, and adorned with precious necklaces. There was considerable devotional commotion, due to the presence of half a dozen Buddhists; but by now I was something of an adept at the formalities, and I chimed in with all the poise of one who had been raised in this country.

6

As we were taking our holy water we heard that the doors of the tomb of the late Dalai Lama would be closed shortly; so we made haste to get to it, if only for a glimpse. This tomb consists of a *chorten* over three stories high. I must explain that one Tibetan story is roughly the equivalent of two of our stories. From top to bottom it is covered with pure gold, to say nothing of its adornments of jade, turquoise, rubies and coral. The top of it is decorated with an immense necklace of jade and coral. Any tiny section of this beautiful golden tomb, encompassing

A young carver immortalizes the life of the Dalai Lama on a wood block

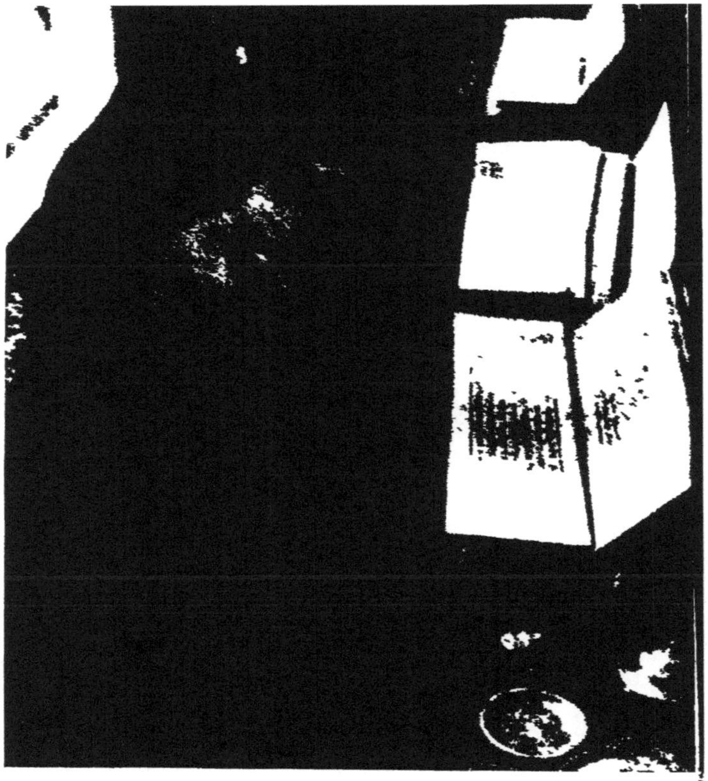

Lamas reading proof

some fifty square feet of space, would exceed the entire wealth to be seen in the monastery of Gyantsé, which threw me into such raptures. The gold alone, mind you, that covers it, is not mere goldleaf, but slabs of gold thicker than a sturdy piece of cardboard. Then consider the countless ornaments which adorn the altar: small trees of solid coral, the loveliest of Chinese vases, images of the purest jade, Buddha lamps of the finest silver and gold. And I must not forget to mention the large offering in the form of a Chinese house standing about three feet and a half, encrusted from top to bottom with pearls. On the floor, in front of this altar, are butter lamps of gold, standing three feet high, large enough to hold a sufficient quantity of butter to burn for three months without being replenished.

From the ceiling down on two sides are shelves holding the precious *Kangyur* and *Tengyur*, all written in gold. In their proximity, in the far left-hand corner, is a large image in gold of the late Dalai Lama himself, in the company of his tutelary image, which is likewise life-size and of the same metal. A wealth of countless small images graced the walls. The large pillars forming the nave in the centre are covered with beautiful silk brocades; the ceiling is also designed on the patterns of silk brocades, woven in with pure gold. Never is the opportunity missed to use gold. Hanging from the ceiling to the floor, but a short distance from the four corners of the *chorten*, is the long royal cylinder or banner, also of the most precious silk.

In the upper stories of the roof, on walls surrounding the top of this *chorten*, they are still in the process of finishing the life-size murals, which will tell the entire story of the late Dalai Lama's life. It is interesting to watch the craftsmen using their small bamboo paint brushes; it must require infinite patience. Just outside the upper galleries the artists are painting sets of *thangkas*, which will also delineate the same life story. These are made by stretching a piece of canvas over a wooden frame, laced with a heavy black cord. At first a rough outline of the picture is drawn; the artist goes over this again and again, each time adding a new color, until the picture is finished. It seems like a very detailed, very intricate process.

7

From this tomb we wended toward the various shrines, any of which would rank among the first anywhere but in Lhasa. We visited the shrines of some of the other Dalai Lamas, who went before, the late Dalai Lama being the thirteenth. Outside of the tomb of the fifth Dalai Lama, however, none of the *chortens* can compare with that of the last. The *chortens* of the fifth Dalai Lama and the late Dalai Lama may be said to compete in the same way that the *Queen Mary* and the *Normandie* rival each other. Actually, the new *chorten* is only a foot or so taller than the other.

Before leaving the Potala we visited the workshop to have a look at a recently printed copy of the late Dalai Lama's *Kangyur*. It was like walking through the stacks of one of our modern large libraries. Each of the large wooden blocks was carved by hand, and its printing as perfect as that done by our machinery. In the rooms below there were the workshops in which the carvers were at this moment making the blocks for the printing of the biography of the late Dalai Lama.

In order to touch on all sides of life, we visited the Tibetan prison, which reminded one of a trap to catch a man-eating lion; it was filled with wretched, withered souls, trotting about with shackled limbs. We entered into a conversation with one poor fellow. He told us that he had stolen a couple of charm boxes about five years ago, and he had no idea when he would be released. What actually happens is that the Government forgets whom they had put in and for how long, which means that once in, always in, unless one day the Government decides to win a

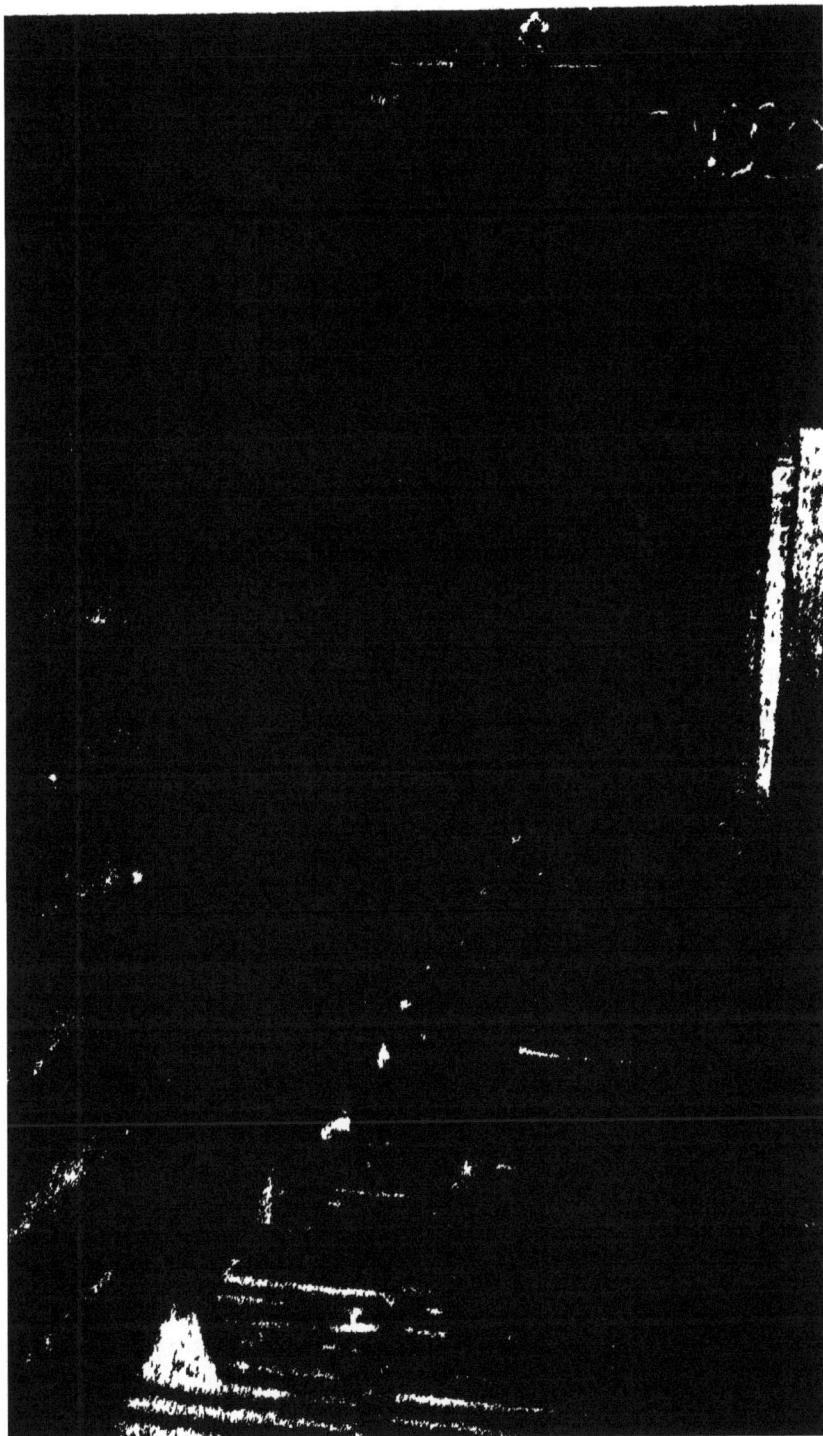

little grace by releasing some of its prisoners; and on so auspicious a day any man may be the lucky one. Just as we were about to leave, we heard faint echoes which emanated from a still lower dungeon, a crying soul was going through the ritual that he might gain happiness in the next life. It turned out to be a friend of Tharchin's, who had once been very powerful, and had the reputation of being a fine scholar to boot.

8

The following day began with an appointment at seven. It is indeed never too early to call on a Tibetan. Our host was to be a young man scarcely twenty years of age. On hearing of our arrival he had come promptly to pay his respects, offering his friendship. I was eager to avail myself of it, for it offered me an opportunity to learn something of the mind of native youth, whose turn would come later to maintain the customs and traditions of the land.

Any time is tea-time here, as I have already said. And one must always take this fact into consideration, that one will drink enough tea to see him through several reincarnations. Fifty cups are a modest beginning, if you go in for it at all. If you are an ordinary tea drinker, you may consume some twenty cups in the course of a meal, which is spread over several hours. And you take a half dozen cups with each brief call you make. To refuse renewed helpings of tea when your cup is empty is regarded as an insult to your host, so if you are clever you learn artfully to sip, and it becomes a game as to how little you can get away with. You'd be astonished as to really how little.

Our young host had a cup of tea in front of him virtually the whole time, as he sat nervously on the edge of an English chair by a Western table, which I had provided, and continually reached for the cookies which we had brought. It was refreshing to see that he was no exception to the rule that all boys eat. He ate because he was hungry, and he consumed cup after cup of tea because he was thirsty. And all the while he flung questions at us, fast, like a child. Unlike the Tibetan adult, who on first meeting will limit his conversation to matters relating to your journey, reserving more serious and intimate conversation for the time when he has learned to know you and trust you, this boy promptly plunged into a frank, natural exchange of questions and answers with an ease which at once established us on a footing of friendship.

No sooner had we left our amiable host than we hurried to keep an appointment at the home of Tethong Shapé. A charming personality, he was, I understood, one of the most influential men in the country. He had made his way from the bottom, as a clerk, to the very top of political leadership. It was quite different during our visit to Pondrong Shapé. In order to finish up all the official calls on that day I contented myself on this visit with the usual formal greeting: I presented my scarf and thanked him for being allowed to visit the Holy City.

He had one of the most enviable house shrines that I had yet seen; it was just the kind I should love to have for my personal use; its size and shape and everything about it gave me untold pleasure. Its images represented a lavish outlay of jewelled wealth, and its carvings were priceless. It must be remembered that a Tibetan will concentrate on his shrine as on no other object. What an infinite amount of wealth is stored away in the form of these jewelled shrines all over Tibet! An important official, he was a tall lean man, full of enthusiasm and vitality. Our talk revolved mostly around my projected tour through Eastern Tibet and China. He had originally come from that part of the country himself, and recently some friends of his newly come from there reported fierce fighting between the Tibetans and Chinese; at the same time bandits roamed up and down the country killing all travellers. But if I insisted on taking that route he said he would do everything in his power to procure permission for me to do so.

The Tethong Shapé's lean and wrinkled face deeply expressed a hidden sadness behind his twinkling eyes. Having remarked about this to some one I was later told that he had but lately lost his wife, a woman he had loved greatly. She had been a close companion of his, and he had grown dependent on her affection.

9

Next we went to the "Cathedral," the *Jo-Khang*, Tsug-lag-Khang, or "the House of the Master," which are the names by which the chief temple is known in Tibet. It was erected in 652 A.D. by King Srong-tsan-Gampo to shelter some images brought in by his Buddhist wife, a daughter of the contemporary Emperor of China, the chief of these images, supposed to represent Buddha at the age of twelve, is actually ensconced here in the Holy of Holies, and it is the aspiration of every devout man in Tibet to make an offering before it at least once in his life.

The entrance of this small two-story building with gilded pagoda-like roof is marked by two large purple prayer-barrels, with the mystical symbol in gilt, and countless devotees storing up their virtue for the next life in front of the doorway. These persons have a wide board the length of themselves with a pad in the middle and bare on either side, with two small hand pads which they use to slide from a standing position to one of humble prostration and then slide back again, only again and again to repeat the process; all this is accomplished very quickly and conveniently. In the matter of penance or the acquisition of virtue they may do this a hundred thousand or ten hundred thousand times in a lifetime. Apart from the entrance, there is virtually no light to be had within the enclosed passageway. There is a large hall that goes completely around the inner room, and down the center of this lane, which is decorated on both sides with religious murals, is a row of prayer-barrels, these barrels being small cylinders of about eight inches in diameter and a foot and a half high, on which is inscribed the mystic symbol. The custom is first to circumambulate this inner shrine and store up treasures in Heaven by revolving these prayer-wheels while repeating the sacred mass. After this you enter the dark inner passageways, guarded by a burning bowl of butter for a torch held at your feet by the monk escort. Incidentally, this inner hall goes around the central image of the temple.

Upstairs the mother of the religion takes the honored place, as does the youthful figure of the Lord Buddha below. None of the images is particularly impressive, and all are filthy and hidden in a thick gloom. Most of the images were of much coarser workmanship than any I had yet encountered. The thing that first caught my attention among the upper shrines was the smell of mice, and when my eyes accommodated themselves to the gloom I could see thousands of these rodents darting in and out among and over the images. One room was filled with weapons of all sorts, such as matchlock guns, spears, helmets and arms of the fourteenth century. Several monks were beating their drums and carrying on the never-ending ritual, while they sat amongst this teeming swarm of mice. And so we left this dungeon of worship and refreshed our souls with a breath of air in the eternal sunlight.

Up on the roof I made the discovery that I would not be permitted to go before the sacred image before I had passed through the ceremony to be held before long. Hurried preparations were being then made for it. It was necessary that I should pass through these ceremonies of purification before I would be permitted to worship in the Holy of Holies.

At no great distance from this sacred place of pilgrimage is a smallpox edict, shaded by a large weeping willow; under the same tree stands the old Treaty Pillar, or *Doring*. The edict which protects one against the horrible disease, which has ravaged so many persons in this community, has his face almost worn away by endless small cuts and marks made by those asking for protection.

Regardless of the time of day that you visit this open market place neighboring on the holy temple, there is an unceasing human stream pouring in and out of the edifice of worship and there are always a number of persons to be found in attitudes of prostration in front of it, even while the rest of the populace dodge in and out among the dead carcasses of dogs or walk around the almost dead humans, in order to look over the wares which are strewn about the street under the canopies of canvas, imported from India. The scene differs little from any Oriental bazaar; only the faces are not the same. The Tibetan merchant is not the aggressive personality you encounter elsewhere; he will not importune you in the forcible manner you encounter in India, and more particularly at Kashmir. The native merchant, whether man or woman, has usually some other occupation besides, and the making of a sale is no life and death matter. It helps, to be sure, and while waiting for a sale he or she will sit around and spin and knit and sew, or smoke, or chat with a friend.

On almost every corner there is a dog curled up asleep, usually a creature with scarcely enough life in him to stir. You have to walk around him.

10

We were late for tiffin. It did not matter much, as I had left word that we might be. In any event, my hosts insisted that I come and go at my own pleasure, as though it were my own home and my own servants.

As it turned out, I was left to dine alone with the Lacham. It left me at a loss at first as to what to do with myself. I had, however, a marvellous meal and a fine conversation, surprising indeed in view of my lingual limitations. And I was mightily encouraged to hear her say to Tharchin, when he appeared after lunch, that we had talked about everything and that I acquitted myself uncommonly well.

It surely meant a great deal to me to live in the home of one of the potentates of Tibet. Not only did it enable me to pick up the language at a rapid rate, but also it taught me all the little things of their life which mean much in any association with the men and women of a country. Who if not the persons in the house in which I was a privileged guest would have taken the trouble to instruct me never to cross my legs in front of a high official? Since I was living according to their customs it was essential that I should observe all such minor details, which seem unimportant yet count for so much. Not that I learned about the management of my legs in front of a high official beforehand. Indeed, I actually committed this gross breach of Tibetan social behavior before I learned of my error. I happened to be visiting an official; I sat on a Western chair with my legs crossed. He was sitting to my right, and I had my left leg crossed over my right knee. All of a sudden I observed his eyes travelling down to the floor. I tried to gather my wits about me, wondering what could be wrong. I could find nothing. Thoughts raced through my mind, for there was certainly something strange in that downward scrutiny. Ignorant of its cause and meaning, I took the precaution of uncrossing my legs, and for the remainder of the visit sat with my feet flat on the floor. Later I made inquiries, and was told that the native custom forbade a person to point his foot toward a high official. It would have been quite proper, however, to have crossed my right knee over my left, and thus have the foot pointing away rather than toward him.

In time, of course, the practice of such native customs becomes a matter of routine. Not less important is it to learn the formalities of religion. It is an education in itself to know how to point one's hand, how to handle objects of a devotional nature, how to conduct oneself in a sacred shrine: indeed, to know all these numerous minor details acquired by cultured Tibetans from their earliest childhood. As I was trying to learn the inner ritual of Buddhism it was absolutely essential that I should know how to manipulate all the necessary gestures correctly, all the more as I was in the precarious position of one who was accepted as the reincarnation of an ancient Tibetan saint, and was therefore expected to have remembered many of the details from my past reincarnation. To be sure, I was allowed the opportunity first to regain contact with the memories of this old soul, and this, it was assumed, would come about by means of the various initiations through which I should have to pass.

II

Tsarong Shape having returned that night, Tharchin decided that it was high time that he began taking his meals apart, so that I might be forced to use my Tibetan upon my hosts. I had a feeling of misgiving, but it turned out to be a pleasant surprise. Though I had a vocabulary well over three thousand words, the great problem was to string together the proper combinations to make sentences—and sense. My trouble was the fear of saying anything at all. Yet I had to talk, and my generous hosts, realizing my embarrassment, helped me along in every manner possible, occasionally, to ease the situation, making the effort to speak a few English words.

I looked forward to having two months at least of this very necessary experience. But I realized that I should have to obtain an extension of my existing invitation of three weeks for that length of time. If I could manage to have the summer in Lhasa I could continue my studies here at the source of Tibetan culture, an inestimable advantage over the alternative of pursuing the same studies in India.

At the same time I was very much concerned about obtaining the permission to continue my journey to Pekin instead of returning to India. There was no record of any one having ever travelled from India to Pekin via Lhasa, and this thought acted as a spur. Moreover, there was the additional incentive of an opportunity to procure copies of the *Kangyur* and *Tengyur* in Eastern Tibet, if I failed to procure them here, at this moment the chances of this seemed slim. I was, in fact, far more interested in obtaining these books than in travel for travel's sake. The end was everything, the means of little consequence. Had it been possible for me to fly into Lhasa and out again without seeing an inch of the country, it would have contented me, provided of course I had been able to procure the things I so much desired, the spiritual knowledge these people possessed. I was here because they could teach me the discipline and the wisdom that were theirs, and to gain this I was ready to walk to the ends of the earth. I wanted to incorporate them into my own life. I was asking for much from their point of view; on the other hand, I felt that as my order had stood me in good stead so far I might reasonably count on my luck continuing. Not that I was unaware that to gain any permission from the Tibetan Government was just as uncertain as the weather. In any case, there was the chance that I might be permitted to go to Shigatsé and on to Saskya in Western Tibet, the original centre of Tibetan culture. As for being allowed to go to China, the prospect was not promising, as the Government might not wish to take the responsibility of my falling into the hands of roving bandits infesting the countryside.

12

Now that the official calls had been made, it was time to make plans for the various religious ceremonies which were to be performed in my honor, making this pilgrimage to the Holy City one of the most enriching experiences of my life. My prime purpose in coming to Lhasa was to carry out the various forms of Buddhistic worship. After consulting with Tsarong, I notified the *Kashag* of my desire, and the *Kashag* sent out an official notice to the various monasteries, which would appoint the auspicious day and make due preparations for the great occasion.

About the same time I paid my respects to the Chinese officials living in Lhasa. They were very friendly. One of them, a very young man, was training to be a Lama. He and I had an interesting conversation on the intricacies of Buddhistic logic. He spoke a very fluent English, and before long we were deep in a discussion of the teachings of Socrates, Plato and Aristotle. This Chinaman learned English in one of the English schools in China, but he also spoke Tibetan and the various Indian dialects. He nourished the ambition of compiling a Chinese-Tibetan dictionary, as soon as he managed to learn all that was necessary in these parts. In most instances it takes the Tibetan about fifteen years to complete his course of study in one of the monasteries, and when he is finished he is usually forty years of age; there is the exception who manages to do it in the early thirties. We in the Western world grudge the years spent in what is thought to be useless study required for a degree, but here almost a lifetime is spent in mere preparation for work. More than that: they are actually enthusiastic about it, and often work their way to it of their will and desire. The old adage "haste makes waste" is no empty phrase here.

The typical Chinese official, wearing a black Chinese robe and black slippers, sitting in a Western chair, with his legs crossed and his hands with long fingernail on the tiny finger, he told me of the historical background of China's control of Tibet, with its various ups and downs. It was to be seen between the lines why they were trying to win their way back through careful diplomatic negotiations. Today Tibet remains an independent nation, isolated from the rest of the world. He assured me that I should have little difficulty in entering China, and that he would immediately send a wireless message to Nanking to secure a visa for my entrance. The only thing left to be done was to obtain the permission of the Tibetan Government. Yet this permission was not a thing to be taken for granted.

CHAPTER VII

SHRINES, AND MORE SHRINES

I

THE new day held the prospect of a visit to the Dalai Lama's *Norbhu Linga*, or "The Jewelled Park," where we had been invited to appear at twelve o'clock. Everything being under lock, it was necessary to give two day's notice to the *Kashag* to make possible the arrangements for our visit. Eager for the opportunity to worship at the private shrine of the late Dalai Lama, I kept an eye on the clock, allowing an hour for the ride to the beautiful park beyond the city, which harbors the home of the Dalai Lama. The matter of time is quite involved in Tibet and Lhasa, for here they have Sun Time, Daylight Saving Time, Indian Standard Time, Calcutta Standard Time, Potala Time, and a mixture of various Lhasa Times; so it was important to start well in advance in order to meet any of the Times, since there is a little over an hour's difference between these various Times.

The park is a little over a mile beyond the city. The countryside surrounding the place consists of a dense growth of willows. Actually, it is a jungle swamp of trees which forms a densely shaded boulevard for about a quarter of a mile to an entrance of typical Chinese design, carved and painted in the royal colors of the native faith. This leads to the old palace, which has been the home of all the past Dalai Lamas but the last, who built a new one for himself. This palace is situated at the back of the large enclosure surrounded by a wall of solid rock of about twelve feet high. I have no idea of its exact size, but I should say that it would require a full day to walk about its spacious grounds; that is, if you did it rather briskly. This great enclosure holds innumerable isolated houses, extensive stables, endless gardens, runways for favorite animals, such as tigers, leopards, bears, monkeys and deer, and a very large bird-cage for peacocks and several other varieties of birds with which I am not familiar. There were also endless winding paths, perfumed by flowering gardens; I warrant you that the great leaders of the faith hugely enjoyed their afternoon strolls. And I doubt if they ever exceeded the most leisurely pace.

The entrances are guarded by a large Tibetan military force, which has an extensive cantonment adjoining the domicile of the most important Buddhist Viceroy on earth. This structure was built by my friend Tsarong, and we paid it a brief visit and offered our scarves to the grounds that the Dalai Lama used when he instructed his military forces and received counsel from his officials. It is a fact worth recording that the Tibetans seem never to have permitted their divine ruler to know of anything but the beauty existing on this material plane, and withheld from his sight the suffering of those souls who were suppliants of his blessings for the next life.

We dismounted outside the rear entrance which leads directly to the new palace at the rear of the enclosure. A short lane bordered with towering trees led from this entrance to the entrance or patio of the late Dalai Lama's palace. Beyond the entrance, a stirring sight, there appeared the even more impressive vision of a modest dwelling, its gilded roof blazing in the sun. This was topped by the conventional tokens that mark the building of such a precious soul, along with the eight lucky symbols and spiritual lightning rods at the corners. Only the roof over the Dalai Lama's tomb at the Potala surpassed this in beauty. The inner patio was paved with stone slabs, relieved by small open-

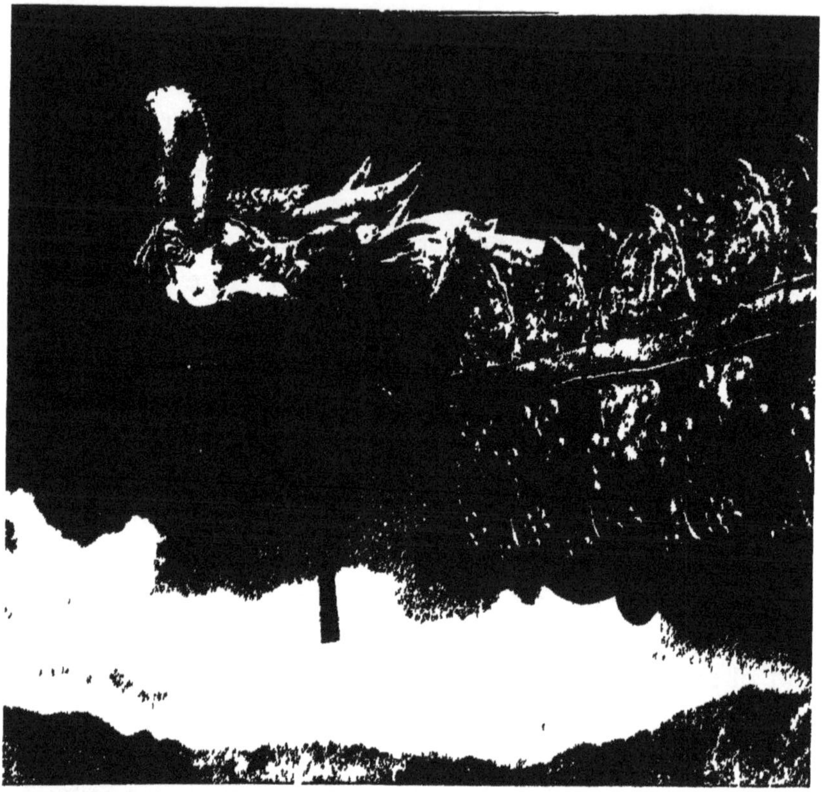

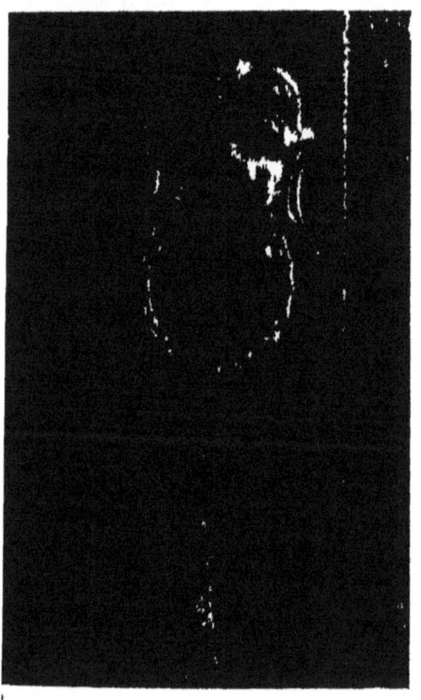

ings for the endless flowers, now in bloom, hollyhocks and roses predominating.

We were greeted by a short, small, rolly-poly, stoop-shouldered monk, garbed in his reddish-brown homespun robe of excellent quality, and also a lay official, a chubby, upright-looking fellow, wearing a yellow robe of officialdom. They both gave us a hearty welcome over inevitable cups of tea.

2

After the restful tea we began our tour of these sacred grounds. Every object used by the late Dalai Lama and every flower lane that had been trodden by his feet was considered blessed, and there was no higher blessing than to be able to touch anything which had a contact with his body; so throughout the visit we were continually placing the precious objects to our heads while repeating our *mantras*.

We started from the bottom, first visiting the stables which were situated in the palace grounds. They were large enough to stall over a hundred of the finest selected ponies, of the small Mongolian type, imported from China. I had visited in India many of the stables of the maharajahs, but these were far more impressive. It was all as clean as the inside of a house, and each stall had a large religious painting on the wall over the feeding-box.

From here we wound our way through the garden jungle, which is gradually covering the flowers almost to the main throne where the late Dalai Lama used to sit. It was his audience chamber, a moderately large room about the size of a small dining hall in a private house, whose four walls revealed one encompassing mural portraying the life of Buddha and the religion coming to Tibet, early Lhasa, and the guardians of the religion; the whole forming a design rich in its blaze of color.

There were various deities cast in gold, covered with silk brocades and jewels.

There was no room in the palace that failed to stir something in that part of us we call the soul. Among these places designed for reflection was a small penthouse built out in the middle of an artificial lake, which was filled with fish and Brahminy ducks. In no instance was any of these rooms large, this one being about the size of the usual waiting room in a dentist's or a doctor's office; there was just enough space to hold the Dalai Lama's floor seat and two *chok-tses* (Tibetan tables) in front and sufficient room for seats to make a couple of visitors comfortable before a small shrine, a gem of its kind, adorned with carved images of coral, turquoise and jade. A small desk, brought, I suppose, from India, seemed incongruous amidst its surroundings. The common hue of all the rooms was that of gold, with deep reds, blues and greens to relieve its brilliance. Every room had its own shrine, and each shrine vied with the others in artistic merit.

When we had finished with the old section, we found a Tibetan lunch waiting for us—a surprise. The Lamas apologized profusely for the modesty of the meal, consisting of a mere fifteen dishes, which we ate on the front porch of the new palace before going through its rooms. We feasted to the chant of a ceremony which is performed daily in the audience hall. The leisurely repast over, I was hungry for more sightseeing, and never was a sightseer offered a finer feast. To be reincarnated into such a majestic station in life as the Dalai Lama had been is surely an unique privilege conferring rare honor, the devotional esteem of a whole people. The Dalai Lama, indeed, is reputed to be the reincarnation of Chen-re-zi. The image of this popular and exalted being is always the central figure usually in the form of chagton-chentog, with a thousand hands and a thousand eyes and eleven heads, but here we found him in the form of

Dugkar, with a thousand hands, a thousand eyes, and a thousand heads, The images were all life-size. A single glance at this figure stirred my emotions indescribably. It gave me the sort of feeling I usually experienced on reaching the top of a mountain or on being struck in the face by a cool breeze on relaxing in a heated sweat of exhaustion to behold the majesty slumbering here below. Here I experienced the same reaction, without the sweat. The room above the audience hall contained the life-sized figure of the Dalai Lama, and beside him were his protectors and inspirers. It would be an experience rare enough in any lifetime to spend one of life's short cycles of light and darkness in any one of these sanctuaries with a fully awakened consciousness. Already I had an inkling that I was being spoiled for any other existence; the desire was growing in me for such a meditative chamber, which by its very nature and design is calculated to induce a human being to collect the inner forces of consciousness.

With this we bade our guides good-bye, and proceeded down the same lane in which the worshipped soul was wont to stroll in his garden, with his great mastiffs chained to their posts for the protection of his holiness. I was told that during his lifetime one never heard the voice of a child here; indeed, it was customary for miles around this sacred park for people to speak in whispers, so that his meditations might not be disturbed.

3

There is nothing that the Tibetan loves more than a feast or a picnic, and all business and work will be called off for such an event. The fact is, I was contemplating giving a party for all the officials of the Government and the other high personages of the Holy City, but I heard that the Regent never attended such affairs. Tsarong, however, did approach him on my behalf, and received the answer that it would indeed be a pleasure, and that, moreover, I could use his quarters for such a party. He would be leaving in a few days for his monastery and would return in about a month or so, when he would give a feast for me. It did not look as if my own party would come off, for I was guest in the Holy City and they all insisted that it was their pleasure to entertain me. Never elsewhere did I encounter such hospitality. Every one in the city insisted upon doing everything that was possible for me, every one was concerned for my comfort.

One afternoon one of our servants announced that a Lama from the monastery had come to see me. I was beginning to be aware that the words "smile" and "Lama" were synonymous; I had yet to see a Lama whose face failed to radiate a smile for which we would gladly pay a million in this country. He was draped in the customary robes of a reddish brown homespun cloth, which left one arm bared to the shoulder. He lent a sense of life to the flowing drapery which was folded into graceful lines about his body. His head was close-shaven, as is the custom of all the Lamas of the Yellow sect. His face revealed definite Mongolian characteristics, while his eyes twinkled with that spark that comes only with years of meditation and the solitude of understanding. He had travelled very widely over Siberia, Mongolia, China, and India, as well as Tibet, and he was very anxious to go on to Moscow, where he wished to learn Russian, having already mastered the languages of the other countries to the extent of being able to write perfectly in their languages. In spite of his travels and erudition, he was extremely timid, but ready to laugh on every provocation.

He left after a couple of hours, as he had several miles to walk in order to return to his monastery, but he promised to return to continue our discussion of his travels and of the spread of Buddhism in Asia. He expressed himself as very anxious to

help me. Why he came was a mystery to me. After his departure I spent some time in trying to fathom as to who could possibly have told him so much about me, and why he was so willing to be my guide. He offered to come and live with me during my stay in Lhasa and help me in all my work. Such things are bound to baffle a stranger travelling in this country, for from time to time some one pops up, some one who seems to drop in from the blue and knows all about you; indeed, knows more than you can possibly tell him. He is fully aware what you want to do, and he makes every suggestion ahead of time as to what he can do to help you. At the moment I merely accepted it as one of the mysteries of the country.

4

Before many days I visited the famous temple of the Rammoche, reputed to be the second most holy temple of Tibet, in which the celebrated image of Buddha, brought by the Nepalese spouse of King Srong-tsan Gampo, was enshrined. The Rammoche was rather less impressive than I anticipated. The only thing of consequence, it seemed to me, was the main image whose cell was protected by a large hanging mesh screen of iron, which is bolted down. The nave was virtually nothing but a continuous aisle of cushions, which would be filled up with monks at the time of my ceremony. After offering my *kata* to the sacred image, which was covered with the customary wealth of jewels, very crudely carved, I circumambulated this enormous cell three times by means of the narrow dark passageway that led around it.

From there I passed around the entire temple, with its endless row of prayer-wheels, which I went on turning, so that virtue might be stored up in Heaven for me.

Then I visited a minor temple near the Tsug-lag-khang, with

Guru Rimpoche as the chief deity. There were many lesser deities at the altar, the forms of which I had not seen before.

More and more I was impressed with the sheer quantity of unstudied material here at the disposal of the scholar who wished to make an intensive study of Buddhist art and literature. And it occurred to me that, with the foundation I was laying for myself, I might some day want to return and do some specialized work for the sake of a world eager for a knowledge of these things. Tibetan culture has a direct relation to the rest of Oriental culture, and it has exercised an influence on world culture, but no one has yet measured the extent of this influence.

For the time being, however, I had no alternative but to stick to the main purpose for which I had come, and this was to acquire the requisite spiritual training.

5

On this particular morning at seven-thirty the room was beginning to be filled with people, and everything was hurry and bustle, in preparation for the party of the day. All objects had been removed from the room, after which the army of servants began piling up great stacks of mats, which were to be spread out on the floor around the low Tibetan tables and covered with rugs.

In the circumstances, it was impossible to continue my work. Besides, I was shortly expecting a barber to come and give me a haircut for the occasion; for I was beginning to look like a jungle man. A certain quantity of hair might be excused, because of my beard, but there is a limit to such things, and I felt that I had exceeded it. The barber turned up, but without his scissors. He dashed out of the room, and reappeared within a few minutes, leaving me to assume that he produced his implements out of a hat. My curiosity as to the nature of these implements was soon aroused, for I felt a tugging around my scalp and a grinding next to my ear. When I finally had an opportunity to catch a glimpse of them I discovered, to my amused horror, that the so-called barber was using ordinary garden shears!

While our own party was being prepared, Tsarong and I, accompanied by Tharchin, started for the Regent's party. I felt the need of Tharchin's presence as interpreter. I was still too timid to try my luck at conversation with so divine a dignitary, even though he expressed the wish that I make the attempt, promising to make allowances for my linguistic deficiencies. He said that was the only way to learn, and offered to correct me every time I went wrong. It was a gay procession. Tsarong was in his best, attired in a gown of gold, seated like a little Napoleon on a very large horse, astride a Tibetan saddle reminiscent of those used by the knights of King Arthur's Court, with rugs and trappings of the most beautiful Oriental design. The horse was as handsomely adorned as the rider, and wore a half crown of jewels as a part of his caparison. A retinue of servants accompanied us. Before the advance of our tiny cavalcade the populace in the bazaars of Lhasa scattered to left and right, bowing graciously at the same time.

On entering the audience hall of the Regent, Tsarong recognized the divinity of his king with the customary devotional prostration of humility, but from then on he was himself, direct, outspoken, and fiery. The Regent had a small table arranged for himself, and a raised row of Tibetan mats next to the wall of glass overlooking his flowering garden. A short distance from this, and parallel with it, was a larger table for the guests, which consisted of our party, a Lama, and two boys, one of whom was quite small. I was under the impression that they were kinsmen of the Regent. This table was covered with yellow silk brocade with a design of black silk. The small boy looked as if he had been playing in a Tibetan alleyway; I felt sure that water had not touched him for months on end; his skin and clothes were far beyond the point of being merely dirty. It is a real experience to dine in such a place, where the best of Tibet is to be met with, and to have the jolt of long unwashed arms stretched out before you helping themselves to the food, but a Lama is a Lama for all that, washed or unwashed, in the Regent's house or elsewhere. The Regent himself wore spotless robes of yellow silk.

We seated ourselves to the endless helpings of Tibetan tea, served with silk napkins. The Regent's napkin was a beautiful yellow silk on one side, and a plain white on the other. This was supposed to be only a light lunch, but the dishes kept coming in numbers that I could not keep up with. I learned, however, how to nibble like a rabbit for hours, without permitting much to enter. This is the only way to survive in Tibet. Nothing could be more fatal than to take a generous helping of anything that is particularly pleasing to the palate, bearing in mind the fact that no meal is ever offered that includes less than fifteen dishes. While there is no doubt that the Regent was a highly spiritual person, with a slender, emaciated body, and stood only five feet eight, he gave every indication of having an appetite good enough for a growing boy.

During the conversation I had with the Regent, he informed me that my request to be allowed to make my exit by way of China was granted. He also told me that they were very anxious to give me every opportunity to secure a set of Tibetan scriptures. If I may put it bluntly, I consider it Hell to live in a place where people would think you had gone mad if you should break out into paeans of joy; I had indeed to content myself by saying very quietly that I thought it considerate of them, after which I proceeded with my meal outwardly un-

perturbed but inwardly afire over my good fortune. The Regent also asked me to furnish him with a complete list of things I wanted, and he promised that he would make every effort to have them found for me. There was every indication that they would be outright gifts, furnished me in order that I might use them in my work on my return to America.

When I left him, the generous Regent presented me with a long white silk *kata*, and also with a small piece of red silk, with which he tied the triple knot and placed it around my neck; it is one of the highest honors that one can receive in Tibet and is awarded only by their most holy Lamas. Then he made me a lovely offering of a small image of Buddha, and of a large Tibetan book wrapped in beautiful yellow silk. It turned out to be a very fine one, with each page inscribed with a design of a different deity. It is the custom to have such images only on the first few pages, but rarely on every page.

Now that I had been allowed to remain here another two months, it gave me pleasure to think that I should be able to see the Regent several times upon his return from his monastery. In the meantime, I had to hurry home, for there was yet my own party before me at tea-time.

6

Norbhu, who had but lately arrived in Lhasa, was already at the house chatting with Mrs. Tsarong. Presently, the other guests began to arrive. Oddly enough, it was a Chinese official who reminded me that it was my own national holiday, July Fourth, and, indeed, he had taken the trouble to bring me a *kata* in honor of the day, congratulating me at the same time on belonging to a free people which had had the sense to throw off the shackles of the outworn forms of the Middle Ages. I could think of no finer way of celebrating the day than by sitting at a table at which six nationalities—Chinese, Nepalese, Sikkimese, English, Tibetan, and American—were represented. Eighteen languages in all were at our disposal, but we confined our conversation to English and Tibetan. The fact is, nearly every one at the table could speak English, a fair indication that English comes pretty near to being the universal language. There were sixteen persons in the party, and the servants brought up the number to over forty. There were pots of tea boiling in all parts of the house, in order to serve all.

Now that the parties were coming to an end I was settling down to work. Lhasa being a literary center of Tibet harbored many scholars and attracted learned pilgrims. The prospect of remaining here for the entire summer was, therefore, a propitious one from my point of view. Lhasa, if you like, was a sort of a clearing-house for all manner of Tibetan knowledge; here it was possible to learn where in the land this or that manuscript was to be found, or in which cave this or that teacher had his abode.

Yet now and again there was a feast day, and something was to be learned on such days too. There was a feast day when officials could be seen hurrying to take part in the ceremonies, and on this day Tsarong Lacham left the house in her finest attire. She could scarcely walk because of the weight of the precious jewels. I held the camera in readiness until she came down, and I took a picture of her in all her glory. Yet she said that she was by no means at her best.

I had an orgy of photography at a neighboring park, in which some of Tharchin's friends were making merry at a picnic. Here in Lhasa, as elsewhere in Tibet, it is the fashion for folks to leave their homes for a few days and have a grand picnic in the park, but a mile or so away. We in the West usually think of such outings in terms of hours, the Tibetans in terms of days. The camping picnickers were greatly amused to see me attired in Tibetan dress. It seemed to put them at their ease with me. As for me, I fully enjoyed the comfort of the roomy native clothing. It was again and again a bit trying for me to be offered the inevitable tea-cup while I was taking pictures.

From here we walked through the grove of trees to the banks of the beautiful Kyi-chu (Lhasa River). Instead of the small stream I imagined it to be, I was surprised to find it a broad river, which would have taxed my strength to throw a stone across it in my best baseball days. On the banks of this lovely river many villagers were washing their clothes, while in the middle of the stream an occasional native boat could be seen floating down the rapids, carrying wares of one sort or another down to Chu-shu, where the river joins the Tsangpo-chu, the mightiest river in all Tibet.

Several Lamas visited me to discuss preparations for the big ceremony which was to come on the following Thursday. This was to be the biggest religious event ever held in Lhasa, and my own modest part in it would be to participate in my purification initiation, which was eventually intended to give me contact with my inner self. A particularly significant fact, and not a little mysterious, too, was that the most learned Lama of Lhasa sent word that he would officiate at this ceremony. It seemed incredible. At the same time qualms seized me. Was I sufficiently prepared to stand the test? Apparently they had confidence in me, or they would not give me the opportunity. It was absolutely essential that I should know all the formalities to the minutest detail, so that nothing might interrupt the ceremony. It was to be another of those days of days, because never before had a foreigner been allowed to take part in a religious ceremony before the sacred shrine of the Tsug-lag-khang, the holiest spot in all Tibet. What was it all going to be like? What would happen to me? What depths was I to sound?

7

My study for the day was topped off with a Chinese meal that I am sure I shall never forget. Indeed, I arrived for the meal at one-thirty and did not stop nibbling until five-thirty, finishing up the thirty-sixth dish around five, after which some rice was brought in and six more dishes of the fudge variety, delicacies of their kind. If my stomach should survive this orgy, which was more than I at the time expected, I calculated that it had consumed enough food to last me all the way to China and back again. The thirty guests, who included three Chinamen and four Nepalese, the remainder being Tibetan Lamas and officials, appeared to have a right gay time. During the meal I had the pleasure of sitting next to Mondrol, whom I have already mentioned as having been one of the first to greet me on my arrival in Lhasa with a gift from the *Kashag*. Speaking a perfect English, he plied me with questions about America, and as I was just as anxious to learn in my turn I plied him with questions about his experiences. Our exchange of talk was constantly interrupted by the arrival of a new dish, and, worse luck, as the guest of honor, I always had to lead the way, and then take a second helping to encourage the others.

During the feast a heavy rain came up and, to our delight, cooled off things considerably, as well as settled the dust, which was getting pretty bad, this being the unpleasant aspect of Lhasa. Of even greater interest was the fall of heavy snow on the peaks which surrounded the city. This heavy blanket of snow on the mountains seemed to have no effect on the climate; the air was not by any means cooler, but it was certainly clearer.

We left the feast filled with pig bladder, chicken gizzards, fish stomachs, sea slugs, cuttle fish, birds' nests, and what not. It all sounds terrible, but it tasted grand. I only wish it were possible for me to set a meal like this before my friends in America.

8

Word came that preparations were being made for the great ceremony to be held on the morrow in the Holy of Holies; moreover, that permission had been granted me to photograph these preparations as well as the ceremony itself. So we made a scramble for our cameras and promptly departed for Tsug-lu-khang in order not to miss anything.

Within the precincts of a very small patio, situated within the innermost part of the temple, some twenty or more Lamas had gathered in order to knead 4000 pounds of barley flour into innumerable specimens of a small sacred object known as a *torma*, which is shaped as though a cone had been placed on a cylinder, the whole not unlike a miniature *chorten*. These are used as offerings at the altar during all the ceremonies, after which they are served as food to the Lamas. The place itself was strongly reminiscent of a baker's shop, for the light was being reflected in all directions by the multitude of sunbeams diffusing the flour dust from these vats, which were being filled from the great bin, into which the Lamas dove clear up to the shoulder in the process of kneading it all into dough. Before they began this process each and every one of them very meticulously washed his hands and arms all the way to the shoulders.

The first task was to measure out the necessary amount of this sacred flour, which was done by one man dumping a sack of flour into a small wooden trough, levelled off at the top with a board, tapered at the end, in the hands of a Lama. The contents of this were promptly dumped into another container, which was used for the purpose of carrying it to the great shadowy flour bins, where the Lamas stood, as white as our own bakers, and were toiling away. They worked with astonishing rapidity; in an incredibly short time they had the entire quantity of flour ready for the mixers and kneaders to begin their task. It took only about five men to do the measuring; the duty of carrying the flour back and forth fell upon the women, who were always brought in to do the heavy work. These women and girls placed hundred-pound sacks on one another's backs and walked away like piano movers. They disposed of their burdens to men who mixed the flour with water, which was brought in large wooden containers—also by women. As soon as the right consistency had been reached, great bulks of it were rolled out in a contrivance made for the purpose. They all puffed and heaved until it was all worked up into large dough-balls of approximately thirty or forty pounds each. The next step was to mould the emblem; this was done in the same deliberate, systematic fashion as all the preliminary processes. When finished, each *torma* stood about a foot high. The hands of the bakers worked as rapidly as machinery on small wooden trays, and as rapidly the *tormas* were whisked away, to make room for the next batch. It took only half a day to complete this task.

This, however, is only the beginning; for there is a like amount of grain coming from over forty sacks, each weighing a *maund*, or eighty pounds; the whole contents are measured out into the thousand waiting copper bowls, which are then arranged on two rows of the surrounding altar. On the lower tier they place one bowl on top of the other, while on the upper tier they stack them up three high and then join them all by placing incense sticks in each at angles, thus crossing the one coming in the opposite direction from the bowl next to it. So they form a holy lattice work, placing a small round flake of a flower at the point where the two sticks of incense cross.

There is a similar time-consuming task in decorating the one

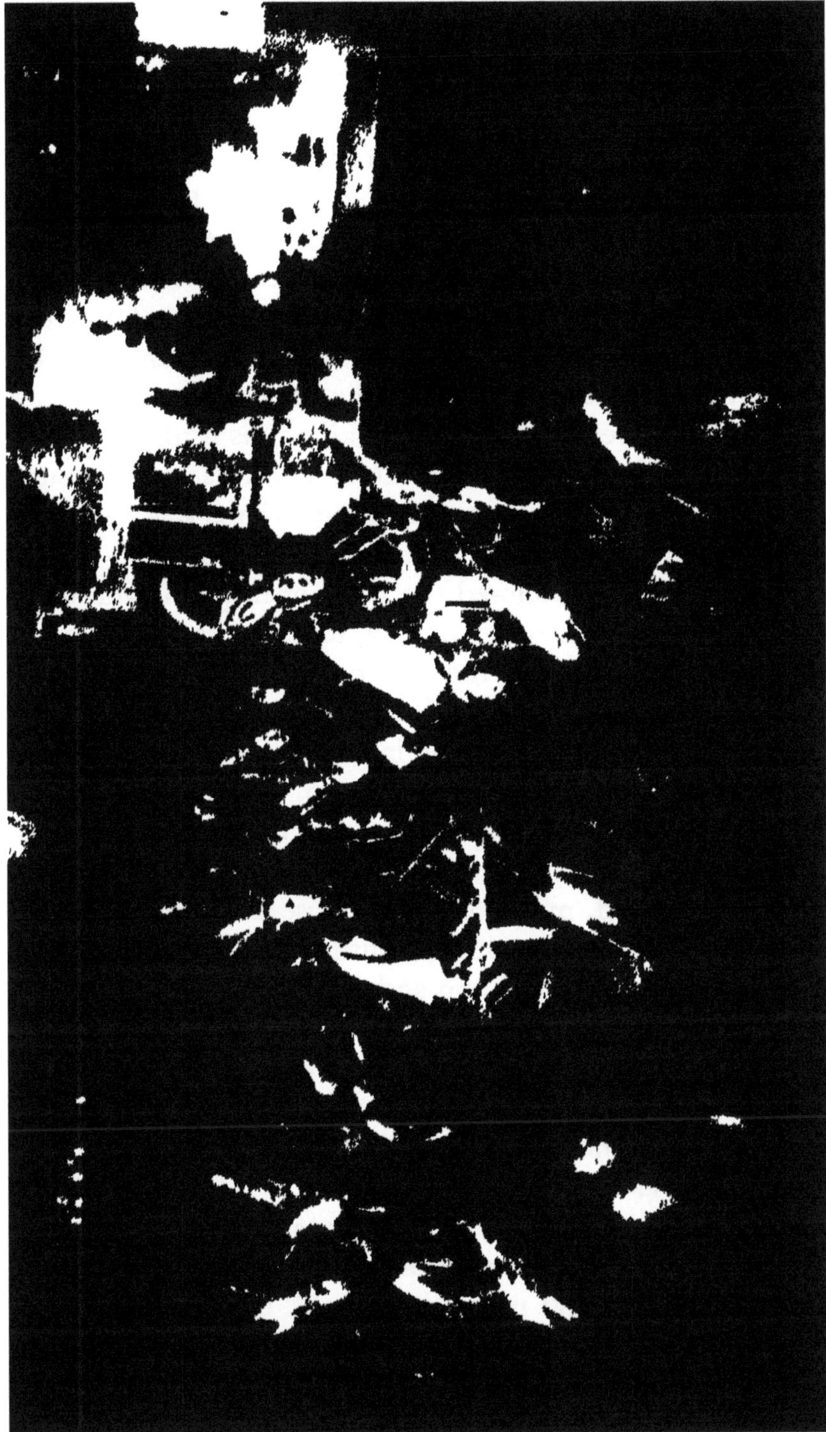

ısand *chortens* with lovely butter designs, after they have ı placed in theır proper positıons. These *chortens*, ınstead of g stuck on top of one another, are placed three deep on row. Before these preparations are finıshed, there must till another row arranged below all this, of a thousand ls of sacred water; and as we were watching them getting *chortens* ready, we came upon a large group of women ered in a circle in sitting posıtions on the floor and polish-ıp the brass bowls to be used for the holy water.

bout five feet removed from this altar was a narrow table ıing the entire length of the altar, this table was to sus- the thousand butter lamps. And the whole was designed ɔrm a sacred lane through whıch only the purified mıght . This sacred aisle enclosed the large open patio, where all nonks would gather on their long, unrolled carpets to have - tea and graın during the ceremony, which would keep ı engaged from the break of day until far into the night. scrutınized the details of the inner temple I thought how ınate I was in that it had an open top, thus making it pos- for me to take photographs. Later in the afternoon, how-, when I returned to the patio to see how far the prepara- ; had progressed, much to my surprise I found that they covered the entire top with a beautiful hand-decorated can- ın order to keep out the rain and also the light.

'n hearing that the butter had arrived at the customary ɛ for its melting in large copper vats, ornate with their lded designs and inscriptions of *mantras*, we sauntered off ıat direction in the hope that I might have a few shots with :amera; but as luck would have it, the rain had come, blot- out the little light that might penetrate into the dark cham- Nevertheless, I did make an effort to record the process of ,hing the twenty and more bags of yak butter. In all they ;ured out over two thousand pounds of butter in order to feed these thousand sacred lamps to last through the entire ceremony. I have an idea that electricity might be far cheaper, because by the time this supply is brought from the great herds of the Chang-tang (Northern plains) over a thousand miles away, the price soars progressively. There was no way of telling how old it was, but I may hazard the guess that the cows that gave the milk for it were in all likelihood dead by now. As soon as the butter is churned out it is all "hermetically" sealed in yak-skin bags and headed toward Lhasa, where it is used for such devotional purposes. Over ten thousand pounds of it are used at this small shrine alone each month.

After it has all been weighed out and the records made, the bags are carried and placed on the floor beside a great oven. Then a fellow comes along, covered from head to foot with encrusted grease and soot, and with a blade in his hand larger than any butcher knife we use at home; with all his might he drives this blade into these black hairy bags, ripping them open. On accomplishing this, he places them on a narrow ledge next to the great boiling vat, under and around which was a roaring blaze of burning cedars. With a large wooden spade he heaves in the butter, then empties the barrel. After it is all melted down, the butter is borne away in small jugs to the temple about half a mile away; here it is poured into containers holding a small wick and used for the lamps.

The only thing that is actually wasted is the butter, for it is all consumed by the holy flame. The rest of the material, however, is distributed among the numberless monks who live at the Rammoche. Some of it is even sold, and the money is used to purchase necessities for the monastery. The grain used in the baking of the ceremonial *tormas* is not wasted; indeed, it is the staple food of the monks as it is of the lower class of Tibet. Often, too, a Lama will take a small portion of this food and walk out with it through the village of the Holy City and distribute it to the very poor. Now and then he might visit a prison and give a share of it to some of the forgotten souls. And so these lavish ceremonies are, in a practical sense, not wholly unproductive of good. They are, in fact, among the mechanisms of society for the taking care of the poor and of their religious fathers.

CHAPTER VIII

I AM INITIATED

I

As an interlude to the events just described we met one of our Tibetan friends and went to his place to have tea. I had been there previously, but this was the first time that I was taken to their sitting room, which was the shrine of their personal deity, Chen-re-zi, that is the deity which guides their personal belief. Besides this, there is always the private temple of the house, and, when possible, it contains a full set of *Kangyur* and *Tengyur*. Here the main image is usually that of Buddha, with Guru Rimpoche on one side and Tsong-Khapa on the other, this to substantiate the prophecy of Buddha that he would bring forth the religion that is known as the Gelupa cult today. If the host belongs to another sect, the arrangement is naturally different, because Tsong-Khapa is the founder of the Gelupas and belongs exclusively to the members of this cult. In the present instance Chen-re-zi is of importance, and his main figure on the altar embodies the principles which are supposed to guide this deity's meditations. On each side of him he is represented by other aspects of himself in smaller images; and there will be other favored deities, notably Guru Rimpoche. Such a shrine will probably cost in the neighborhood of five thousand dollars. The cost, of course, wholly depends on the size of the main image, the amount and quality of the hand-carving, and the gold and jewels used. We spent the entire tea-time discussing the various deities of the different sects, and my host appeared anxious to impart all possible information to me, since he considered me as one who would carry the seed of truth embodied in their teachings back to my country. Already regarded as a Buddhist by them, I enjoyed their confidence, and all information, asked and unasked, was freely forthcoming.

I had worked at top speed that morning to get things out of the way so as to keep an appointment with Mr. Richardson for an early dinner; he had promised to show me the finished picture of Lhasa which had been taken by the British Mission during the past winter. And in the evening over a leisurely meal I had a long discussion with Mr. Fox concerning the various teachings of the East, in which he was intensely interested. He was a Catholic, having been converted to the faith after much unsatisfactory searching around among the different interpretations of Christian spirituality. He had lived in India for over seventeen years and always held a lively interest in native thought, though he had never had the leisure to delve into its depths. A tolerant man, he seemed astonished and not a little impressed when he heard about the beliefs held in this section of the world. The rumor having spread that I was a Buddhist making a pilgrimage to Lhasa, he was eager to talk with me and to hear what I had to say about the teachings of the faith. I remember stressing the fact that the ancient King Asoka had about 250 B.C. contrived the most effective means for exploiting these teachings, so that today we have forgotten the philosophy which gave them life and are held in fetters of emotional ignorance, maintained by ritual and organization. The truth of the matter is, the mire of sanctified formality is so deep today that it is next to impossible to find the original gem that gave lustre to the faith.

After the meal there was a showing of movie films. Movies in Lhasa seem incongruous. Yet the fact must be recorded. The most interesting aspect of the showing was the large crowd of Tibetans who filled the room. "Like sardines"—this old image should do. They were teeming at the door when we first came down, and when the door was opened they swarmed in like an army of migrating bees. The guests arranged themselves in the chairs in the large dining room, while their servants flocked in on the floor, crawling forward until they were sitting directly beneath the screen itself; against the wall in the rear they clambered over and upon one another's shoulders and stood up on chairs or on any other piece of furniture within reach. It was impossible to open enough windows; the atmosphere was stifling. Mr. Richardson told me that these servants had seen the same pictures on several previous occasions, yet every time he showed them there was the same eagerness to be admitted. They always enjoy seeing themselves in the picture, but it is the Charlie Chaplin reel that brings the roof down, with Rin-Tin-Tin as second favorite.

2

The day of which I am writing, being the last day of the Tibetan month, was considered auspicious for the ceremony of Tsug-lag-khang; it was to mark my first purification ceremony. I hoped it would enable me to gain contact with my inner self, which in this instance meant with that part of me that had already lived before this life; it was now commonly accepted that I was the reincarnation of an ancient Tibetan saint and had, therefore, come to them not as a disciple but as an adept whose duty it was now to brush up the old subconscious memory that would restore me to my real self returned to this earth to continue my predestined mission.

At first their meaning eluded me, yet something within me gave me a glimpse of the truth, and I knew that there was no escape for me, that I could not but follow the inner urge which would force the unconscious to break through the shell that held it back from the mysterious hidden knowledge. I was as excited about it as I had been over my first visit to school during my early childhood.

The monks had started at daybreak the repetition of certain required chants, preliminary to the ceremony. These chants had to be repeated a definite number of times, ranging into the thousands; and a strict count was kept of the reading of the particular formula. I imagine it was quite an ordeal. This formula was one which I myself had requested, it being optional, and the ceremony connected with it, according to my own desire, demanded that the monks abstain from meat, and limit their diet to tea, *thukpa* (porridge) and rice. It is the custom that a portion of the food prepared for the ceremony be sent to the devotee, and so early in the morning large quantities of it began to pour in. The containers sent would easily hold ten gallons. A like quantity of tea was sent along. I am sure the boys of the house had all they could hold for a few days. I personally had no desire to begin the diet at that particular moment, though I must admit that it did not taste half as bad as it looked. Indeed, I am convinced, one might get fat on it, and that it contained sufficient nourishment for the maintenance of health, once the palate got adjusted to its odd flavor.

It remained for me an unaccountable mystery why the great T'ri Rimpoche himself, the precious holder of the throne, should have chosen to officiate at my first initiation. He was commonly accepted as the most learned Lama in all Tibet; he had risen to this position through sheer effort of application, and without the aid of a fortunate reincarnation. This one chair is always open to candidates, and only the industrious are ever able to attain its prestige; it ranks the holder only next to the Dalai Lama himself, often officiating in his place when the other is absent or indisposed; he often becomes the Regent of Tibet.

That he should conduct the service for me was an honor I had not anticipated. To give some relative idea of its significance I might compare it to a marriage or some other ceremony in the Christian faith being performed under the personal direction of the most noted bishop in the land. The T'ri Rimpoche spent most of his time in study and meditation and usually took charge only of the most important ceremonies. His own training consisted of satisfying all the requirements of a *geshe*, which is equivalent to our Ph.D., with the difference that it takes about forty years on an average to attain it. Once he has mastered these requirements, he is permitted to take up the *Tantrik* teachings, which are the most guarded of all revelations in Tibet; hence, one is never able to study them until rather late in life.

The ceremony which awaited me was wholly of a *Tantrik* character, and was therefore of the greatest interest to me. Ceremonies of this kind are never performed in the monasteries. This temple, as it happens, is one in which people convene for different types of service. Since it is the Holy of Holies, it is considered the most sacred place in Tibet for any service. Any ceremony held here demands the presence of an officiating Lama. The formula which was being repeated by the Lamas throughout the day contained some *mantras* which were reputed to hold certain designated power which, after the devotee had been fully prepared, would be practically instilled into him, even though he might not be fully aware of it at the time. The realization of the effect of these various psychic endowments was supposed to come to him from a later ceremony, for which all of these were but preliminary steps. It was a great mystery to me why the Lamas came to me, and why they arranged that I should go through all the ceremonies.

3

Shortly after breakfast the Tsarongs hurried me into a Tibetan costume, so that they might inspect me before my departure for the ceremonies. It was as if I were their child going off to school for the first time, and they were anxious that there should be no fault in my appearance. Their interest was truly touching, for I was forever bothering them with questions and appeals for help. In the end, however, they thought I looked ship-shape, whereupon I took my departure in the company of Tharchin, and my two "boys," Lhare and Norphel, who carried my photographic equipment, I thought I might have an opportunity to make some sort of record of a part of the ceremony, and I did not want to miss the chance.

One matter to which I had to attend before leaving for the temple was the writing of a long prayer, wishing health, wealth, and happiness to all the world. This had to be composed according to a set formula, and my name and nationality had to be inserted. It was important to have it ready early, so that the person who was to read it could have an opportunity to practice reading it beforehand; for they are so meticulous with all the details of their ritual.

Full of excitement I left the house for one of the most absorbing experiences of my life. I had not the slightest notion of what was going to happen. I must have felt as a Baptist feels on having to go to a Catholic service. I was full of confidence, however, having gone through a lot of mental rehearsing.

We entered the dark alleyway leading into the hall which circumambulates the sacred shrine; here I made my three devotional rounds, turning the prayer-barrels and repeating the sacred formula: "*Om! Ma-ni pad-me Hūm!*" There was a throng of wondering onlookers, who never before had laid eyes on a European turning prayer-wheels in humble devotion. Because of my beard they could not quite guess my nationality, and I detected the repeated whisper: "Who is he?" Outwardly, at least, impervious to the attention I was attracting, I continued my devotional perambulations.

The T'ri Rimpoche had not yet arrived, so all the monks—about eight hundred of them—were having a brief respite from their discipline. The entire patio, so bare yesterday, was covered today with long lines of red homespun mats. The altar next to the wall was attractively decorated with the vessels of water, and with the *tsampa chortens*, which we had watched in the making yesterday. The small altar in front made a narrow aisle through which one might pass between the towering offerings and the glowing flames of butter, which induced the exuding of sweat if you ventured to linger. At the head of the lines, under an immense canopy of canvas, was the high seat of the head Lama, usually shut off when he was on it, so that he might not be seen. A short distance in front, on both sides, were the seats of the next four highest Lamas, two on either side, one pair facing the other. The setting itself inspired awe. It was very unpretentious and austere; its very simplicity induced a subtle reverence.

A large mat was arranged for my seat; it was just a trifle higher than the seats of the other attendants. And here for a little while we relaxed over cups of tea until the head priest arrived.

The intense silence of the empty assembly hall was broken by the deep vibration of the melodious gong which had been struck with a mallet. This was the signal for the monks to assemble, for the Lama had arrived and was already in his seat. There was a muffled rush, and the rustle of homespun, as the multitudinous monks hurried to their respective seats in their silent shoes and expeditiously donned the red cloaks which they had left behind during the intermission. As soon as they were wrapped in these spacious garments they seated themselves almost as one man, and in an instant they were a disciplined unity; the room promptly began to vibrate with the low mumbling of their prayers. Immediately upon the completion of the first prayer—the Tea prayer it was—the younger Lamas sitting at the extreme end on either side began to stir. These barefoot servers were running to the rear of the room. Here, at the entrance, there were women who brought large earthen jars of prepared tea, which they poured into empty barrels bound by bands of brass.

After all had had their tea the Lama who had been all the while sitting at the rear of the room on a small raised platform was now advancing to the center of the room. After performing the three customary devotional bows he began to read my petition supplicating that I be given the opportunity of having this ceremony and requesting the consent of the Lamas to the repetition of the secret *mantras* which the T'ri Rimpoche had ordered. To this a low rumbling response of consent came forth, whereupon he produced my prayer and read it to the assembly.

This marked my entrance. Leaving my camera in the hands of my companions, I advanced to the center aisle, where I likewise made three devotional bows, then walked forward toward the esteemed soul sitting on the divine throne of wisdom, where I made the same offerings as at the Regent's place, and obtained on the spot. Indeed, I was hardly aware of what I was offering, so quickly did the different objects flash past my vision. The first put into my hand was an object whose nature eluded me, and it was followed in quick succession by a small prayer-book, an image of Lord Buddha, and a copper *chorten*. After this I presented my *kata* and bent forward to receive the blessing which would come to me through a moment of silence, with my head bowed, touching the sacred throne upon which he was seated. From behind this closed chamber came a *kata*, which was given me with his blessing. Then, backing away in humble respect, I offered my *katas* to the four high Lamas, who likewise gave me their blessing after reverently placing their *katas* over my head.

A long period followed, while I sat in silent meditation below a small shrine which had been erected for the purpose; at the same time the monks continued to repeat the formula which was to bring me so much virtue. Simultaneously the high priests were filling the room with mystic waves; they twisted their wrists, with fingers placed in various positions, and they rang a small prayer-bell and held the *dorje*, thumping on a drum made of a human skull. During this part of the ceremony endless cups of tea were brought to me, and I had to consume them for the sake of friendship. Then came the time for me to make a round of inspection, after the offering to the monks had been made. Again I followed to the center aisle, where I demonstrated my humility; then, with burning incense, I walked up and down the lines of endless Lamas, who were seated in humble respect on the carpet. Afterward, *tsampa* and rice were served to the monks.

By this time several hours of the day had passed by, and I am sure that some of those lost tones of the underworld brought forth their subtle effect, for never before did I so intensely experience the feeling of being consumed with a fire within.

After we all had had a bite to eat they were to continue the repetition of my *mantra* throughout the entire day, until they had completed the book, which would probably hold them in assembly until about seven that evening. Before that time arrived, however, they would probably have had three more servings of tea, which would make eight in all, with one serving of *tsampa*. Each Lama carries his own cup and bowl in order to receive his share of tea and *tsampa*. With this they will also have one generous helping of rice some time during the day. With the setting sun I had to return to the meditative chamber and once more repeat the sacred syllables which had been given me and to reflect upon the symbology of the shrine which had been erected for me; and this marked the end of the beginning, and also made me aware of how hungry I was. I had not been privileged to eat as were the other Lamas, as I was the one to receive the effect of those mystic words; so little time was wasted in returning to the Tsarongs, who were waiting dinner for me.

4

It may be of some interest to note that the Chinese, who lost all influence over Tibet in 1911 and have been trying to regain it ever since, still labor under the impression that Tibet belongs to them and that the Tibetans are a folk inferior to themselves. Actually, the Tibetans have taken good care of themselves since the expulsion of the Chinese. The Chinese have the notion that there is only one supreme intelligence in the world—and that is of the Chinese. If they condescend to admit that the Western world has surpassed their wildest imagination in mechanical and industrial advancement, they qualify it with the comment that does not necessarily imply great intelligence but rather that the Westerners have merely given greater application to matters to which the Chinese did not attach undue importance. If this is their attitude towards us, it is easy to imagine as to the importance they attach to the Tibetans, who have done nothing but preserve the Buddhistic scriptures for themselves.

For some years the British had been keeping a representative travelling back and forth from Gyantsé to Lhasa. One of his apparent duties was to keep an eye on the possibility of Chinese intrusion, which might have consequences of a political and commercial nature. The British desire Tibet to remain a closed country and to continue its speculations in religion, with the attendant isolation which enables the British to maintain what is practically a commercial monopoly.

These reflections are in no small measure due to the fact that on this particular morning, very early, I set out to see the political officer, Mr. Richardson, take his departure from Lhasa. The party which saw him off was a large one, and the affair bore an official character. The Lhasa camp, from which the departure was made, was a little over a mile from Tsarong's house. I took a short cut which led me around old Chak-po-ri (Temple of Medicine), situated at the opposite peak of the same rocky ridge that helps to enclose Lhasa. I had never been around this way before, my usual custom when going to the political offices being to go through the city and the passageway leading under the enormous *chorten* which forms the entrance gate to Lhasa, built at the lowest place of the saddle between Lhasa's architectural wonders. The medical center is built on a precipice of solid rock, and it reminds one of the castles of Germany. Along the narrow ridge over the gently flowing stream leads the narrow trail around this rocky ridge. This trail forms a narrow ledge along the side of this natural wall, on whose sheer face endless carvings are to be seen; virtually all the deities of the Tibetan pantheon are depicted here. The gods are painted in their respective colors, forming a vast fresco for the traveller to admire. For almost a quarter of a mile the cliff is one solid mass of rock carving.

It is certain that one of the things one learns from such an experience as living in Tibet or in any other remote place in the world is that it becomes absolutely essential to find recourse in one's imagination for any possible pleasure, and it creates the ability to extract a deeper joy out of the simple few diversions than from the endless shallow pleasures of our infinite ostentation. The need to discover diversion in myself led me to this

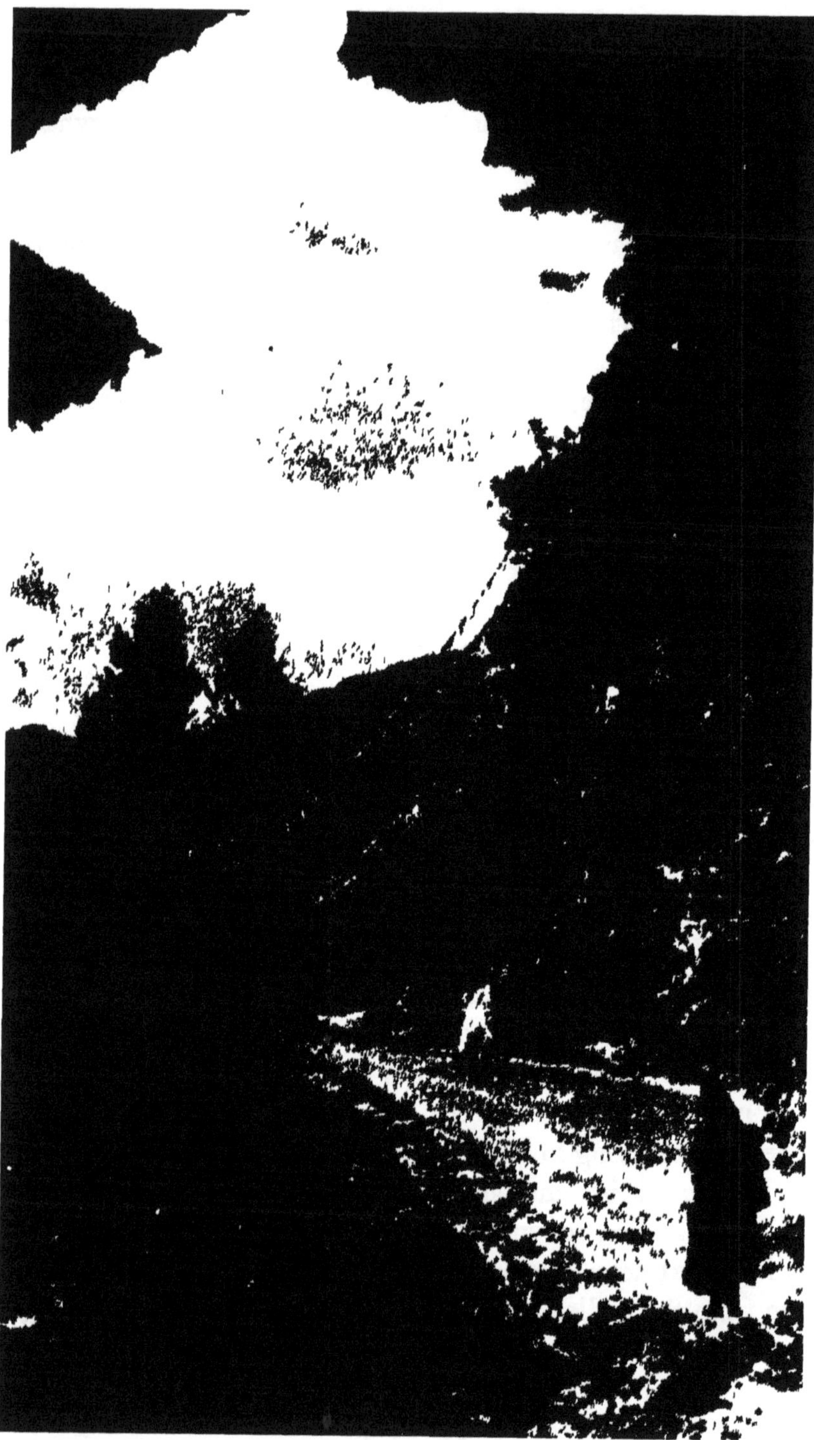

repeated discovery. Remember, the usual things are absent, there is no one to whom one may even talk for relaxation; there are no books, no shows, no fashionable amusement. It is true, I learned to talk with the mule boys, the servants, and even with myself, and I must confess that I failed to experience many of those moods of despondency and boredom which tend to come my way when living in the world to which we are most accustomed. The fact is, I found a deeper joy than I ever experienced in my life, and at no time was there any sense of missing anything that I had had in the past and did not have now. I must add that I did not suffer a single instant of loneliness.

As it happened, I met Richardson and his escort just coming out of the gateway. I rode along with him and we engaged in a last-minute talk about the beauties of the scenery and the enchantment of Lhasa. About four miles down the road the Tibetan army was on parade and offered him its salute, after which it passed inspection. This took only a few minutes, and we were off again for the next stop about half a mile away, where at a table of honor in a large tent he went through the ceremony of exchanging endless scarves and had a cup of tea. He also partook of the auspicious bowl of rice, which was offered him for a safe journey. It is the custom to take only one pinch from this bowl, putting a couple of grains in your mouth and throwing the remainder over your shoulder. From here we went another mile or so down the road where he bade goodbye to his guide and personal escort of natives whom he was leaving behind. Then we continued to the new bridge of Tsarong's, which was another four miles distant; here Tsarong was waiting to have a last cup of tea with Richardson, after which we were to return together to the city, eight miles away.

During this brief return ride I had the urge again to be on my way to almost any place, if only to be on the move, travelling over desert lanes and through fertile valleys. The heavens were banked high, and color was to be seen in every direction.

I had marvelled over Tsarong's bridge in a country so devoid of the mechanical enterprise. It is a remarkable example of modern construction. And yet you wonder how it could have ever been accomplished without a single instrument of precision, but by accurate natural surmises. I doubt if a better job could have been done in our own country with all its perfected instruments and trained experts.

5

The *Kashag* was having a great festival which had gone on for eight days and had still four more days to go. It is the custom that each year a different Shapé should have his turn at entertaining, and this year the honor fell to Tethong Shapé, who had just finished building his new house in the city. It was generally agreed that this house was the best in Lhasa; but my chief envy was its shrines and the gorgeous array of *thangkas* which adorned the sitting room.

I received an invitation to attend this festival, and I started for the house about eleven in the morning. I knew that in its way the entertainment would be an ordeal, for I should be expected to stay hours and go on eating the whole time. As an honored guest, I could scarcely avoid going. If I could get away by eight in the evening I should consider myself lucky. But many Tibetans would stay on until midnight, and actually if they showed an inclination to stop the night there, and, for that matter, for several days, making one continuous meal of it, they would not consider it anything out of the way. How they stand up under this sort of thing is quite beyond me.

The house is three stories high, with the best places at the top, where one can have a view and fresh sunlight. There at the top was an exquisite sitting room with large bay windows with beautiful awnings over them to keep out the glare of mid-day. You climbed up to it through the usual dark passageways and Tibetan ladders. And there was a feeling of cleanliness about the whole place.

I found the house full of guests. Every room through which I passed had a small party going on. Both high and low participated, it being the custom to entertain the servants as well as the honored guests. My host said that he was able to accommodate only sixty guests at any one time, with any comfort; so he had to take on different groups each day. On the day of my visit, this entertaining had already gone on for ten days.

What principally held my attention in the beautiful private shrine was a set of nine *thangkas* portraying the life of Lord Buddha, all hand-embroidered. My host had another set just like this one, but which was painted; he sent it to China, where they made a duplicate set of hand-embroidery. It was by far the finest thing of the kind that I have seen. The room itself was of a typical Tibetan design, with the poles carved and painted blue and gold on a red background, and the main part wrapped in beautiful silk, where the average shrine has only bare red poles upholding this cornice of lovely carvings. The ceiling differed from the standard pattern, for here were blue beams placed a short distance apart with the ground of the ceiling painted green, covered with hand-painted flowers of a rather subtle color, characteristically Chinese. This design was broken up by a thin body of blue worked out in a very symmetrical pattern, too involved to attempt to describe here.

On arrival I was promptly served with several cups of tea with cookies and figs. I dared not branch out into the harder spirits there at your disposal; like all who have had experience, I knew that it was the better part of valor not to want anything until it was forced on you, as before long you were sure to get more than you wanted of everything. Indeed, food soon began to pour in, following the regular course already described in an earlier chapter. All I need say is that nothing was omitted on this occasion. It was the finest cooking I had yet tasted in Tibet; for all that, I thought it best to finesse my way through. Yet at the end, when vermicelli soup was served, I had to consume five large bowls of it, not a small amount on top of all that had gone before.

I was congratulating myself on having gotten through with it all with a minimum of discomfort, when the *chang* girls came in and every one began to shout "*Tashi deli!*" which is equivalent to saying "Bottoms up!" So I had to drain cup after cup of their *chang*, which is a beverage made from barley flour, containing possibly half a per cent of alcohol. This is really like drinking a toast of health to one another. One would not mind a few glasses, but when it gets up to around thirty he begins to realize that it is not water, that there are limits to one's capacity if not to the supply.

The tables were cleared for Mah Jong, but some persons amused themselves with other games. The Chinaman was there in all his glory, showing the boys how it is possible to lose their money in a hurry. He had really an extraordinary facility in handling the ivory squares, but this did not stop the beer which continued to come in without interval of respite. Seeing that I had no restraining influence over the *chang* girls, who seemed to have an eye on me, I thought I had best for the time being become something of a nomad. There was one very charming girl in particular, a buxom Tibetan lassie, who reminded me very much of a well-fed farmer girl, no matter where I turned up, there was she, with sparkling eyes, holding her keg of *chang* and insisting that I have another glass. There seemed to be no way of saying No to them; they simply didn't understand the word. Politeness in this country is entirely different from ours, and you must learn how to take it. Indeed, they go so far as to stick you with needles if you refuse, and by this time the eyes of every one are on you, begging you to have more—so what is one to do? I finally fled to the roof to have a look at the scenery of Lhasa.

The rhythm of the music I had heard all that day persisted in my mind, and with it the picture of the three lady dancers who danced to it, making movements very much like those of the geisha girls of Japan. The orchestra consisted of a long wooden fife or flute, a fiddle and a banjo; the instruments were actually different from our own known by these names. The girls marked time with their feet as though tapping, and at regular intervals they swung their arms, with their sleeves hanging far below the ends of their hands. It was a pleasant rhythm, and again and again you found yourself waiting for it to resume. This went on from the time of my arrival until I left, and it may still be playing for all I know.

The air refreshed me, it was the first time that the digestive apparatus had had a chance to catch up with itself, and I was anxious to remain on the roof as long as possible, for the dinner soon to follow would prove yet a greater ordeal than the one which I had just survived, and it would be to the tune of a continuous stream of *chang*.

After watching the children at play in the tent provided for them in the garden below, I rejoined the party. On the way down I stopped off in a couple of the other rooms and watched the guests at their gambling games. Here all were men, the women were on the other side of the house having a party of their own. There seems to be no mixed companionship in this respect, even though there is the most intimate companionship between the Tibetan and his wife. But the array of jewelry, of which I caught a glimpse as I passed a room full of women, was enough to make one gasp.

I also had a chance to meet a few Lamas and officials at the party, and to exchange a few thoughts on the subject of religion and of my studies in it. Every one was naturally cordial, and I was made to feel at home with all, in spite of the size of the gathering and all its members being strangers to me. I feel that this speaks well for the Tibetan character, as I cannot say the same about my own people; hence, my fondness for the people of Tibet continued to increase.

And so the last meal was brought on, and I tried to hold up under it, but must confess that we had all to yield honors to the Chinaman when it came to drinking *chang*. We finally wound up playing the old Chinese game of calling the total number of fingers which would be shown; the penalty provided that the loser drink more *chang*. The enthusiasm of the Chinese official was that of a small child—for he never lost, and therefore he never had to drink—and so, filled to the neck, we called it a day—and a night.

CHAPTER IX

I ESCAPE WITH MY LIFE

I

IT WAS another very sacred day, and all sorts of things were going on in the village. Great masses of people were making short pilgrimages to the small monasteries in the neighboring hills, while the rest of the Lhasan populace were out in their best clothes to see the crowd on their return. They all love to dress up and look at one another, and as a crowd they act very much like any other crowd in any other place.

After a hurried snack I went out, and was joined by Tharchin and the "boys." First we went to the Tsug-lag-kang, where the Government had put on a ceremony for the day. It was not quite as large as the ceremony in which I had lately taken part, but it had a very attractive addition of color in the shape of *thangkas* and images brought by their owners, in order that they might acquire special virtue from the blessings offered in the temple. So all the wealthy persons of Lhasa sent their religious objects here; they crowded the nave, two and three deep.

Afterwards I went to the end of the village to watch the great crowd and take such pictures as struck my fancy. I counted without my multitudinous host, for the crowd, on seeing me, surged around me. Apparently they were even more interested in me than I was in them. I was having an exuberant time weaving my way in and out of this seemingly endless, seething mass, and trying from time to time to take a picture of a face or a character that caught my interest, when all of a sudden I found myself backed against the wall, with the crowd growing denser and the pressure heavier. For a few instants I felt panicky. And on top of that, without warning, there was the sudden impact of something weighty against the side of my head and a feeling of dull pain; it was a stone the size of a baseball, aimed at me, unfortunately with only too accurate aim, by some one in the crowd.

Almost instantaneously I realized that in no circumstance must I show any sign of fear, or even of anger. It is true, however, that my first reaction was to start beating down every one around me. Luckily, the prompt thought that followed held me in restraint. To have used violence at the moment would have been fatal; that great unruly mass would have disposed of me more quickly than a can of T. N. T. might have done. While I was trying to gather my wits about me, four more stones came hurtling in my direction with effective aim, hitting me on the shoulder and the head. My eyes sought for Tharchin and the boys. They were not in sight; doubtless they were lost in the mob which spread out over an area as large as a football field.

Immediately, I bethought myself of my aura, the aura which I had been coached to assume as a preliminary to my Lhasan pilgrimage, and now I assumed it. I straightened my shoulders, lifted my head high and directed my eyes straight ahead, and, with the air of a great dignitary of the faith, I advanced with a rapid, firm stride, tramping down any one who did not stand aside. I turned neither right nor left, nor looked at any individual, nor said a single word. The crowd opened before me, and in the effort to draw back some persons fell, and I without much ado merely walked over them. This, in a psychological sense, did the trick; for immediately others came forward and beat the crowd back and forced them to make way for me and saw to it that they did not once touch me with their defiling hands.

Maintaining this mood to the end, I walked straight to where our horses were chained and Tharchin and the boys were waiting for me. With this experience immediately behind me, I thought it was time to call it a day, so I went home to give my head the opportunity to regain its original shape.

2

Having added more details to my daily discipline, it was necessary to begin the day before the break of dawn, in order that most of my daily study might be finished by breakfast, as there were endless things to do between breakfast and late in the night. I was now preparing to continue my translation of the *Life of Padma Sambhava*, begun at Kalimpong, and I wanted to finish it before it was time to leave for America. To this I hoped to add translations of the Lives of Rechung-po, Dag-po, and perhaps Tsong-Khapa. All of my earlier hours were now being spent in carrying out the meditation discipline which was given me together with some studies in the language, so I was able to crowd in at least three hours before any one else began to stir for the day. There is such a gap between the literary and the colloquial in the Tibetan language that I decided to pursue an intensive study of the former under the guidance of a teacher, as I foresaw the difficulties of trying to study the language by myself upon my return.

There was a morning when I was able to continue my studies after breakfast until tiffin, and I managed to sandwich in a brief period of reflection on all that was happening to me, and on my inward reactions. In this inner inspection of myself I must admit to having felt a strong mood of warmth, the warmth that comes from the glow of the creative imagination, stimulated by all that was to be had and experienced here, and it was my hope that I should be able to absorb it deeply enough into my system so that I might take it away with me as a part of my make-up, as a part of my integrity. Truly, I knew no other feeling of happiness that gave greater contentment; all other ways sooner or later let you down, but this one promised perpetuity.

This particular morning I happened to be reading the life of the saint Milarepa with considerable envy. I could not help agreeing with him that this life is so brief and so transitory that it is a pity we must waste so much of its precious energy on misdirected externals, even while the spirit of the eternal is within, and, once the awareness of the rise of our inner consciousness has been experienced, all doubts as to the purpose of this life can be forever removed. Yet it is true that these infinite external manifestations have their place, inasmuch as they afford the needful experience to bring about this awareness and this kind of meditative mind in a person not of that reflective nature in the beginning. Indeed, speaking for myself, I should need no encouragement to follow closely on the footsteps of Milarepa, yet living as we do in a social order wholly incompatible with any such scheme of existence, it is scarcely possible at this time to take any practical steps to launch the program it involves. Let us hope that before the end has arrived it will be possible for those who feel that this is the way of life to climb over the confining walls and to realize some of our cherished ideals.

At the beginning of my experience I could not have thought it feasible, but since I first entered my new environment during the past winter there developed in me a growing confidence, until now I had the assurance of being able to forge ahead alone, without the aid of a teacher, into the wilderness of Maya (illusion), which surrounds our subconscious. Nevertheless, there were still a few principles of which I was anxious to acquire knowledge before I could feel wholly confident of being able to go through the gamut of complete isolation, but even without it I felt sure of enriching my life in every aspect.

In going over this experience in my mind, while sitting during my ultimate initiation in the cave of solitary confinement, I came to the realization of the meaning and purpose of all that had seemed so mysterious at the time I was passing through the experience. And I arrived at the conclusion that as soon as it becomes possible for one to consult with the inner consciousness, all else loses its importance, and books and the like become superfluities; for all things in this external world are only extensions of that infinite intelligence which is to be found in the innermost being of every living soul.

When it is said that the world is moving at such a rapid pace, and that it is impossible to keep up with it, the inevitable conclusion is erroneous; for human nature itself is by no means changing at that rate. Indeed, the very fact that our world of name and form is admittedly moving ahead at a pace with which man is unable to keep up is in itself ample evidence that he is not changing, or at any rate not changing sufficiently fast to keep up with the constantly accelerated existence. When the true principles of life are properly understood a complete insight can be had into any problem offered as soon as the essential facts are known. After all, even if we knew all the latest traffic laws, what has that got to do with the purpose of life? We must learn to distinguish between those things which appertain to man and those concerned with the mechanism arranged so that he can function at his fullest capacity.

And so my thoughts continued to pile up, and a strong longing was growing within for the light of contemplation and of reflection as the result of past experiences, and for finding a way that could be adapted to the everyday life of the individual in the world of affairs who cannot give up all of his time but will be able to carry on his activities with a deeper joy for living gained by this means: the establishment of a contact with the flow which is the essence of his soul.

It may be asked, does the average Tibetan get any of this from his teaching? It is probable that he gets little more from his ritual than does the devotee of any of the great faiths of the world today from his. That does not mean, however, that what lies behind the ritual is wrong. The world is changing, and conditions are very different from what they were at the time of the great teachers, but the truth remains the same eternally. It is only the name and form, or the crystallization of that eternal truth, that changes. This change is one of the very laws of the universe, for they teach here that the truth is like the sun, ever the same, ever radiating its light, yet that if we look at its reflection in the water as the wind stirs the waves, we find that it is ever changing, ever moving. We know that it is only the reflection we see, and so it is with us, the world of name and form in this world of Maya (illusion), it is only the reflection of the truth, and it is that that goes on changing, while the truth is the same eternally.

What the world needs today, it has been said, is not one to reveal the truth, as that can be found, but a leader who can show the people how to advance these teachings to accord with the new set of facts with which we are living. They appear to be irreconcilable at times. What is required is a thorough understanding of both sides of the problem, and the establishment of an equilibrium between them, which means the avoidance of either extreme. The main problem is essentially the reconciliation of the internal with the external. The thing I was seeking, I realized, was an understanding of life, such an understanding as could grapple with the problem of relating the intelligence gained from the inner revelation to the practical aspects of our Western life, and if I could lay a few seeds, so that in time some one else would carry on the quest, I should consider the little I have done with unbounded satisfaction. The first thing needful was to gather the facts, so the problem might be seen in all its clarity; then there was the hope that a genius would arise who knew how to use his gifts in solving the problem shrewdly and practically, or at any rate start it on the way to solution by steps taken in the future by other individuals through perpetuity.

3

I spent a good part of the day in making out lists of rare books which I was trying to find to take back with me to America. I learned that all the printers had been engaged by the Government to work on the *Sum-Bum* (Biography) of the late Dalai Lama, making it impossible to find some of the books which otherwise would be easily obtainable in Lhasa. As I have already indicated, a book in Tibet is not merely a book, but is looked upon as something to be worshipped. Hence, as soon as a book is published and sold to a person, it is next to impossible for him to pass it on to some one else. I was determined, however, to make every effort to secure all available literature on such subjects as the native deities, the Tibetan liturgy, medical science, poetry, astrology, philosophy, logic, as well as descriptions of the monasteries and the lives of the saints; indeed, on everything that makes the Tibetan civilization and culture. I was particularly anxious to obtain two very scarce books, which are the lists of all the block prints to be found in the printing establishment at Narthang, and of books published at Derge, in Eastern Tibet. I was intent on leaving no stone unturned in order to bring back to America a collection of books which, once translated, would give the outside world a deep insight into the thoughts of the people of this land, where spiritual growth is considered the most important thing in life. I realized that it would be an act of God to be able to obtain these books, and I had been so lucky so far that I felt that my luck must hold out even in this.

The blocks used in the making of these books are all hand-carved, and it is usually necessary to find the printer who knows about the desired book; it is for him to dig up the old blocks and run off an edition for you. Before printing, however, the paper has to be made, and this again is a slow and tedious process, since everything is done by hand. Today the best paper is to be had in British Bhutan, about 350 miles away; this makes the price very high, owing to the long trek in transporting it. It comes in oblong sheets of about four or five feet long and two and a half feet wide. The printer cuts up these sheets to the size of the manuscript and pastes several of the small sheets together, and after the paste has been generously applied and the paper ironed out, the book is ready for printing. But there is still a lot of work ahead. Little wonder, then, that it is difficult, if not impossible, to make any one part with a volume, once he has obtained it.

Tsarong had a complete set of the *Kangyur* and *Tengyur*, printed for him at Kham, for which he was at this time having the boards made which are used as covers. He said that he would eventually find a set for me. But until the book was actually in my hands I could never be certain; in this country ten or twenty years means absolutely nothing. The distinguishing feature of Tsarong's set which differentiated it from all others was that, instead of being printed in ordinary black ink, it was all printed in red. There was a proposal before the *Kashag* that a special printing be made for me from blocks of Narthang, with particular care that a good and clear printing be executed. From what I knew of these blocks, however, the prospect of a good printing was not at all bright.

The making of illuminated manuscripts is a highly developed art in Tibet. A large manuscript will often cost thousands of rupees. In fact, the present Maharajah of Nepal has one which is reputed to have cost one lac, or 100,000 rupees. Now

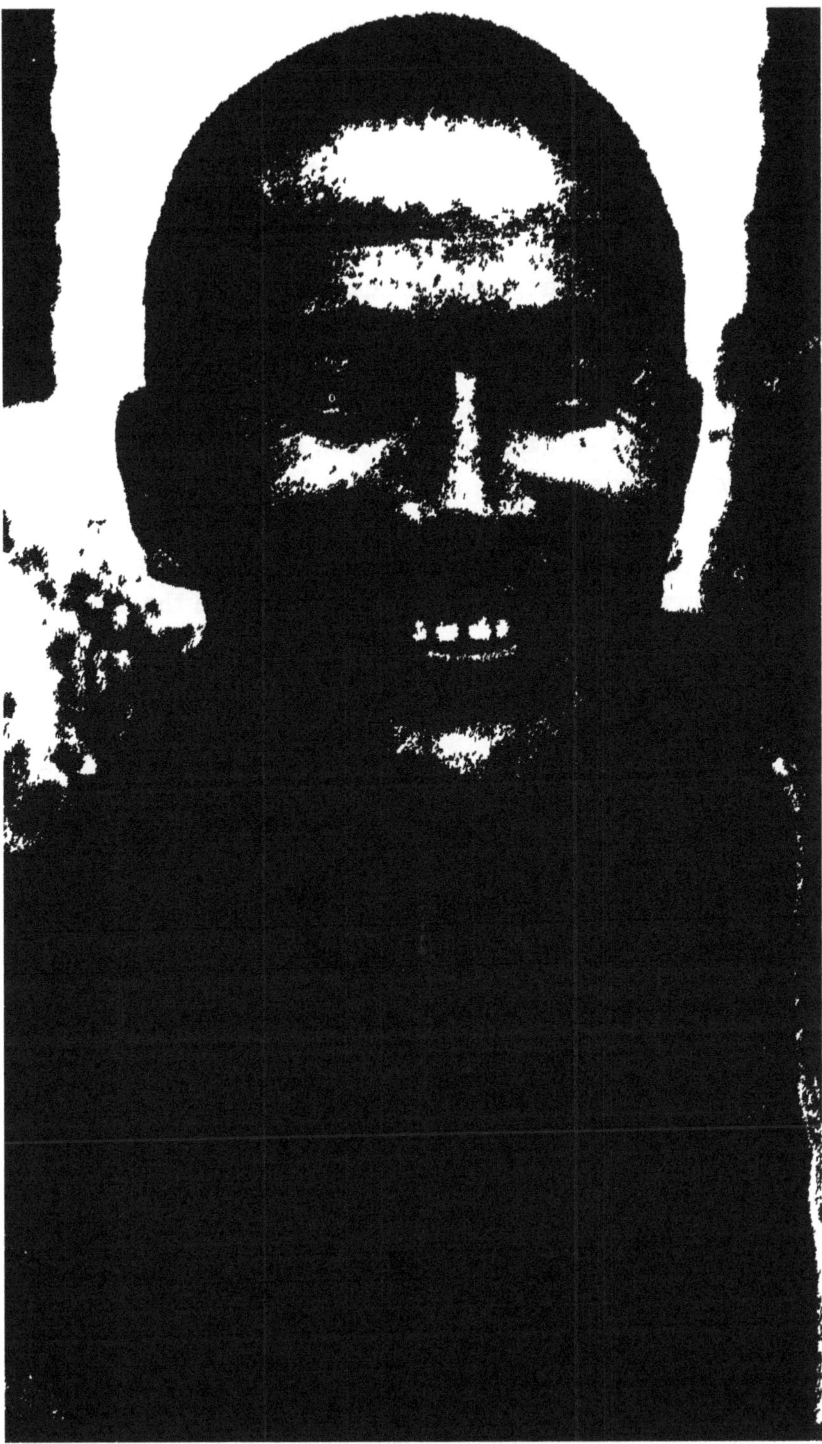

and then the entire *Kangyur* and *Tengyur* is printed in this fashion for the Dalai Lama or some other very high priest. Tsarong showed me some *de luxe* editions of small prayer books of perfect workmanship, with high-raised gold characters set in a thin wooden frame, to which the paper has been pasted. The frame itself was exquisitely painted, and covered with a strip of red silk with a layer of yellow. The rest of the book revealed alternate lines of gold and silver, something I had not seen before. Usually, the first two or three pages of such a book, and perhaps the last, have hand-painted deities at each end as borders. This gives only a brief description of the effort and care which go into the preparation of a fine Tibetan book, but there is no way to convey its beauty or give any idea of the hours of patient toil necessary to produce the sanctified results.

In this connection, I must add that for some time I had been spending no little effort in having a Christmas card printed in order to show my friends at home a modest specimen of Tibetan manuscript making. Even so, I had four persons and their assistants engaged in the task, and I had to use no little persuasion—and offer no little remuneration—to prevail upon them, especially as the Life of the late Dalai Lama was at this time engaging the effort of all the writers and artists of Lhasa. It was only after I pointed out to them that I had come a mighty long distance in order to make their teachings known on the other side of the world that they condescended to assume the task I set them, that of whetting the appetite of the West by a glimpse of the art of the East. As it was, I had still to figure out how I could provide the necessary English lettering. I was sure, however, of being able to devise something in good time.

4

I spent the rest of the day in making a review of the rise and spread of Buddhism from the time it entered China in 61 A.D. and Japan in the sixth century, until it came to Tibet in the seventh, and flowered there in its own fashion. This event occurred in the reign of King Srong-tsan-Gampo who, as I have already told, had been converted to Buddhism by his Nepalese and Chinese wives, both ardent adherents of the faith. He was given the Chinese princess, Wench'eng, by the Emperor of China, T'ait-sung of the T'ang dynasty, in order to induce him to forego his military pursuits on the border. The Nepalese princess, Brikuti, daughter of King Amsuvarman, was first taken in marriage when he was only sixteen; so the Tibetan annals report. When the Tibetan King asked for this princess, he is reputed to have said:

"I, King of barbarous Tibet, do not practise the ten virtues, but should you be pleased to bestow on me your daughter, and wish me to have the Law, I shall practise the ten virtues with a five-thousandfold body . . . though I have not the arts . . . if you so desire . . . I shall build five thousand temples."

The Chinese assert that there was no religion in Tibet at this time. As a result of his conversion the Tibetan King sent Thon-mi Sam-bhota to India to acquire the teachings, and this gave rise to the Tibetan alphabet. The Chinese princess became the White *Tara* ("Lady of Mercy"), while the Nepalese princess became the Green *Tara*, but this was as far as it went, and nothing was done for the religion. It was not until the reign of his powerful descendant, Thri-Srong-Detsan, in the eighth century, that the real foundation was laid; it was he who brought Guru Rimpoche, also known as Padma Sambhava, to Tibet. On the advice of Guru's brother-in-law, Santa-rakshita, who was made the head Abbot of Samye, the first monastery of

Tibet was built in 747. The first Lama was Pal-bans, who succeeded Santa-rakshita, and the first ordained monk was Bya-Kri-Gzigs. The most brilliant follower was Vairocana, who translated many Sanscrit works into Tibetan. This marked the beginning of the Nyingmapa sect. The same King founded many other Lamaseries and gave a strong impetus to their literary efforts. Consequently, his era is looked upon as the Primitive or "Augustine," followed by the Mediæval, then by the Reformation and the Modern, to the beginning of the line of King-Priests of the Dalai Lamas of the seventeenth century.

It was in the reign of Ralpachan, Thri-Srong-Detsan's grandson, that the translation of the scriptures and commentaries of Nagarjuna, Aryadeva, Vasunbandhu, etc., was prosecuted. Because of the great devotion of this King, he was murdered; his younger brother, Lan Darma, on assuming the throne, did all he could to uproot the religion, and he, in his turn, was assassinated in the third year of his reign. His efforts had merely served to give greater vigor to the faith.

The last-named episode gave rise to the famous Black Hat dance, of which every visitor to Tibet must have heard. The story is that a dancer came performing outside the palace walls to win the interest of the King and the opportunity to perform within the walls of the court. He had hidden under his robes a bow and arrow, with which he hoped he would be able to dispose of the King who was destroying the religion. It was not long before his skill as a dancer gained him the favor of the King, and he was invited within, to entertain and dance. At the first opportunity that arose he drew his bow and arrow from their hiding place and shot the poisoned arrow deep into the King's heart. Then the dancer fled on his horse, which was covered with soot. When the rider came to the Lhasa River he removed the soot, and turned his own black gown inside out, thus transforming the appearance of himself and his beast and making escape possible. Since that day to this, the story has been enacted by the dancers of Tibet, who go through all the motions of the Black Hat dancer in the drama of his rise to favor, his assault on the King, and his escape from punishment, having saved the religion from destruction.

In 1038 came Atisha, and started the Kadampa sect, which later developed into the Gelupa and gained the principal power of the state under the leadership of Tsong-Khapa in 1407. It was not until 1640 that it became the ruling power with the rise of the fifth Dalai Lama. With the advent of Atisha and the reformed Kadampa sect came the semi-reform sects of Kargyupa and Sakya, the latter gaining the dominating control through the great Chinese Emperor Khubla Khan, a descendant of Ghenghiz Khan, who captured Tibet in 1206 A.D. In searching for a religion for his people, he took over Lamaism and made the Abbot of Sakya head of the church in much the same manner as Charlemagne created the first Pope. During the Ming dynasty in 1368 the ruler deemed it advisable to raise the heads of the other sects to the level of those in Sakya, in order to eliminate quarrelling amongst them and thereby make it easier to rule the country.

In the fifteenth century Tsong-Khapa reorganized the work of Atisha and created the Gelupa sect, which took the lead in 1640 under the fifth Grand Lama, Nag-wan Lo-zang. He induced Gusri Khan to capture the country and make a present of it to him; in 1650 he was given the Mongol title of Dalai, or "Vast as the Ocean." He held himself to be a God-incarnate, and built the palace temple on the hill in Lhasa; it was named the Potala, after his divine prototype, Avolokita, "The Lord Who Looks Down From On High."

So we have Buddhism coming to Tibet with its final perfected Theocracy, which continues to rule the country to this day. Now its power is on the wane, and the prediction is that it will not be many more years before the civil authorities will have taken over the country.

5

Tsarong generously offered to do everything in his power to procure for me not only the sacred scriptures but also the desired deities and *yidams* (protecting deities of the religion) for the shrine which I was planning to erect in America, though I had not yet decided whether it would be private or semi-public. He also promised to have it carved in Lhasa and shipped to me, so that it would be authentic from beginning to end. The Regent was trying to secure for me my main deity; as he was a dependable person, I considered the matter as good as settled. As for the books, Tsarong practically promised to turn over his own set to me. He said he would order another set for himself, which meant that he could not possibly have it for another three or four years. Indeed, it had taken him five years to obtain the set he promised me, because he first had the paper made in Lhasa, after which he sent it by his own animals with his own men all the way to Derge, he also despatched his own printer from Lhasa to do the printing. During the winter it is so cold that such work is impossible, and the summers are short. In any case, one never hurries here. And every page must be proof-read by the Lamas to check every word of it. Then it must be transported back to Lhasa, which is a thousand miles away.

On its arrival in Lhasa the high Lamas from the great monasteries came to his private temple in his house and after the dedication ceremony had the books placed on their permanent shelf where they were expected to remain forever. It was the custom never to remove the books from the shelf of the temple, once they had been blessed by the Lamas, except for the purpose of reading and studying. It was argued, however, that in such exceptional circumstances as their use in propagating their teachings to the world, their surrender to me might be allowed. Indeed, the prospects of an exception being made in my case were good, for there was the prophecy of Buddha that eventually the Law (*dharma*) would spread throughout the world.

6

Having gone through my one pair of trousers, and with an extended stay in Lhasa before me, it had become absolutely necessary that I get some clothes; for if I now started to wear my one and only Tibetan gown it would be worn out before I returned to the West, and I was very anxious to show to others how Tibetans dressed. So I took up the problem with Tsarong. He responded by bringing out bolt after bolt of the most gorgeous silk that I had ever seen. Overcoming my reluctance, he gave orders to have several Tibetan robes made for me. He sent out a servant to fetch his head tailor in order to have these made to my measure. Then I went out to buy some "accessories"; I found shopping as much fun as at home. I only wish the men in our country would adorn themselves with a little more of the material and color used in these parts.

While we were going over my need of new garments, the conversation was switched to the subject of jewelry used by Tibetan women. Very popular is an article called the charm box, made to hang from the neck. It is a small square box about the size of a large compact, with another square pattern within placed as to resemble a four-cornered star. For the most part made of gold, the back of it is often of silver. The design on the box is usually bordered by turquoise, the rest being of other precious stones, according to the wealth of the owner. The box is usually about half an inch deep, and contains charms to ward off evil. During our talk Tsarong brought out a large bag filled with turquoises of the finest quality, and not one with a blemish, all of the most exquisite blue. What the diamonds are to us, the turquoises are to the Tibetans. Not content with his wealth of turquoises, Tsarong was interested in the possibility of importing more of these precious stones direct from the American mines, and he was anxious for me on my return to investigate the prospects of this, and, indeed, I should like to render him service in appreciation of all that he has done for me, an unheard-of stranger.

Tsarong was equally interested in the possibility of importing silks from Russia. It seems that in the past the Tibetans imported a great deal of silk from Russia; indeed, the famous silk brocades to be found in Tibet today all came from that country. After the Revolution, however, all such trade stopped, chiefly because they did not want the Reds to meddle in their affairs. He was anxious, however, to find out if these silks were still being manufactured and if there were some way of being able to procure them again. A small fortune might be made in Tibet in trading in turquoise and silks. All of the *Shapés* made inquiries of me as to the possibility of procuring Russian silks, held in such high regard by the wealthy Tibetans.

7

A messenger was sent to inform me of preparations being made for the ceremony at Rammoche, and that my presence would be welcome. The ceremony on the morrow was to be similar to the one in which I had only lately taken part, with virtually the same monks officiating. The fact is, they lived at Rammoche. Accompanied by Tharchin and the boys, I made my way on horseback through the flowing sewers of Lhasa, for it had rained heavily the night before, filling the streets with water which floats the filth. The country all around is incomparably beautiful, but the streets of Lhasa after a rain are incredibly unsightly. Indeed, the better-class Tibetans complain of it, and are frankly apologetic before a stranger. I usually tried to put them at their ease by telling them that it really didn't amount to anything compared to the way our country used to be in the early frontier days.

The Rammoche is situated just at the edge of the town, and the way that leads there offers an interesting spectacle of Tibetan life. The grand houses we pass reveal the general living conditions, the shops show how the various crafts are carried on. The streets are filled with donkeys, yaks, dogs, sheep, goats, horses, Lamas, beggars, men, women, and children. The last two hundred yards offer the greatest interest in the never-ending pageant of travellers passing over the road which leads out of the town. Just before reaching this long, straight stretch you pass a *mani* (sacred wall) about a hundred yards in length with the usual throng of beggars squatting beneath its sacred emblems. I do not believe there is a place in the world which can compare with Tibet for its herds of dejected travelling mendicants who pass through this life clothed in tatters and with begging bowls in their hands. Mendicancy is considered a respectable profession in this land, though the lot of the beggars at best is far from an enviable one, to judge from the ones you see, with scarce a real flicker of life among them.

Our jaunt was not without its pathetic touch. We joined a rapidly increasing crowd, attracted to the sight of a human being taking his last breaths while prostrated on the kerb, with almost the entire calf of one leg eaten off and the heel of the other foot gone; and there was all the gore that colors such a scene. It appears that one of the dogs had become a little hungry and helped himself, and the fellow was now the recipient of gathering sympathies and of unheard-of aid. We tried to make arrangements for him to be taken to the Mission physician, but it did not look as if our efforts would prove successful.

They do not have much faith in doctors in these parts, and, moreover, the attention the man was getting meant the promise of Tibetan copper coin, which is worth even less than our pennies. Our efforts unavailing, we continued our way to the temple, where the monks had been busy decorating the *tormas*, which had been made and arranged before our arrival.

At the previous ceremony I had not been able to see them decorate these *chortens*, so I was particularly interested in seeing the systematic way in which several Lamas carrying large trays with ornaments hurriedly slapped the decorative bits on to the *tormas*; it was all done rapidly and effectively, with almost the automatic rhythm of machinery. They went through the same procedure with the next decoration. I observed all this from my mat, while I was drinking tea and having a few pinches of sugar-rice, which is done for good luck. Then, after making my turn around the inner temple and revolving the prayer-wheels, I went into the courtyard, where the butter was to be melted. Several large copper vats were boiling away with the butter, which was then poured into the large earthen jugs and carried over into the monastery and used to fill the thousand butter lamps.

Within the courtyard there was a spacious clearing, bordering on a dense growth of large trees. At one end there was an enclosed platform, generally used by one or another of the learned Lamas when instructing a young student. One of the Lamas in charge wanted his picture taken and had selected a background, a large grove of hollyhocks which should make a perfect frame for that saintly face. I did the best I could under a heavily clouded sky.

On our return in the late afternoon I ran across our beggar acquaintance, who had dragged his mangled limbs to a more advantageous spot and there gave up in despair.

8

The next day was to be another memorable one for me, for I participated in the ceremony of the *Sa-wang duk-pa* held at the Rammoche temple, which was erected in the seventh century to enshrine the image of the Nepalese wife of Srong-tsan-Gampo. The monks greeted me as an old acquaintance, having officiated in the service held during the past week at the Tsug-lag-khang, the Rammoche being their permanent headquarters.

I had asked that different deities be propitiated this time to give me an insight to other services. The general externals were the same as far as the order of events was concerned, but different ornaments were worn. The *mantras* and the prayers were also of another nature. The service held more fascination for me than the previous one, since it provided for an invocation to one of their secret gods, which called for the *mandala* (mystical diagrams) as the main decoration hanging from the high beam at the head of the nave just a short distance in front of the head Lama of the day, who was the same who had conducted the previous service for me. This particular deity is supposed to abide in the center of the *mandala;* so the ceremony revolved around the intricate passageway to his abode of bliss. Again, it is an object to awaken the imagination concerning the Maya of life.

All this ritual was devised by the learned ones who compiled the *Tantras* countless centuries ago, aware of the incapacity of the human animal for seeking strength and solace within. From these works have originated all the ritual practised by all the original sects of India and Tibet. To be sure, India will not admit certain practices, such as the endless *pujas* of propitiation. But the Tibetan grants everything its place, and the *Tantrik* teachings make up the bulk of their sacred literature. This is not surprising, when it is considered that Padma Sambhava, who brought the religion to Tibet, was reputed to be one of the greatest *Tantriks* of his time. The Tibetan sages realized that there is nothing that brings out the emotions of man so effectively as poetry and music, so endless *mantras* have been devised for the purpose of this emotional awakening. Before the individual can receive the blessing of his devotion he must first be awakened, and they are fully aware that nothing is bestowed upon him from the outside, that everything must come from within through this emotional awakening. By employing an image representing the supreme power of life the individual has something tangible to which he can cling; to keep before his mind the transitoriness of our physical existence, these endless themes have been devised portraying the different aspects of the futility of life.

The chief shrine was that of Dorje-Jig-je, who is believed to be a metamorphosis of the moral and merciful Chen-re-zi, the patron saint of Tibet. His life-sized image copulating with his spiritual counterpart was all in blue, while the human heads above his bull face draped with human skulls were in red, as were the flames which make up his aura of power. His sixteen hands all held sacred objects. His spiritual aid was in a hue of gilt beneath silken wraps of blue and red. Before this image we stopped to reflect and to contact the flow of life, and thus glean understanding of life's passing nature through the feelings as well as through instruction revealed in the scriptures. Here they accept the duality of externalized nature and they always reveal the hideous aspects of their deities rather than try to convey the impression that all is perfection. These endless fiends shown in sexual embrace are only used to remind one of the union of the positive and negative aspects, which ultimately are revealed in the unified perfection of the Godhead.

The low and the ignorant never look upon these images but to comment that the religion of Tibet is nothing but the most degraded form of idolatry. They are oblivious of the rudimentary facts of symbology which lie behind these external forms used only to aid the weakness of a fleeting mind. Once the individual has gained inner power of his own nature, he can dispense with all such forms and continue alone. Here is where The Gelupa differs from the Kargyupa, for the latter advocate hermitages where the individual may retire for silent meditation, once he has gained the power through the physical forms of the ritual, which adheres strictly to the principles of *Tantra*. The Kargyupa has gained supreme unpopularity precisely because man always wishes to choose the easier way, dear to his own incapacity; so high and upright principles as an ideal to live by are offered, leaving the power of salvation in the hands of the high priests of the country. And thus we find the rôle of ignorance holding popularity.

So much of the ceremony at the Rammoche followed the order and ritual of the ceremony described in the previous chapter that I shall refrain from repeating such details as I have already given. Again, the highest and most spiritual Lama of Tibet honored me by conferring his blessing upon me. Upon their heads the Lamas wore a crown of about two feet high, made of black velvet, graduated to a point like a *chorten*. It had a high border consisting of five silver sections shaped like the charm boxes worn on the backs of the traders. This was supposed to represent the dress of the particular deity to whom they were making the offerings of imagination which went on throughout the day. The chants, begun by the head chorister who filled the room with the unending roll of thunder in the heavens, were picked up by eight hundred Lamas, only to be relieved by the tinkling of their bells, for every Lama had his bell and *dorje*; the latter being constantly used. At times they would pick up the *dorje* with the pointer-finger and little finger extended, while grasping it with the rest of the hand, and wave their twisting wrist in the air, along with the bell held in the other hand.

With the first part of the ceremony completed, various offerings were brought forth in the form of beautiful silken scarves in deep reds and blues; these were placed over the laps of the Lamas, and various *mudras* (mystic positions) were assumed while grains of rice were tossed from little piles in front of them. At times they would place red scarves on their foreheads and, after other *mudras*, they would be removed. The process of putting these offerings away was followed by a procedure just as deliberate.

Then came the repast of tea and rice. Once they had their bowls filled with tea, they all made small *chortens* and other odd twisted objects, which were placed beside them in the course of the ritual. I observed one quaint note. After the tea had been poured and they took a few minutes to sip, they all began to blow back the froth of the floating butter and to drink, but the head Lama tasted only a little, after which an attendant took his bowl and distributed small portions of the remainder to the monks, until all was gone.

It being past my usual lunch hour I was grateful for the food brought me by attendants. I had yet to make my tour of inspection with the large bundle of burning incense, which I was supposed to distribute to all the monks in the temple for their service in my behalf. Shortly after eating I had to prepare *puja* before the main gods of the temple as well as the fierce forms, which were hidden away in the dusty gloom of their sanctuaries dimly lighted by flickering butter lamps. It seems to me that these forms are horrific enough to protect themselves in the light where humans can appreciate these creative shapes. The main reason for their concealment, however, as I previously indicated, is the dangerous influence they may exert on the untutored, ignorant of their true meaning.

So this day marked another historic episode in my unprecedented experience in forbidden Tibet. I and my companions returned home under the gaze of all Lhasa; there seems to be nothing that arouses the curiosity of the mob more than to see a bearded Westerner marching through their streets in native dress. From the time I came out of the temple until I reached Tsarong's I had a mob running ahead of me trying to figure out what it was that permitted such an event.

CHAPTER X

FURTHER EDUCATION OF A LAMA

I

I HAD a visitor in a Lama from the Drepung monastery and we made arrangements for a daily call from him to instruct me in the inner ritual of the monasteries and methods of training. He was a *Geshe* who instructed aspiring students at the monastery. It seemed something of a mystery why he was sent to me. In any event, it was quite evident that they kept track of an individual. Your history was an open book to them, they knew what you were doing, and they could almost tell you your future. As for me, I accepted these facts for all they meant to me, no longer surprised at anything that might happen to me in this strange land.

On the following day I had a visit from a Lama, who had been the spiritual guide of Thrimon Shapé. He came at the suggestion of Tsarong to have a talk with me, with the idea of giving me instruction. We met in the courtyard, and exchanged the customary *kata*. Few words were said on either side, yet a mood of understanding possessed us both. We seated ourselves Buddha-fashion near the low Tibetan table, and his servants soon came bringing his offering to me, as was the custom on making the first call. His gift was a small image of the Guru Rimpoche, the founder of the order, and a short Tibetan prayer. In silence I placed the image to my head, in accordance with tradition. As a follower of their teachings I was supposed to know all the gestures of respect and humility. I confess I found it rather trying to keep up with the endless ritualistic forms. This Lama whose growing faith revealed the countless years he had spent in study and contemplation was deemed by all as being one of the most learned in the esoteric aspects of doctrines of the *Tantras*. To meet him and receive instruction from him was a rare privilege I scarcely expected on entering Tibet. He was reputed to hold what might be called the mystic key to life, to all the teachings written in the form of stories. To possess this key is to gain profound philosophical insight, which permits an individual to meet all the adversity of life with the fortitude of understanding.

The Nyingmapa and Kargyupa sects, of which this Lama was a follower, are more liberal than the Gelupa in their regulations of discipline, they proceed on the theory that you should develop understanding through the process of experience; hence, they allow their followers a measure of worldliness. This particular Lama, for example, had long hair, in contrast to the shaven head of the ordinary Gelupa Buddhist. Marriage is also allowed, and wine is permitted as well as women. It is argued that until you know these aspects of life, it will be impossible for you to surmount them. Indeed, it is one way of getting these things out of your system, and only after you have done so can you gain the higher understanding. To insure understanding, however, instruction is provided simultaneously with your living the experience. Ultimately, liberated from such worldly concerns, the individual is ready to have the secret teachings of the *Tantras* imparted to him. This calls upon him to turn within, and extract the wisdom hitherto hidden in the depths of self.

Thus, with the Gelupas, they strive to place an unattainable ideal before themselves, and then, with the sublime thought, wallow in the mire of life, which externalizes itself, in the case of the monks, in the teeming hives of religious devotion. The circumstances would seem to indicate that it may be better to yield to the ways of life and not be quite so virtuous and thereby have life devour one.

The teachings of the Gelupas are mainly based on the Sutras; those of the Kargyupas on a mixture of the Sutras and the Gsan Sngags or esoteric *Tantras* (secret *mantras*); while the Nyingmapas virtually practice the *Tantras* in their purity. The essential differences between these three main sects are illustrated by the following story:

There was a beautiful park in which grew a deadly poisonous plant. One man came along and suggested that the plant be wholly uprooted. Then another man came along and suggested that by pouring boiling oil over it the bush would be killed. Then, still a third man came along, a doctor, who, knowing the chemical properties of this plant, took its leaves and by mixing them with other things showed them the plant's value—this is the Kargyupa, while the sect symbolized in the previous suggestion is the Gelupa, and one before that represents the teachings in India. During the conclave an ostrich happened to be by, and he began feeding on the vine, resulting in a greater richness in the color of his feathers and in an increase in his vitality—and here you have the Nyingmapas symbolized, for this cult knows how to utilize the facts of life for its good. All the three, however, are linked up with the same goal, and differ only in their disciplinary methods. It would seem that the Kargyupa would be the most popular since it advocates the acceptance of life and the living of it. The human mind does not, perhaps, like to admit this. The problem is to receive a spiritual response in holding up the moral idea of life, and at the same time to live in a fashion contrary to this idea. In no event will they give up their way of living, but their cult does not offer them that sense of mystic security which can assure them justification for their acts even as a lesson or an experience. They follow the psychology of the typical drunkard, who advises his young friends never to take up the vice, but you will never catch him directing any one on the right path by example. They all want their drinks even while they "pass out" so to speak, thinking of the virtue to be gained in the hereafter if they could only do what they think should be right during this existence. Then, too, the Kargyupas have one other drawback, as far as popularity is concerned. They advocate the hermitage and teach that every devotee should at one time spend three years, three months, or at least three days in a cave with the object of silent meditation. This usually works out with the most ardent in a period of three months and three days. And there are some who stop at three days. Nevertheless, Tibet does have its faithful hermits who spend a good portion of their life in these caverns of withering ignorance. Indeed, there is a chap in a cave near Gyantsé who has stayed there for twenty years and more; today he is barely more than skin and bones, assuming that the spirit of life is an addition. He will remain there until the life is extinguished, when his attendants will break through the encased cell and remove the shell that remains. He has only a small hole in the wall through which he can pass his arm in order to receive the daily ration of grain that is passed on to him by those who patiently wait for the fateful moment.

I have almost come to the conclusion that wherever one finds a strict adherence to external rituals and discipline and devotions, everything coming from that source can be discounted 99 per cent; these adherents know no more of the inner life of man than does a cow—indeed, not as much.

To come back to my friend of the Mystic Order of Ignorance. I must admit that I relished the story told me by my new Lama instructor, who was opening up a new vein of Tibetan knowledge for me. It took him two hours to tell it, never stirring from his Buddha posture. He did not reveal so much as a twitch of the body as he sat there motionless, only his lips moving below his sparkling eyes. He had a comprehensive knowledge of Tibetan literature, and he had a pleasing personality, even though he may not be reaching Nirvana in this life. He was like a regal human being living a normal sort of life, yet not neglecting an opportunity to develop his spiritual side.

To begin with, unlike most Tibetan monks, he had long hair. Then, he had his own private home, where he lived with his wife and family and practised his daily discipline of study and meditation, in accordance with the methods taught by his group. There was no aura of sanctity about him; he was filled with laughter, saw the drift in all things, and pointed out how foolish certain beliefs were when considered from the point of view of their philosophical foundation. He was always ready to pull my leg about Christianity, about which he admitted to have no vast understanding, having read only the New Testament in a Tibetan translation. Yet after talking sense for a long while he would suddenly come out with the wildest tale about sacred objects of some old superhuman spiritual masters and saints, who always lived in some remote corner of Tibet. One finds the same sort of thing in India—just when you have a fellow before you with a little common sense, and you are willing to agree with him as to the foolishness of certain practices, when out he comes with the wild desire to run and take a bath in the sacred river, the Ganges.

2

I had an appointment at ten o'clock to call on Thrimon Shapé, one of Tibet's ex-potentates, the same whose former spiritual guide had now become mine. He held the reputation of having been a Shapé for a longer period than any one else, and, having held the throne of power during his long term, his present reputation was that of being just a little mad. The beauty of it—so I understood—was that his slips usually came at the most convenient time, and he seemed to be a perfect artist in carrying them through. There is the story, for example, of his running through the streets naked, which, when you get to know him, sounds rather incredible, as he is a most sedate gentleman. Indeed, he was dressed in all formality to receive me when I paid him a hurried and informal call, which followed his sending me gifts of barley, eggs and green vegetables.

The large courtyard of his house, which sheltered the stalls for his horses, was extraordinarily immaculate, as was everything else about the place. In front of the entrance to his house there were large squares marked off with powdered chalk to indicate the places from which the animals were barred. In accordance with the usual custom, I climbed up the dark ladder staircase, but here again everything was clean, from the landing to the top. His servants were also exceptionally clean, and the house throughout was spic and span. There was not a thing to be found out of order. On the small tea-table, which he had arranged for my visit, was the finest linen which he had imported from India.

As for my host, he was as mild and reflective as his age, and dressed to perfection, which is usually the case with high officials. Even among them it is not so uncommon to find a greasy spot on a projecting undergarment, but not so with him. I venture to say that he even took a daily bath. According to formal custom, he wore his official hat throughout the visit; it was stiff and shaped like one of our straw hats. The crown was not so long, but a bit higher, and the brim was wider. It was all made of silk and felt, the silk being the "Regal Blue" of Tibet. His face retained much life, and his manner was slow and deliberate, with all the precision of a long disciplined life. There was not a moment that you did not feel at ease with him, and just for the fun of it I deliberately at one time lapsed into silence, to discover how such a personality would handle the silence of embarrassment. I did not have a chance to try that for long, for he promptly launched into a series of penetrating questions which stimulated me to the marrow and made me talk as I never talked before; and his reaction indicated an intense interest. With the end of his life nearing, his personality had grown reflective and his imagination had a very mature quality, with a definite sympathy for the host of youth for whom room and opportunity must be made. Yet he would like to leave a stone along the path that would indicate to those who follow which road he felt the best after his long trek.

And so a very pleasant hour was passed, which whetted a taste for more. It is the sort of personality that wins me over more quickly than any other.

3

My Lama came the next morning at ten, and we spent four hours together, after which I had a hurried lunch and did a bit of writing, before responding at four to an invitation from the British Trade Agent to join in a game of Badminton, which incidentally gave me a special opportunity to meet other Tibetans and increase my growing circle of friendship. On the other hand, since on visiting a new acquaintance there was the need of bringing a gift with you, the situation always promised embarrassment. The fact is, as often as not I found my cupboard shelves empty. I was given, however, every consideration; and forgiven were many of the oversights on my part.

Remembering the joy of my previous trip over the trail leading behind Chakpo-ri I decided to try it again. Once I left the city a short distance behind, the air became fresh and stimulating, stirred by the gentle breeze of approaching evening. The natives were sitting around small camp fires or winding their way back to their homes. Everything tended to induce an undisturbable inner peace and made me want to linger a while. I had to forego this pleasure, as they were waiting for me. Nevertheless, I was able to tuck away a few thoughts that will always hold this horseback ride in my treasury of feelings. Likewise, the narrow ledge around the sheer cliff below the medical college brought forth related thoughts; for again I saw their symbols of worship hewn in the rock from one end to the other, with the deities painted in color as an extra touch. About twenty or thirty feet below, on my left, a small stream flowed through a dense area of trees and low shrubs, and the sight of this and the sound of running water added to my mood of ecstatic peace.

From this spot it was possible to look down upon the animals grazing, and, much to my surprise, I saw a large herd of light-colored Mongolian camels. Of all the places where I had expected to find camels, Lhasa was about the last. But then I remembered that these camels had been used to cross the great Chang-Tang (Northern Plain) of Tibet. These animals had belonged to the late Dalai Lama, and were now having an opportunity to rest. Until the Divine Ruler appears again on earth there will be no need to use them.

I found every one at the party in white ducks having a good time, so I took a racket and joined in the game. We were just lining up for it when a Tibetan guest and his family arrived. To my surprise, he was greeted in English, and when we were introduced he conversed with me in perfect English. Indeed, he was one of the four Tibetans sent to England twenty years before to obtain an English education; today three of them are still living in Lhasa. The name of this one was Ring Gang, and he was in charge of the Electric City of Lhasa. He was full of ideas, which he expressed in a lively fashion. He removed his Tibetan gown and revealed the typically English sporting ducks he had on underneath. He joined the game with the remark

Sounding the trumpets from the top of the Potala at noonday

that he had not handled a racket in fifteen years, but I noted that he certainly caught on quickly. With him came his brother, a man weighing about 300 pounds, who had been in charge of the army in Kham for a long time. He felt considerably relieved when I told him I had given up my plan of going that way; for he confirmed all I had heard of the dangers which confronted travellers; indeed, things were getting much worse. He offered to try to obtain the *Kangyur* and *Tengyur* for me in the city. It did not look promising, all the more as I had heard lately of efforts to obtain these books by Italy, France, China, Japan, Russia, Germany and India.

Along with the men came their women, fine specimens of Asiatic beauty, adorned with pearls, turquoise and rubies over the blue and red silk blouses, worn beneath their gowns with their rainbow aprons.

While waiting for dinner to be served, Mr. Fox turned on the radio, and there was good music. Some one made the suggestion to a small child of Ring Gang's—he was only about five—that he dance for us. Much to our surprise, he came forward, and what is more, he gave a performance which would bring the house down even on Broadway. His footwork and hand movements were simply perfect, and with a little training he could certainly become a dancer of note.

Throughout the meal we listened in on Java, China and Hongkong. Afterwards we retired to a large room downstairs and were shown a movie. The room was crowded with Tibetans who wanted a chance of seeing themselves on the screen. As on the previous occasion, the audience provided more interest than the picture; it was fun watching their fervent childlike responses.

The day came to a close with one of the loveliest rides that I have ever had, returning in the moonlight along the lane with barking dogs, beneath the Potala.

On my arrival from this ride at Tsarong's I was too much worked up inside to sleep, so I stayed up for hours and thought over matters a bit. It is hard to say whether it is the inner nature or the things I have been doing during the past year that have brought about such a close feeling of contact with life. Undoubtedly, the sort of life one must live in these parts has something to do with the creation of this mood, for one is ever in touch with the world of the spirit. At home we are usually carried to our destination by means of some mechanical contrivance, while here one either walks or rides, both of which bring you into closer contact with life. The pony I rode was one of Tsarong's finest. It was a very high-strung horse with all the pride of the best of his race. Again and again, he flung his head almost back into my lap. No matter how slowly he had to go, it was nearly impossible to keep him from prancing with his head among the clouds and their world of dignity. Regardless of how dejected and tired his rider might be, I do not believe it would ever be possible for one to sit on such a bounding spirit without partaking of a little of it.

The diffused light over that magnificent palace stimulated every pore of my body. The architectural gem of Asia was wrapped in a midnight veil with which my inner spirit merged; there was a flow and a diffusion of life, of which I was intensely conscious. I could not escape the awareness of the importance of living in a closer contact with that innermost self, which is of the essences of life. One does miss a great deal of this side of existence in the great centers of today, where everything has become so mechanical and matter-of-fact. He even begins to despise his fellow man, as he likewise despises us, and shuts himself up in that chilled shell of reserve. This worldly mood is spreading so rapidly today that it is almost impossible to have a human, or humanitarian, interest. Despite the crudity of it, every one in the old forgotten Wild West was regarded by another as a friend; the outlaw was the exception. I think that it is still possible in our modern hubs of civilization to retain something of the old friendly spirit, while clinging to the mechanism. I have many friends who say that this is impossible; it has been invariably their experience that after six months in New York they no longer have that contact with the flowing energy of life; or else, to avoid becoming automatons, they have to flee to the silent groves of nature. Yet I have the strong feeling that it is a matter of a little discipline, and that it is possible to yield in some measure to the requirements of our social machinery and yet retain the inner contact. A pretty tall order perhaps, yet then and there I resolved to learn something of the methods for establishing the union. If a reconciliation of the two ways of life is at all possible, some means must be found to bring it about. It is not reasonable to think that there can be 150,000 million beings striving for happiness, with no chance to salvation ahead. I knew then that my first test of all this training would come after my return to the world of external action, when I should discover how much of this life of the spirit I personally could retain. People today carry on at a terrific rate. It all appears as a superhuman ambition, but where they are going, and what it all has to do with their real selves, they do not know.

4

When I went upstairs for lunch I found a rather large party, for there was a Mongolian Lama who had just arrived from Pekin, and one who had come here originally as a chauffeur of the late Dalai Lama, who was very modern, having purchased a Baby Austin and a Dodge and had a road built for himself from his summer palace to the Potala. It was he who had sent the four Tibetan boys to England, and they have more than repaid all that was ever spent on them. It was also the

Dalai Lama who introduced no end of flowers into Tibet, and today all the flowers of sunny California are to be found flourishing in the Holy City. The Tibetan takes great pride in his flowers and has them in almost every room. Cut flowers are an exception; potted plants are used almost exclusively for decoration; the Tibetan is loth to cut flowers, whose beauty thus passes away only too quickly. The flowers of Lhasa are one of the things which must impress the newcomer, and for this beauty alone the late Dalai Lama is deserving of the worship and devotion accorded his memory.

Another guest at the party was a strange Tibetan woman of fascinating charm; and she had a large measure of character unusual in Tibetan women. Had she been of our world we would probably find her doing the work of Eleanor Roosevelt, but here all her talents will die in the rôle of motherhood, unknown to herself or any one else. I never learned her identity. For a while I suspected that she might be a sister of Tsarong Lacham, for she was nursing a child of a couple of years. If this be the case, the child is the son of Tsarong, it being a good old Tibetan custom that a husband may live with any of his wife's sisters, if he so desires. The younger sister has a child by him, a charming little girl who probably will begin her English schooling at Darjeeling very soon. Tsarong himself told me about his other children with a smile, adding the comment that it was "not an American custom."

We still had our daily discussion, of how to secure a *Tengyur*. I must not leave Tibet without one. Here was one of the world's greatest collections of literature, the storehouse of knowledge of a whole race which has preserved the wisdom of the ancient sages. It was becoming a bit absurd that I should have to put so much effort into finding a set of books whose contents should be known to a world eager for knowledge. Even if I were saved the seemingly insurmountable task of finding the books so necessary to me, there would still be the vast task of translating them—a mere matter of 333 volumes! If I could have my way, I should like most of all to select a staff of Lamas and secretaries to begin this terrific work of translation; for as yet I have not met any young students walking over half of the globe to extract the secrets of the mines of the religious spirit, whether they exist in Tibet or elsewhere. And, with so many volumes to translate, it seems a pity to waste so much time in the mere preliminaries. If the translation were actually started, and all arrangements were made for its publication, it might be twenty or thirty years before the dream could become a reality!

5

It was necessary to start at three in the morning for the Drepung monastery in order to be there at sunrise, the time set for the ceremonies in which I was expected to take part. Drepung is about four and a half miles to the west of Lhasa, and the ride there at the break of dawn, with the birds of the valley trilling their scales of joy, was exhilarating. At this hour the Potala's inspiring majesty assumed a new aspect, its serried roofs being touched with the first glow of the rising sun. The valley itself lies East and West, with a very low depression in the ridge at the upper end which forms the path, permitting travellers to pass on their way through to Eastern Tibet. At that point the heavens were still a misty mackerel, with the early morning colors visibly changing, and adding to the quiet ecstasy, which seemed to be in the very blood. The streets were as yet almost desolate of human beings, and the beggars were not yet at their posts. Here and there, on the kerb, some one was performing his morning ablutions, without the slightest concern for the passer-by. After we had passed through the *chorten* gateway leading into the Holy City we began to pass the donkey and yak trains bringing their wares of grass, butchered beef, green vegetables, wood, and cow dung to the market. The markets here are busiest between five and seven in the morning, and again during the last couple of hours in the evening after the workers have returned from the fields.

We were received at the gate of the monastery by several Lamas, one of whom was distinguished for his prodigious stature. He was at least three and a half feet across, and all of six-foot-six in height. He wore a bright red robe and the regulation Gelupa headdress, strongly reminiscent of the bright headgear of the knights of the past; it was a brilliant yellow, and its effect in the early morning light was superb. Before him walked his escort, who carried a heavy iron bar about five feet long and two inches square with a thin spike at the end, extending the bar another several inches, and on its tip a yellow hat had been placed. This iron bar, decorated with carvings, symbolizes the authority of the sect. The high official before whom it was carried had a little neophyte walking beside him to hold up his gown and prevent it from dragging on the ground. From the gate we followed along a path which ultimately led through steep, winding, narrow passageways, often up still narrower stone staircases; and all of it a labyrinth more confined in space than the streets of San Francisco's Chinatown. The leader was continually shouting, heralding the approach of authority, before which all had to make way. It is the habit of every one in this country to escape the presence of any high official, before whom you must show every formality of humility and respect. And so, given the warning, any poor fellow will duck into the nearest alley rather than go through with it. Indeed, Tsarong himself once told me of how he usually fled in the opposite direction when he heard of a higher government official coming his way; otherwise he would have been obliged to get off his horse and wait until the potentate had passed before remount-

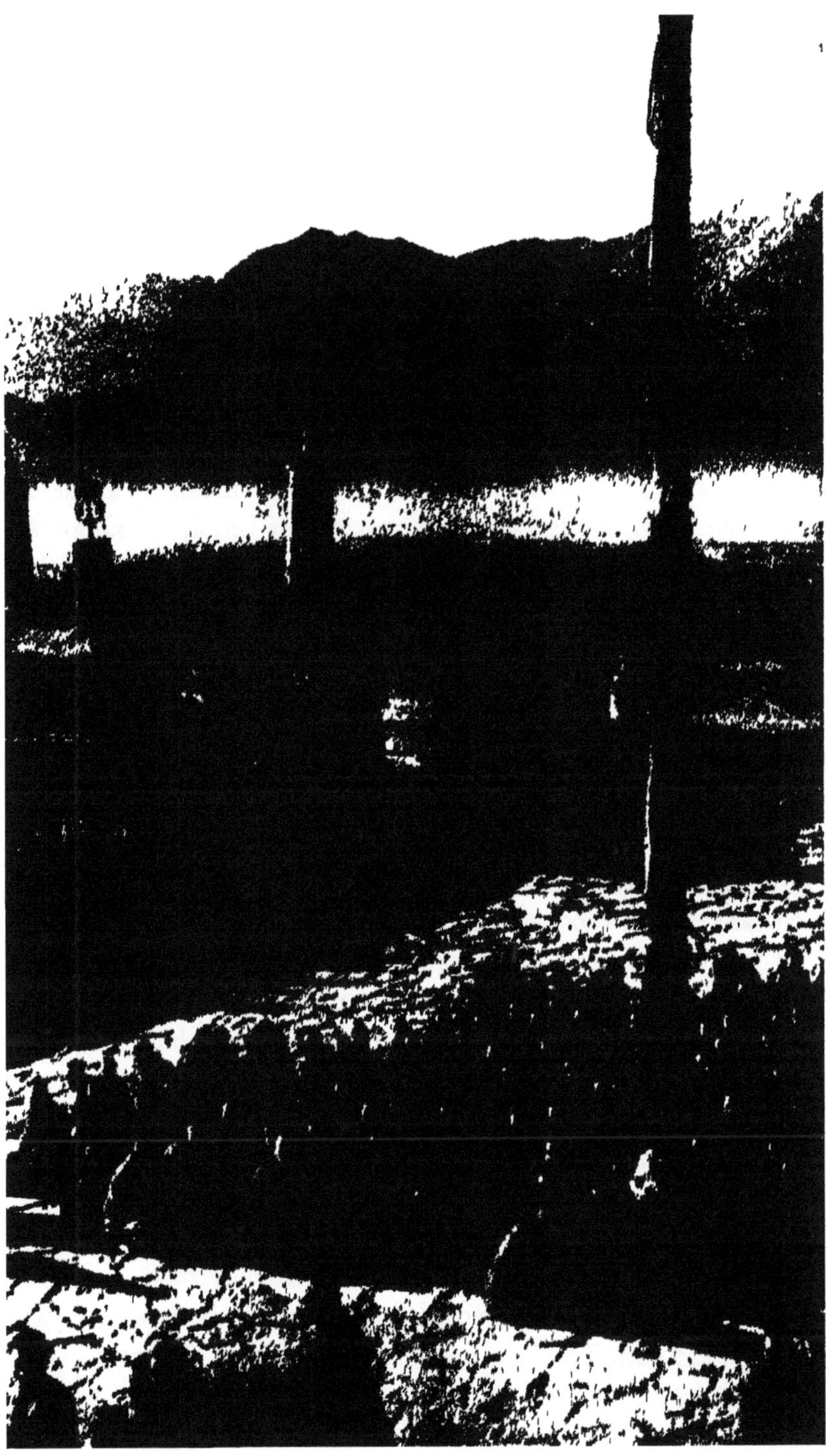

ing. And members of the lower class acted in a like fashion towards all officials, high and low, to whom they owed obeisance. On this particular morning, however, a couple of monks, having failed to dodge in good time, hovered together in a dark corner, with bent heads and stooped shoulders, holding their hats in their hands, scarcely breathing; for such is the custom when a high official passes by.

This immense Buddhist monastery is situated in the upper part of a deep nullah, among great masses of tumbled-down boulders of sandstone, appearing for all the world like an Arizona hillside. It received its name, Drepung—meaning a pile of rice—from the famous *Tantrik* monastery of India, Sri-Dhanya-Kataka, to be found at Kalinga and identified with the Kalachacra doctrine. Its three or four stories of whitewashed dormitories give it the appearance of a pile of the auspicious rice—that is, if you see it at a proper distance. My own excitement bore a more intimate character, since I was shortly to be a participant in an early morning mass performed by thousands of monks. While the official number of monks housed in Drepung is 7700, that of Sera 5500, and that of Ganden 3300, these numbers are mystical rather than factual; the real figures in each case exceed those given by thousands.

It was a long hard pull from the great stone entrance to the large rock-paved assembly grounds in front of the main temple, where all the monks from the four colleges which made up the monastery had gathered for this mass. With each step we ascended another few inches, yet I must admit that the way was clean in contrast to what I had been led to believe from the reports of others who had visited this place. The buildings were all very close together, leaving canyons wide enough for two persons to walk abreast or a single pack-donkey.

The monastery was erected by Geshe Rabsen-age Gyal-Ts'ab-je in 1414. The final ascent to the Central Cathedral with its glittering golden roof, which can be seen for miles from the surrounding countryside, was a steep, rapidly rising ascent. It was the thrill of a lifetime to arrive at the top and find all the monks seated in long lines on the paved pavilion waiting to catch the first glimpse of the rising sun. The general effect of this seething mass of bareheaded men in reddish-brown homespun was that of a swarm of bees, for they were mumbling their precious mystic formula and counting off their beads, as with a furtive curiosity they observed the arrival of the bearded foreigner in Tibetan dress. If there had been any way to catch the racing thoughts that passed behind those endless eyes focussed on me, as I walked slowly up the steep stairway of the cathedral, they would, I venture to say, have provided material for a fascinating volume.

The first rays were to be seen on the distant peaks, and no sooner had I settled down in the seat arranged for me than the Lamas came around with the incense which I was to carry. By now I was at ease. No longer was there any fumbling or hesitation on my part; for I knew my ritual and had had some experience. Promptly I was up, and off with my handful of burning punk. I entered the great temple, which to my surprise was likewise filled with monks, who were all chanting in the gloom of early morning. I turned over the incense to the assistant and made my devotional, as if I had done it all my life. Then I began the tour of the holy lanes, in which the sincere were reciting their sacred formulas and the weary were sleeping with nodding heads. Before the various shrines I left my stick of incense, and after the customary ritual received the blessings symbolized by these golden deities.

With the break of day the trumpets, the horns, the conch shells and the cymbals burst into sound and continued until the sun had drifted out of its shining crib. This was followed by the deep rumbling of the chants, which, I warrant, would send quivers up any one's spine. Within this great hall was another of their chief potentates, this time carrying his own emblem of authority, and after each chant it came down with a thud, which made the entire room vibrate with submission.

The time taken was scarcely more than an hour, yet the experience will live with me until the end.

Word had come that they had prepared food for me upstairs, so I took up my photographic equipment and moved along to partake of it. This time there was a regular monk's breakfast waiting for me; it consisted of dough prepared from barley flour poured into a half-filled bowl of butter tea. After this has been thoroughly mixed, something made of other grains and mixed with water and sugar is moulded into the dough, which you proceed to break off into small portions until you have had your fill. A bowl like this is devoured by them without difficulty. How they manage it I do not know, for though I was hungry in the beginning I found it difficult to finish it along with the pieces of dried raw meat which go with the meal. It is certain that a Lama never dies from starvation. Indeed, they eat far too much to gain that spiritual insight which they are all seeking. The truth is, only one out of every thousand is sincerely striving toward that end. During the meal the head Lamas honored me with the presentation of their scarves. They were all dressed in brilliant red robes, decorated with golden designs of heavy silk embroidery.

After I had enough to eat and had taken pictures of the ceremony, a sacred tour of inspection began, lasting over four hours. I will not speak of the army of images—gods, goddesses and *yidams*—which greeted me during the first hour. But I cannot refrain from mentioning the set of Tibetan *Tengyur*, whose covers were of carved sandalwood, and whose boards were decorated at the ends with beautiful intricate Chinese ivory carvings. Again, I must speak of some of the books, which were printed in red on one continuous sheet of paper printed only on one side and folding up like an accordeon.

On our way to one of the holy shrines we passed a large group of monks busy at the task of sewing garments for the deities, which are always dressed in the very finest silk. It is surely a fine thing to be a god in this part of the world. There were young and old at this work. A large population of boys under fifteen years of age are kept busy at endless jobs within their powers of endurance, when they are not engaged in studying the scriptures, whose endless pages they must recite by heart on the day of official examination before all the inmates of the monastery.

The next shrine was the most holy place within the cloister, full of golden deities, and we had to go through a number of purification rites before crossing its threshold.

Four different colleges make up the monastery, and these are again broken up into small subdivisions for the purpose of personal instruction. Each takes up a somewhat different aspect of things, and persons tend to join the one most in accord with their temperaments. There is one which all Nepalese attend when they join the monastery. Then there is another devoted entirely to *Tantrik* ritual, with Dorge Jig-je (Vajra-Bhairava) as the chief deity. He is reputed to be the fierce aspect of the merciful Chen-re-zi, and it was in a similar temple that I took part in the ceremony to this fiend at the Rammoche. He was represented here by an enormous image; his main head is that of a ferocious bull, and he holds his counterpart in a consuming embrace of flames with a single pair of his sixteen arms, the multiple hands clenching weapons of war. Beyond the main nave was a dark cell lighted by the dim flare of butter lamps; here was another image of this fiend, along with many other such *yidams*, decorated with human skulls. One large figure was firmly chained in the corner, and there was an inscription to inform you how dangerous he was, for he had caused a lot of destruction and, finally, had to be imprisoned.

The chief college of the four has the finest temple, which is beautifully carved and decorated at the entrance, and well draped within with endless *thangkas*, many of which are fifteen to twenty feet long, hanging from the beams of the high ceilings. There were endless sets of smaller *thangkas* of minor interest. It has been my experience that the finest examples are nearly always found to be owned by individual Lamas or rich believers in the faith who spend all that they have for perfect workmanship.

I returned for lunch to the place where I had had breakfast, and after I satisfied my hunger I made a call on a learned Lama whom I hoped to induce to give me instruction. He offered us endless cups of milk, an ordeal to be endured. His dark cell was about thirty feet long and eight feet wide; it was lighted up at one end by a small window, where he sat on his mat among several pots of lovely flowers, mostly of carnations in bloom. After a long talk he promised that he would come and live with me and instruct me in the various problems which I was eager to know. He had a very pleasing personality and bore every token of an arduous student, living the modest life of one seeking the truth.

From his place we walked around the entire monastery among the desert shrubs and large boulders of sandstone. Here we were able to glimpse another aspect of the monks' lives, that of work, for there were endless monks and women carrying jars of water from the adjoining stream. There is no water within the monastery; everything must be hauled in. If you could but see the immense copper vats used for the making of the daily tea, you would think it almost impossible to bring enough water each day to keep up with the demand.

A visit to the temples of the four colleges revealed nothing new in the way of idols and objects of worship, with the exception of a small tutelary deity whose shrine stood in front of the finest figure of Buddha that I have ever seen. It was that of the Coming Buddha, and to the right and left of him were shelves about thirty feet in height which held sets of the *Kangyur* and *Tengyur*. The small image was almost wholly covered with *katas*, which devotees had offered it during their pilgrimages. On either side were various instruments of war, signifying protection. These consisted, on one side, of a sheaf of arrows in a bow, and a couple of spears along with a symbolic spear of over three feet in length, their points being elaborated according to custom with an adornment intended to represent a burning flame, beneath which, forming a cross, was a *dorje*. On the other side were similar instruments, except that in place of the *dorje* was the representation of a flame with its points going out in three directions. Then against the point in front of the deity was a large iron arrow of about ten feet in length, with its end extending beyond the shaft for about a foot and a half, being six inches across the widest point.

In wandering around these various shrines we followed the sacred direction of the clock, finding our way up and down the paved alleyways leading between the countless houses, which were all built out of hewn rock, and throughout the entire morning I did not observe one bit that was filthy, as I had been told it would be. All was the quintessence of cleanliness, a mark in their favor when one considers the many monks living here and all lack of a sanitary system save for the small house with its hole in the roof. This method works fairly efficiently in this part of the world, owing to the extreme dryness and the cold weather.

The monastery commands an excellent view of the fertile valleys below; for it is spread out about half way up in one of nature's amphitheatres, with a very rocky trail leading up the soil-eroded hill of crumbling sandstone. The main path which we followed in the morning was bordered on either side with white slack lime, or something of the sort, to indicate the royal way. Most of the buildings run from three to four stories, but there are a few which go up to five. Everything is white, while the windows, protected by canvas canopies, have a wide black border, which seems to be the custom in these parts. The large canopies, which are spread over any desired patio to afford protection from either sun or rain, are rather striking with their extensive sign in the middle; this sign usually comes in dark blue or black strips. In many of the windows are to be observed boxes filled with potted plants.

The hard, hot pull around the monastery had its rewards in the views it offered of the country in which the ancient predecessors of the Lamas had tried to isolate themselves for the purpose of religious devotion. The trail, about five feet wide, was worn clean by the countless footsteps that have passed over it. On the west side it ran along a narrow ravine, sheltering the stream which serves as the water supply. Its banks were teeming with life, for those who did not carry water were washing their clothes or were just having a sunning. To the right of the trail was the high rock wall which surrounded the park of the monastery, filled with a variety of trees, including endless apricot trees laden with ripening fruit. Some of the monks retire to this quiet spot for instruction from the head Lamas, who lecture to them, and they also sometimes do a little studying out-of-doors. Most of it, however, is done within the confines of their small rooms. After you have climbed to the upper trail you obtain a fine view of this large monastic compound, as well as an extensive panorama of the valley threaded with endless small rivulets branching off from the main Kyi Chu (Lhasa River).

Immediately below us, at the foot of the hill, could be seen the small group of houses where all the butchering is done for the monks. Its name in Tibetan means "skin-flag," for it used to be the habit of the ruler of days gone by to have the disobedient killed at this place and flags made of their skins, which were then flung out to the wind.

6

The horses met us at the bottom of the hill. We rode on to the small monastery of Nechung, only a few hundred yards removed down a beautiful trail of trees; here the chief oracle of the Government resides. The story of its founding is that one of the past Dalai Lamas captured an evil spirit, which was causing considerable destruction. After placing the evil spirit in a box, he flung it into the river. One of the Lamas of Drepung, having heard of it, sent a young disciple to fetch it, with the admonition not to open the box. The temptation, however, was so great that at this spot, immediately below the monastery, he opened it, whereupon a pigeon flew out and lighted on a tree. When he went to catch it, it vanished. On returning with the tale to his master, the latter said that wherever that spirit was kept, there prosperity would always come. So Nechung, built in an oasis of trees, will always be a cloister of happiness, and the chief oracle who lives here is in contact with that spirit, whom he consults in order to be able to apprise the Government on whatever problems may arise.

All that could be seen at first of the monastery was its golden roof emerging out of the verdure. The trail to the building was marked off on each side, but in red chalk, not in white as was the case at Drepung. Immediately in front of the door leading into the home of the chief abbot was a large swastika, which looked auspicious. There was the usual food awaiting us, too much of it, as always. The abbot was a very pleasant personality of about sixty some odd years, with an Oriental braided beard consisting of a limited number of hairs that you might easily count.

We walked about, while he pointed out endless things of interest. Finally, we somehow drifted to the question of suicide. He said it happened only rarely, even in great monasteries, and that the usual method employed was that of hanging. An occasional man dashed himself against the rocks below a high cliff or flung himself into the river. The act is usually attributed to the intrusion of some evil spirit, and whenever it happens, certain rituals are promptly carried out in order to drive it away and prevent others from putting an end to themselves. It was impossible to dwell on the subject, since a ceremony was to be held on the following day, and such talk was not considered auspicious. It is more than likely that the night was spent in ritual to banish the evil effects of the discussion.

About the time of my visit they had just secured a new oracle, for the previous one had made the wrong guess when he predicted that the late Dalai Lama would survive his last illness; the Government informed him that he no longer had the power over the spirit, and it chose a successor to him. The method of choosing and retaining the oracle is as follows: The candidate all of a sudden begins having fits, and claims to have been entered by the spirit. After a great deal of ritualistic investigation, they decide if he is telling the truth. The method of summoning the spirit is by retiring to the room in which the spirit resides, and then, while others are performing the various appropriate rituals, the spirit enters the candidate, and he promptly begins to be the spokesman of this ethereal soul. As long as his predictions are verified, he retains the position as official oracle. But let him once be wrong, without a perfect extenuating circumstance, then out he goes. He is wholly incapacitated for a couple of hours after his performance, during which interval the attendants take the very best care of him and help him to recuperate.

This monastery shelters about 160 monks who act as internes from ten to fifteen years, learning the various rituals, after which they can take charge of private temples or conduct services wherever they may happen to be. The special function of this school is to train monks in the ritual.

Of all places that I have ever visited I must confess that it would be difficult to find more inspiring surroundings; the place is one solid grove of trees forming an almost impenetrable shade.

CHAPTER XI

MORE SIGHTS, MORE CEREMONIES

I

THE most interesting diversion of another day was a performance given by four men and four women, the women providing the vocal accompaniment, while the men danced. One dancer in particular gave you the tingle of his inner experience with the grace of his movements; you felt like floating in the air with him. This group of travelling dancers had been across the length and breadth of central Tibet, even finding their way to Kalimpong during the winter months. I could not resist the temptation of making an ample photographic record of this wandering dance team for the benefit of my friends at home. Even though the sky was dark, I took a chance on a few rolls of colored film, to add to the realism of the record. They were real technicians at beating the drums with the curved drumsticks which followed the drums tied on behind them; they danced and gestured with their arms while dancing, never missing a single beat. The men added to the chorus with small hand cymbals, which clashed to the rhythm of their footing. The dancing was followed by a few musical numbers on their two-stringed violin-like instruments erected on a gourd head, and a small stick was manipulated to stretch the string.

The main event of the day was the ceremony held before the tomb of the Dalai Lama at the Potala; it was tremendously impressive, and I thought myself infinitely fortunate in being permitted to take pictures of it. I had to operate quietly and unobtrusively, as they are very touchy and would prefer it not to be done at all. But I was given special consideration, because of my having gone around the world to make this sacred pilgrimage; so they granted me the privilege of making a Memory Album of interiors while the ceremonies were in progress. Many are the records to be had of the outer dead wall, but it was given only to me to take impressions of the rooms filled with the Lamas dressed in their black conical hats and waving their *dorjes* and thunderbolts to the rhythm of drums and droning horns.

The Potala is only about a mile away from Tsarong's home, and as I approached it on horseback I was impressed anew with the magnificence of the edifice towering hundreds of feet into the heavens. Its rhythm is that of a rapid rhapsody, with no two lines balancing, but forming a perfect composition by uniting in the glittering roof of the gods. The entire structure is protected by an inaccessible wall of stone with a walled barrier in front of the entrance forming a short maze through which one must pass under the guard of well placed slits for the purpose of shooting without being shot. These guardian eyes are placed at regular intervals all along the ever rising stone stairways which one must mount before finally entering the sanctuary. At the foot of this soaring structure of windowed rock we left our horses, and began to climb, zigzagging back and forth in order to gain the necessary altitude. As a rough guess I should say that the building is around 500 feet high, or as high as a fifty-story New York skyscraper, spread out in length to three football fields, placed end on end. The sensation of staring into space and peering into the clouds is for all the world like trying to comprehend the Rockefeller Center on Fifth Avenue. But there are no handy elevators here to facilitate your ascent and descent if your time is limited and you are in a hurry to keep a luncheon engagement. You simply have to walk up, or stay down. The stairways of solid rock are about twenty-five feet wide, with a stone railing about breast-high; they rise in long steps of several feet. As you work your way back and forth to reach the entrance of the building proper, you are able to get a beautiful panorama of the fertile Lhasa Valley, from the towering Chak-po-ri at the western entrance of the city to the low divide at the eastern end of the valley.

We passed through endless halls, ever rising into the higher chambers of sanctity, on our way to the tomb where the ceremony was to be held. All the way we marched to the unceasing sound of trumpets, of the blasts of horns, of the clashing of cymbals, and as we came into the opening of the courtyard, we saw two enormous drums hanging from the ceiling on either side of the door, and these appeared to be the only instruments about the place that were not used to make a noise.

We were led through the kitchen, which appeared exactly like the old kitchen dramatized by the Baptist in his Hell of fire and damnation. It was about as black and seething a dungeon sweatbox as I ever hope to pass through in any lifetime. Over the vast ovens of earth were immense vats of steaming tea far above your head, and the only light to be had was from the glowing coals of the fire. We got out of this in a hurry by means of another flight of stairs to a small cubbyhole just above the spot where the trumpets were being sounded. Here I learned that the oracle was about to receive the particular spirit which resided at this place, and as there was ample time before the ceremony to be performed before the tomb of the Dalai Lama, I promptly hurried downstairs and around corners to slip into the temple room, so that I could have the privilege of witnessing this event and, perhaps, of receiving a blessing from the oracle.

The din of the instruments did not let up. It sounded a very slow and low pace. It was as if they were working up what we should call a fitting "atmosphere." They were preparing the place for the spirit—as it were, coaxing him in. He seemed to be a very temperamental spirit. The oracle came in, dressed in a gorgeous array of yellow brocade, with a sort of witch-hat. He seated himself Buddha-fashion, on the floor in front of his throne. Four men held him in a mood of greatest tension, as if to be ready for the moment the spirit made his entrance; for them, the oracle was no longer a human being, but the recipient of the spirit's confidence, and its spokesman. While he sat there in silent meditation, in order to relax his nerves and yield to whatsoever manner of convulsion this never-ending din would induce, two rows of drums continued their beating on one side, while on the other side trumpets went on with their unceasing blast; at the same time about thirty seated monks were chanting their sacred formula. At last he began to quiver, and the drummers and the trumpeters drew closer and closer to him with an increasing volume of mystic sounds, finally drumming and blowing directly into the ears of the oracle in order to prevail upon him to stay. After an hour of this unceasing rhythm—even I could not resist it and felt my emotions merge with the vibrations of the room—the spirit must have entered the oracle, for he began to vibrate like a G-string on a base viol, while his four attendants were trying to hold him down. His strength grew terrific, and they were forced to yield in the end, content merely to keep hold of him to prevent bodily injury. With this he suddenly sprung from the floor, still in his cross-legged position, far above the heads of all in the room. He repeated this several times. Then he straightened out, and stood up, pacing the flor back and forth before ascending the throne reserved for the Dalai Lama. During this exercise he appeared to be keeping time, and made a strange sort of noise very much like a hiccough. Then he made way to his throne, where several cups of some kind of drink were offered him, he consumed it like an accomplished heavy drinker. An attendant held a large number of short red scarves, which the priests placed around the necks of those making offerings to him. A congested line of Lamas formed; they held the *katas* in readiness to offer them to him as soon as they could work their way to his feet. During all this time he continued his hiccoughing noise, and reciting whatever the spirit would impart during the emotional fit. Persons from all over the place were rushing to the windows to witness the scene. Shortly he spoted the onlookers and, reaching for a silver cup and anything else that came to hand, he flung them in their direction with the splenetic fury of a hysterical wife or husband.

Thus, I had to come to witness one of the greatest spectacles of all Tibet.

2

By now it was time to go into the tomb of gold and make my offering. Today they were performing the ceremony of Dorje Jig-je, which was just a little different from the one performed at Rammoche, different only in the matter of detail. It took place in the uppermost part of the building, added on at the late Dalai Lama's request. The monks had already assembled, and the officiating Lama was the lifelong teacher of the Master whose tomb this was. The space in front of the tomb was limited, permitting only about a hundred monks to crowd in, and leaving but small space for me to carry on my ritual. After stumbling over black hats, bordered with mystical symbol Sanskrit letters, I made my way to the central aisle at the head of which was the priest in charge. I made my offering and received his blessing. I felt an unaccountable excitement in standing before this golden memory, while the chamber vibrated with beating drums and clashing cymbals, and the low mumblings of the chants.

It was here that I observed the first example of nude phallicism in the protector of the *yidam,* who was in heated readiness to embrace his female counterpart who, with responding passion, was mounting his extended leg in eagerness to be possessed. Above the group was one of the finest *thangkas* that I had yet seen; it represented this deity in the serious aspect of Chen-re-zi, the patron saint of Tibet, the God of Mercy. His image was very common, as the late Dalai was reputed to be the reincarnation of this Merciful One.

The altar was alive, and all the lamps were sending forth their small yellow flames, only to awaken a deeper feeling in those who had come to express their devotion. Once you fall wholly in tune with the mood of the room, you begin to experience the most agonizing pangs of yearning for an intenser devotion.

The ceremony coming to an abrupt end, I continued my tour of inspection, my first stop being in the shrine of Avalokitesvara, where I had expressed devotion during an earlier visit of the tombs of the other twelve Dalai Lamas. I saw some exceptionally fine *thangkas*, representing various demons. All the *yidams* revealed different forms of sexual embrace with their *Dakinis;* power and action are the two chief demands of these protectors, and there is nothing that symbolizes this more forcibly than the sexual aspects of life, with the consuming flames of destruction. In every instance that I observed, with the single exception already pointed out, one never sees the sexual organs, as the *yidams* are always portrayed holding their counterparts in a standing position, while the female clings to her consort with her legs locked around his waist, pressing her heavy breasts into his chest and entwining her arms around his neck. Her customary hue is red, while he is usually black. I noted a few exceptions to this combination; sometimes they are both of the same color, and in one instance he was painted blue. Almost invariably, if you peer into the dark, you will see him crushing human forms beneath his feet during his intense exultation of passion in an aura of leaping flame.

The tour concluded with a walk beneath the eaves of the golden roof of this newly-erected shrine for the late Dalai Lama. A photograph I took of it gives a better idea of its beauty than any description it is within my power to give.

The hour was now twelve, and the Lamas were on the edge of the Potala roof, blowing their twelve-foot horns, so that the villagers far below might be brought to a short halt for silent prayer. The deafening rumble of these horns lasts about five minutes in all. Every now and then one of the blowers pauses to get rid of the accumulated saliva, then resumes his task, giving his neighbor a chance to do likewise.

Thence onward my journey developed into one continuous orgy of photography. The environs of the residence of Buddha's viceroy on earth surely deserved every indulgence of the camera. The approach of the park is a long boulevard bordered with tall poplars. It was along this road that the Precious One was wont to be chauffeured in his small Baby Austin when attending to business or ceremonies at the Potala.

On our way we were able to watch the Tibetans at the task of rejuvenating the top of the old *chorten* which crowns the entrance to the Holy City. There was a scaffold all around its crown, upon which workmen could be seen painting and mending.

The entrance to the palace grounds, which are surrounded by an enormous wall of rock, is of typical Chinese design in a Tibetan variation, far less generous in the use of dragons. The Tibetan does not use so much of the Chinese combination of gold and green, but he does not spare reds and blues, and in many places he uses gold extensively. To the left of the twenty-foot gateway was a small guard-post cell with three soldiers, who presented arms as we entered. The two swinging doors must be all of fifteen feet high, with six yawning lion-handle grips on each. They are made of brass and carved rather lavishly in keeping with the Tibetan tendency to embellish everything they touch. They rarely leave material in the nude, but always clothe it in handsome ornament. The roof which covers the entrance has the appearance of green tiles, and beneath its far-projecting eaves is the typical tiling of Chinese blocks, with dragon gargoyles at the end, decorated in the royal color. On the inside a small protective enclosure is formed, with four large columns supporting the massive roof. Two of these are of chiselled granite; they were the first pillars of the kind that I have seen here. As might be expected, they were not left bare, but were nicked up in artistic fashion. The two wooden ones were painted red, according to the common practice, and striped with three finely drawn yellow lines. In very many instances, within the temples, these are wrapped in heavy reddish-brown homespun cloth. At the top, where they spread out for several feet and support the cross-beams, they are always carved in some intricate design of flowers, or symbolic flame on the sides, while a lotus, a lion, a dragon or a lucky sign graces the center. As a rule, all this is placed against a background of red, with designs painted in red, green, and gold, and all bordered with blue. The ceiling of this small waiting space was covered with a design which had a large lucky *mandala* in the center.

The large gateway leading into the old place where the Dalai Lamas were wont to receive their court differed but little from the gateway I have just described. There was the customary row of yawning lions over the doorway, beneath which was an auspicious inscription. This appears to be about the only way in which they try to take care of the future, they seem to feel that if things are kept auspicious at all times, there is little need to worry. A small courtyard of about thirty feet leads directly into the audience chamber. Just outside and under the well-decorated porch were long, raised platforms on each side, where visitors could wait on the large mats provided for them. Just in front of the door as you entered was a small decorated screen to give privacy to the interior; here the officiating monks were sitting on the floor in two lanes facing one another, beating their drums that the good spirits might always be in the room. At their head was the chief Lama, who sat in front of a skull cup, sounding his small hand drum, which was beaten with two mallets attached to a string and struck by the twisting of his wrist, as the drum was held between his thumb and forefinger. In the other hand he turned and waved his *dorje,* while his lips chanted the sacred *mantra* of the service.

From here I returned to the garden, where I took a short path through the patio, where lectures used to be held under a canopy of unbroken shade. A short distance beyond this clearing was a large bird cage which held a pair of some rare feathered creature, whose Tibetan name as far as I can render it in English was something like "A pretty bird with a long neck."

The path led to the small pond, which is formed like a large rock reservoir, with a tiny rock path leading around it beneath the bowing willows and stately poplars; there is a low stone railing to prevent the unstable from slipping. In the center is the Dalai Lama's small garden house, connected with the mainland by a well-constructed bridge. Some water fowl, for the most part the colorful reddish Brahminy ducks, disported themselves in the sun. The house, decorated in dull gold and black, with all the usual Oriental intricacies, is set back from the endless flowering plants, small trees and rosebushes. At each of the front corners is a large iron lion from China to protect the Precious One. I have already told of the beauty of its interior, with its small shrine of jade and coral. In all of India, including Kashmir, there is nothing to compare with the beauty of this spot; here you could settle down with your books for the remainder of your life and forget there was a world beyond.

After inspecting the stables and the grounds of the former Dalai Lamas, being dazzled by the brilliant glow of the sun on a golden roof, I decided it was time for a little refreshment. Our anticipated small lunch turned out to be a complete Tibetan dinner, provided by the *Kashag*, which apparently had ordered that nothing be spared. By now a Tibetan meal is an old story to the reader, and I shall not attempt to dwell on its details. It lasted over two hours amidst the finest natural surroundings to be had anywhere. Before we had come to the end the sky was black, and soon there was a light thunder shower. I had to forego further attempts at photography for the day.

3

It was evening as we were returning to Tsarong's after a day filled with excitement and beauty. The cattle of Lhasa were winding their way homeward ahead of the weary herdsman who stumbled along over the dusty way. It was one of those pastoral scenes of forgotten history recorded by poets and painters and unknown in real life to the bulk of our city dwellers. All along the road leading to Lhasa we wove our way in and out among the strolling herds, and so with the setting sun we arrived at Tsarong's, too thrilled to find expression for our mood in words.

During the lunch hour on the following day the tailor brought my new Tibetan gowns. They were too beautiful ever to think of wearing, but what with my regular clothes worn out there was no alternative but to put them to use. Not that there is any comparison between the loveliness of our clothes and theirs. Such a profusion of silks, colors, and designs was revealed before me as to leave me gasping with astonishment and admiration. I found that the Tibetans were delighted over my readiness to wear the native dress, and it at once broke down whatever barriers still existed between us.

My effort to concentrate on my studies was constantly interrupted all that morning and afternoon by the almost unceasing singing of many women who were working in the courtyard laying stones. No sooner does the Tibetan—man, woman, or child—begin to work than he begins to sing, and this does not let up until he finishes his tasks at the end of the day. It's not a bad idea at all, but when you think that it begins as early as five in the morning when the flower-pots are watered, to sundown and later you cannot help realizing that it is too much of a good thing.

4

The following day began for me at three-thirty, and hasty preparations were made to leave for the Sera monastery, where the monks were assembling for the ceremony scheduled to begin at daybreak. It was a cool and brisk ride under a lowering sky, between high dikes of sand and brilliant fields of yellow mustard waving in the early morning breeze.

We were caught in a heavy summer shower, which soaked us to the bone and made of my clean silk shirt a disreputable-looking rag. But that made little or no difference in my spirits, and I proceeded as though nothing had happened, my mind reflecting on the compensations awaiting me at the other end. In any event, I realized that it was the spirit that mattered, and that the value of the entire ritual which I was making my own depended wholly on the measure of feeling I put into it, and that if I held the right thought good would be forthcoming in many lives to come, even as similar endeavors had a like effect in many lives in the past. Or else how was it to be explained that I had wanted to come to Lhasa to take part in these sacred ceremonies? Who is to say how right the Tibetan teachers were in offering this explanation? Who is to deny that they were right? For the scientists cannot disprove it, and the Yogi has his own answer for all actions of man; he does not believe that things just happen to him. Everything is governed by a law of which he can gain understanding, and thereby learn the meaning behind all unfathomable answers.

The monks greeted us just outside the monastery. The path was laid out with auspicious signs all the way to the entrance of the main assembly hall. Because of the rain, most of the monks from the three colleges which constitute the place had to go inside. In the course of an hour, however, the rain had ceased, and about three or four thousand monks gathered in the large paved courtyard just in front of the temple, while the rest filled the dark aisles of mystery within the nave of the temple.

I was escorted to a protected corner, where they were planning to keep up my spiritual advancement with a constant supply of tea and food throughout the day. By the time I had some tea and a typical Lama breakfast of *tsampa*, which one kneads into a nice piece of dough with the addition of butter tea, I was more than satisfied. But you continue to eat, out of a bowl large enough for a horse, and by the time you are halfway through you are surprised to find out that you have developed a taste for it. From then on I looked forward to being able to knead my own breakfast. I must confess that it makes living a very simple affair. Indeed, the kneading—I have already described it earlier—is done even while they continue their chants. During the whole time of the breakfast they were murmuring their long tea prayer, with the wielders of authority thumping their heavy iron bars on the floor as they walked among the faithful.

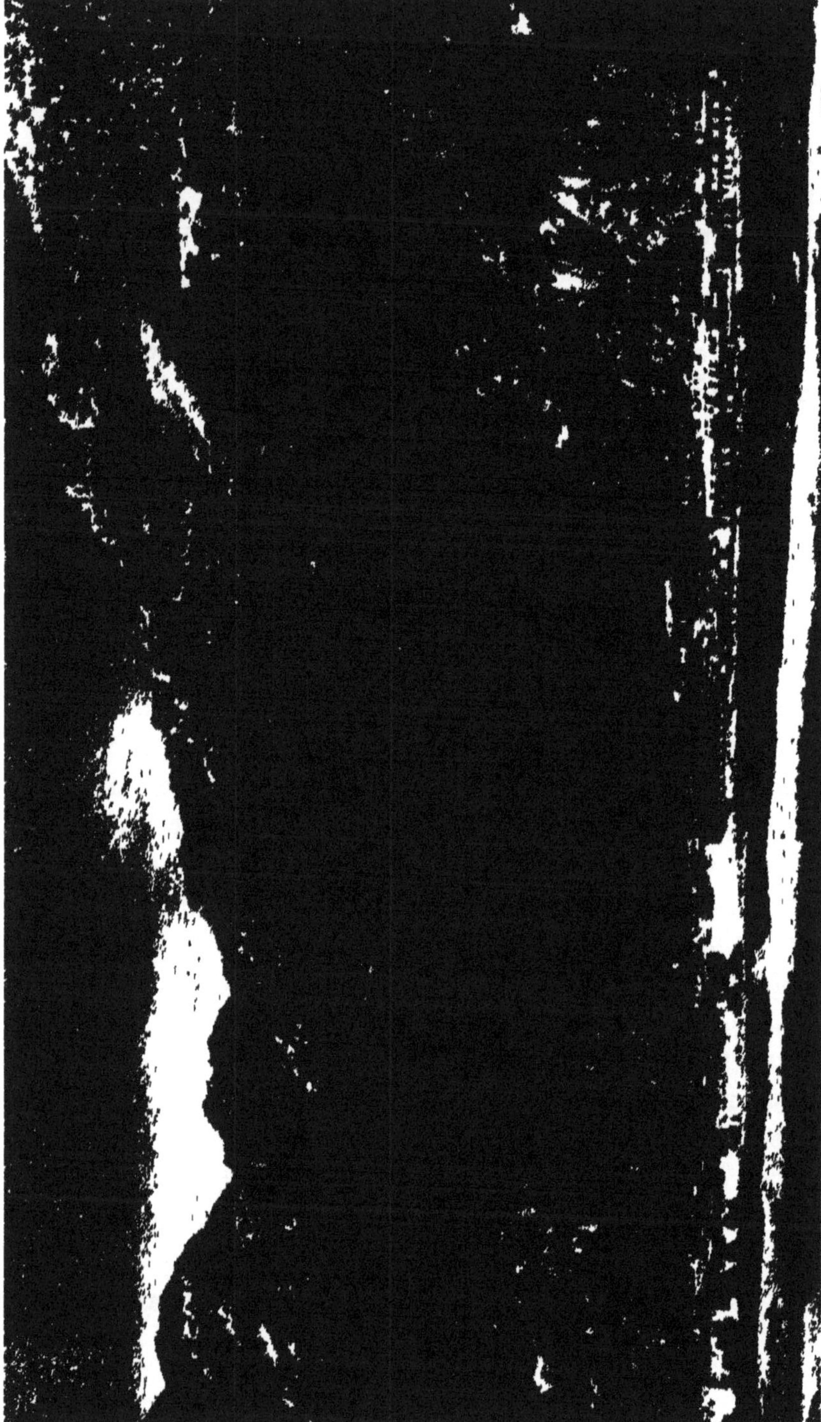

The inevitable moment came when I took my place at the head of the central aisle and, in my drenched gown, went about my ritualistic tasks, differing but little from those of the previous ceremonies, already described. After visiting the shrine of the large Coming Buddha I went to the more esoteric shrines with their small glowing butter lamps beneath the butter *chortens*, which are symbolic of the Buddhistic world, so entirely different from our concept of the world. Indeed, they believe they are right, and cannot understand why it is night-time in America when it is day-time here. This is one instance of many. I can scarcely convey the difficulties I got into every time I tried to explain a single fact in the light of accepted scientific research.

Well, the time came around to eat again, as it inevitably does. The head Lamas from the three colleges had convened in our dining-hall, situated in a small area between two buildings and sheltered from the weather by a canopy. On the ground there were carpets, upon which were lovely Tibetan mats, placed before low tables from which we were to eat. The head Lama of the monastery, who had previously given me his blessing, joined us. Now that we broke bread together as normal humans we had a jolly good time, and he was filled with laughter. For contrast, there were two here that were lost to the world about thirty years ago. One of them found life far easier to sit with closed eyes and mumble the password to heaven, while counting off his beads. The other forgotten soul had toured China in his youth, but that was so long ago that he could no longer remember it; not for him to give a thought as to whether the earth was round or flat—it had long since been decided for him by Buddhist literature, which says that it runs straight up and down. Indeed, he was ready to point out the folly of modern mankind—just imagine them trying to fly! God had given wings to birds, but he had not given wings to man, who should be content to remain in the station assigned to him. There is little to do in such circumstances but live, learn, and be happy, and let others do the same. It is to be remembered that these people have had no contact with such world forces as have acted upon us; there has been no stimulus to cause the thoughts of the Tibetan to function in any other channel. Yet a change is inevitably coming, and I fear within my own lifetime, which means that my next visit to Tibet may be entirely different, unless I can make it very soon. I may say in passing that Tibet has escaped the world-wide depression, and that all its people are employed. Indeed, there is need to implore and to bribe to get the more indolent Tibetan to work; for he is usually too busy with religion or something else to be able to waste his precious time on such worldly things as work.

And, again, the inevitable tour of the holy shrines. This, I must remark, is a privilege. Any one may visit the main temple, and while there is general willingness to extract a little material aid, no amount of money will buy a pass beyond the massive doors protecting the sacred shrines of the inner religion. The way is open only to the brotherhood, to whom all the doors are thrown open; but once you have entered, there is no escaping the duty of visiting every shrine and no way of avoiding the stories of how this deity spoke and that one grew toe-nails or finger-nails, and this one sweated and that one performed some other function of the human animal. There is always one of these deities who has had a few words to say in their dark caverns of contentment. I would speak, too, or do anything in order to escape, but the Tibetan with his endless tales of talking deities would buttonhole me and hold me there very much in the way that the Ancient Mariner must have held the Wedding Guest. I must mention one special shrine dedicated to Guru Rimpoche. The room was filled with small images and an endless collection of ancient weapons of defence. I venture to say that this was the first time in histor that any one ever attempted a flashlight picture in this room, an during the entire time of my attempts they were carrying o prayers and burning incense in order to purify my defiling ac tion. The room was totally dark, with the exception of the dir light thrown by a single small butter lamp and a very tiny win dow in a remote corner at the very top of the room. Differen from anything I had seen before were some excellent wal paintings of seven lucky *Dakinis*, who are so frequently see copulating with their favorite deities; this time they were alon standing in all the vigor of their womanhood.

Then followed the walk around the monastery. The trail le high above the monastic world to a small building in whic the founders of the monastery used to study during its erection And some way up the steep mountain was another small mon astery, a part of Sera, which was used by monks who felt th need for a little solitude; there were about thirty of them stay ing there at the moment. Along the way amidst the wildernes of crumbling sandstone we passed a couple of caves to whic individual monks retire for study when the monastery is to much for their concentration. The summit of our trail com manded an excellent view of the Lhasa valley as well as of th roof-tops of Sera. It is when you reach such places that the ide of monkhood digs its way deeper into the consciousness of th restless human being.

5

Many a time and oft I pondered on the singular fact tha there seemed to be no more fitting place for sleep than Lhas where all should be peaceful and the element of time elimi nated; actually, this was far from the case. I am, of course, re ferring to my own relation to the matter. These days held bu little leisure for me to think of either sleep or peace. Alread

I had to think of my approaching departure, of the thousand and one details demanding my attention before I could set out again on the homeward trek. All this, indeed, left me but little time for study.

I had a piece of marvellous news. Tsarong had finally decided to give me his *Kangyur* and *Tengyur*, because he feared I would take the chance of leaving Tibet by way of China. His attitude was that my life was precious and that I should not take any chances. Having already dedicated these books on the shelves of his private temple, he ran considerable risk in permitting me to take them; here, as elsewhere, persons are ever ready to criticize on the slightest provocation.

Yet, having secured the books, the work only just began. I had arrangements to make to obtain the necessary silk for their markers, on which are indicated the contents of each volume; these markers generally project over the edge of the shelf. Again, the books are supposed to be wrapped in silk, but I decided to have this done in America. There were also the board covers to be made, and this too I decided to have done at home, all the more because they would increase the weight and cost of transportation. I could not avoid, however, calling the carpenter to build the boxes for packing the boxes, or finding sufficient yak-skin for wrapping the boxes; this to prevent any possible damage by the rains of India on the way to Calcutta. All this, Tibet being the sort of place it is, involved far more of my effort and time than would be supposed; and, literally, it was to reduce my already diminished sleep to an uncomfortable minimum.

Indeed, the following several days were to prove an ordeal and a vexation, tinged with not a little entertainment. There was, for example, the selection of the silks. The man who came discussed and re-discussed with me always the same point, driving me on close to madness. It was just the Tibetan's way.

They simply cannot do business in a businesslike fashion. Yet without their help I could do nothing. They enjoy making the most of trifles. We talked and talked, like a couple of temperamental nitwits; I certainly felt like one before I was done. Tsarong sent us his own head tailor to hasten the task of preparing some covers for my Christmas card, which he admired hugely. The tailor sat cross-legged for an hour and a half, cutting out as many covers as possible from the sample of material which we had on hand, while I sat patiently and looked on. In the meantime he had sent some of his men to the city to find samples of different silks, and again I had to sit and wait for their return, which of course took another hour or so. On their arrival they had the silks, but had failed to get the prices. Just a little too polite to mention such trivialities, I finally convinced them that I did not have the slightest idea as to my choice, for it was to be the price and not the design that was to be the deciding factor. So one of the boys was sent back, and we waited patiently for another long while. It is not all as bad as it sounds, for a lot of fun can be had with them, since all Tibetans have an excellent sense of humor. At times I have seen Tsarong double up on the floor like a child with laughter at a good joke, and the Lamas can make the beams vibrate with their low-rolling roar of delight.

Any one coming to my room would have thought that I had opened up a tailor shop to see yards upon yards of silks strewn around the room, and the tailor and his assistant marking it off. The custom for taking care of the precious sacred volumes is to wrap them in large pieces of silk, after which each book must be marked and indexed from the outside, so that one might find the desired volume without having to unwrap each one. Three royal colored covers are placed over the mark for decorative effect; beneath them is the plain yellow piece of silk on which is inscribed the alphabetical number of the volume. With three hundred and some odd volumes, it is possible to see how many markers must be made, of course, they will promise them in a week, but that means at least two weeks. It seems to be the Tibetan way of calculating time.

I have mentioned the fact that the tailor spent hours in my room yesterday cutting out covers for the Christmas cards, and I thought at the time what a waste of time it was for me to have to stick around. And now I discovered the reason for his insistence on doing the work in my room. It is the practice to cut silk in presence of the owner, since the workers are not above stealing a couple of squares of silk, so the more honest ones will insist on doing the work before you, so you will have no cause to complain. He was with me for the entire day, and when I went upstairs for tea, he also went out for tea.

6

There was a short discussion at tea-time about the Tibetan custom of spelling and counting, which is always done by singing, much as we used to sing the alphabet as children in the old days. There is perhaps nothing harder than their method of spelling, which is a long devious task of repetition and pronunciation of each letter of the word before proceeding to the next letter, which wholly alters the sound of the previous letter, which must then be repeated in its altered form. This you keep up until you repeat the whole word as it should be pronounced. There is only one Tibetan in a thousand who is capable of any simple process of mathematical calculation. Usually he does it by singing to a tune, which from a distance is rather pleasing to the ear. It made me laugh at times to watch them try to figure out a simple problem and promptly break into song. Even Tsarong used to be vastly amused by it, and roar with laughter at such unnecessary antics. In olden times they more nearly approached our silent method, and made their calculations on a slate, using the little finger to inscribe in the dust upon which they would write. By the way, the Tibetan holds the pen between the ring finger and the little finger.

I have already spoken of Tibetans singing at their work. When twenty or thirty of them are working together at the same task they produce something that is worthy of being recorded. It seems they have a different song for every occupation, whether working in the field, plowing, sowing, harvesting, or loading for market. Again, there are separate songs for rock breaking, road building, sewing, weaving, grinding barley. Indeed, there is no occupation without its own song. Once I put the question to some one as to what would happen if a new kind of job were to be introduced into Tibet, such as, for example, the stringing of electric-light wires, or the like. The answer was that they had such a large repertory of occupational tunes that one of them was sure to fit in as the proper rhythmic accompaniment to the new work. It was explained to me that the word content of the songs mattered less than the rhythm, which must accord with the speed and manner of the work; and it was claimed that these songs kept the workers going for longer periods without exhaustion. I must admit that it is a pleasure to watch them at their work with such a joy of heart. Having tasted rather deeply of the moral oppression of the long-endured strain of labor myself, I can well appreciate what it means to them to carry on their burdens in such a blithe fashion.

7

Tsarong and I had a talk on Buddhistic art. He argued that the outside world failed to comprehend the principles of this art. He contended that this art was based wholly on philosophical principles derived from religion. Art, as other infinite manifestations of the spirit, has its only source in accepted truth. The Tibetan artist cannot violate the principles of this truth by doing something which does not emanate from the one and only source. In order to understand their art, said Tsarong, it is essential to be familiar with Buddhist teachings and to be thoroughly acquainted with the symbolical meanings which are deeply imbedded in their almost forgotten ancient tradition. With beginnings in China, its Tibetan development led to new adaptations, in art as in other things.

Now, however, the outside world only deals with the external facts with which they come into contact on the border. It would be found that all of their art is based on some religious belief, even though it is only superficial. Thus, in working up a design they will usually include all or some of eight lucky signs: the golden fish, the umbrella, the conch-shell trumpet of victory, the lucky diagram, the victorious banner, the vase, the lotus, and the wheel. Or they will use something from the Seven Gems: wheel, jewel, jewel of a wife, gem of a minister, white elephant, horse, or the gem of a general. Likewise, with the seven royal barges: the precious house (palace), the precious royal robes, the precious boots (embroidered), the precious elephant's tusks, the precious Queen's earrings, the precious King's earring, the precious jewel. Or they may choose from the Seven Personal Gems: the sword-jewel, the snake-skin jewel, the palace-jewel, the garden-jewel, the robes, the bed-jewel, the shoe-jewel. Often the eight glorious offerings are used: the mirror, the intestinal concretions, curds, darwa grass, the Bilva fruit, Li-khri, the white turnip. Then, again, the five sensuous qualities: the pleasing form (rupa), sound (sapta), perfumes (gandhe), luscious eatables (naiwete), pleasing touch and feeling (sparsa). Then there are various symbolic diagrams and triagrams which are formulated on astrological beliefs. With the Chinese, they use the Tortoise, the Phœnix, the Dragon, the Horse-dragon, the Tiger, and the five bats of fortune (Luck, Wealth, Long Life, Health, and Peace). Along with these symbols there is the constant use of various flowers in conventional forms, each with its own degree of importance. The colors, too, carry their own meanings, which have developed from esoteric understanding. Often they are used to indicate moods. White and yellow represent mild moods! red and black—the fierce aspects; blue—things of a celestial nature.

It is possible to go much deeper into these matters, but all such material is already recorded in books, so I leave it to be found there when wanted. All that I wished to indicate was that the main point in these modern representations has been lost. It is, for example, of little importance in itself that red stands for a fierce mood; what is important is the knowledge why this is so, and the answer to the question: is it universal? The same applies to the rest of all this symbology. For if these things are universal, the inevitable conclusion is that they must apply to us equally with the ancients. In the teachings of the *Tantra* it is possible to discover where they originated, and through the application of Yoga it is possible to apply their universal origins to oneself. There is no real need to read a fairy tale and then "take it or leave it." It is possible to dive down into this universal flow of life and comprehend all of its changing and stable colors, as well as all the forms which are manifested in it. In the beginning there was an origin, a source where all the strength lies, but with each succeeding readaptation something has been lost, until today the symbol scarcely gives a hint of its real significance. Without a comprehension of source values, modern investigators and commentators go astray in interpretations which have no relation to the only thing that matters. It is not the question here whether a wheel or some other external design is used to represent a certain aspect of life, but rather that the lines of certain things induce certain rhythms, creating universal moods; the inference is that such knowledge could be used deliberately and with effect, instead of leaving things to chance.

It is not reality that we should seek in art, but the fleeting glimpse into the incomprehensible beyond, a glimpse over which the ideal of every heart is wont to linger in the effort to escape from the unhappy reality which chills the emotions. It is the nature of man to feel conscious of a power behind him bound to no fetters. Sure of his limitations at every turn, he has devised countless mythical tales inhabited by dragons, giants, heroes, etc., last of all thinking of his saints, which the world has not ceased to produce even to this day. We take pride in our vast knowledge. We like to feel that there is nothing that science cannot accomplish, but our greatest idealists are our most successful scientists, a fact not without real significance.

CHAPTER XII

SIDELIGHTS AND INSIGHTS

I

During the day there were frequent interruptions of the dancing Aché Lha-mo, who are the professional lay actors, to be differentiated from the Lamas, who also put on performances. Groups of them travel throughout Tibet, and some of them go as far as the border at Kalimpong, where I first saw them. From the first to the eighth of the Tibetan seventh month they are permitted to play in the city, at which time they go from house to house, usually to those of the big officials; during the rest of the year they are not allowed within the walls. On the twenty-sixth of the sixth month they gather and put on a small dance behind the Potala outside the city. On the twenty-ninth they perform in front of the Potala, and on the thirtieth in the courtyard of the palace, where the fifth Dalai Lama was wont to stay when he went to the Drepung monastery. These actors appear before the Dalai Lama, if living; then before the Regent and the houses of the most important officials. They keep this up for the full eight days allotted to them, and are amply compensated. It is probable that they can live the rest of the year on the rewards earned during this brief period at Lhasa.

At this time of the year—the first part of August—the weather is at its best, and this dancing and acting period is known as *shel-tön*, or *tü* which means "dancing time." There were five different groups that came the day before; I understood that they would be coming at that rate every day until the festival came to an end.

The performances consist of the enactment of various native tales, which are the stories of the famous persons and saints of Tibet, and are devised to entertain and make people laugh. The attire of the actors does not undergo any change with the different rôles. They wear small attractive triangular masks, covered with long white hair, which runs clear down to the middle of the back. The brown skirt is draped from the waist with long tassels all the way around, with a small white ball at the end of each; and all of it goes up in the air fully their height when they perform particularly rapid gyrations, which are certainly graceful. The performance is carried on to the beating of a drum and the clashing of cymbals, with an increase of rhythm to accent the high spots and to intensify the speed for the rapid whirl for which one is always waiting.

Early the following morning I was again interrupted by the Aché Lha-mo, who put on a show of the dancing wild yaks, and I must confess that I got an uncommon lot of fun out of it. Indeed, I yielded to temptation, for I had made up my mind that nothing would take me from my studies. As I heard the beat of the drums and looked out, I saw two enormous representations of wild yaks. Two pairs of men dressed up in yak skins took the parts of the front and the rear of the beasts. Each animal was covered over with the skin, and the head of a yak made it all appear very authentic. The leader beat time with a stick like a drum major, and demonstrated excellent control over his animals, who seemed marvellously trained. At no instant was any part of the body still, and an occasional convulsion of the rear evoked responsive convulsions of mirth from the onlookers. Now and again one of the animals would make a sally into the crowd, which scattered like a flock of feeding pigeons. The performance lasted fifteen minutes in all. Other dancers continued to make their appearance throughout the day, but nothing equalled the early morning show.

2

Then came another day, dark and rainy, with the streets of Lhasa resembling running streams of sewage and human flith. It was the kind of day on which Lhasa is the filthiest place on earth. And there was a party to which I had been invited—at Ring Gang's. I left at about lunch time, and though the way to Ring Gang's was but a five minutes' ride, I was so splashed over by the time of my arrival, that I must have presented an unpleasant sight. The British Mission, with Dr. Morgan, had arrived a bit earlier; and I sat down with them to a cup of tea and trivial chatter. Then all the Tibetans settled down to a game of Mah Jong, which left bridge for the rest. At first I escaped, but when, finally, some one had to leave, his hand was forced on me to play. I had not played bridge in many years, and now I was in the game from about lunch-time till ten-thirty in the evening. Ring Gang joined us, and was my partner. It was fun to be able to beat two Englishmen.

There were several women present, lavishly dressed, with their breastplates of turquoise, diamonds and rubies set in red-gold boxes hung around their necks by strings of alternate coral and a stone they call "eyes," and pearls. Large coils with such pearls and these stones with three "eyes" will run into a thousand rupees or so, while the box runs into several thousands. One wonders how they can afford such an adornment, as it is impossible to obtain a complete set under 10,000 rupees. They love jewelry here, and seem willing to pay any price to have it. The wife of a wealthy official, when fully dressed, will represent several lacs.

After endless dishes of tasty Tibetan food, we resumed bridge. The Tibetan seems to be always at home, for right in the middle of a card game a basin of water was brought, in which Ring Gang washed his hands with the greatest deliberation. In our society this, of course, wouldn't be *comme il faut.* But this was Tibet, and we all liked it.

3

The best thing the following morning was a visit by the dancers, who still had a few days in Lhasa before taking their final departure.

It was a busy day, and one of confusion, due chiefly to the arrival of the finished boxes for the transportation of the *Kangyur* and *Tengyur*. It looked as though I should need fourteen such boxes for these books, and an equal number for the miscellaneous books, without taking into account the many odds and ends collected within recent weeks. Their transportation threatened to become something of a problem, because they were asking fifty rupees per mule from Lhasa to Kalimpong. (There was my own personal transport to be considered as well.) It is easy enough to make a calculation of what these fifty animals would cost, figuring the rupee at forty cents. After some bargaining, the price was brought down to thirty-five rupees, but I came to no decision, hoping to get it down closer to thirty. It is amazing what can be accomplished here by persistent complaining and bargaining.

To avoid the waste of time, which I badly needed for my study and investigations, I hired two Lamas to classify the books.

About the same time news came that the person who had been sent to procure the sixty-four-volume set of books containing all the *Tantrik* teachings had arrived in Lhasa at last. I had about given up hope of his return, for he could have been back weeks ago. But there was no saying what a Tibetan would do. Along with this we received the *Sum Bums* (Lives) of two very important figures. One is Pu-tön, who compiled the *Kangyur* and *Tengyur* in their present form. The other is Mar-pa, who brought the religion to Bhutan. The latter set of books presents a complete history of the religious development and teachings of the Kargyupa sect. Each set embraces over twenty volumes. Twenty-five volumes wholly devoted to Tibetan medical science were also on the way. Moreover, I was in possession of numerous manuscripts, some of them in three and five volumes.

At the moment it did not look as if we should be ready to leave next month. I was hoping, however, that once the *she-tu* was over and the people returned to normal life, we should be able to make some progress. A tour of inspection I made with Tsarong provided much interest. There were at least fourteen tailors working at top speed on the silks, which lay in lavish profusion about the room, flaunting their reds, blues, and yellows. Both the markers and the covers of the Christmas cards were taking shape, and if the dozen artists would do their part I could count on their being finished in fair time. The writers and paper makers were also making some headway. It is really interesting to watch Tibetans at work, and again and again one marvels how on earth they are ever able to get anything done with none of the equipment which we seem to feel is absolutely essential. If you will but feed them tea all day they will go on turning out work. This is rather a good notion, for it certainly keeps up their spirit. It is always understood that no matter what the nature of the work, those who hire them will provide them with at least one meal and serve them tea all day long. In many instances, the hire consists only of feeding them during the job, so they simply come and live with you until the job is over. In any event, a small wooden table about seven inches high is placed beside a group of workers, and small drinking bowls are kept filled with butter tea throughout the day. A large teapot is set over a bowl of smoldering dung, and it is always near by. There is a constant attendant to see to it that the cups are filled. When you consider the fact that the pay is next to nothing, you begin to realize that the cost of the tea and the service is a mere trifle.

We left the tailors to pay a visit to the carpenters, who were making the boxes for the *Kangyur* and *Tengyur*, as well as the other boxes for books and personal equipment. There were eight of them sitting cross-legged on the floor, buried in shavings and working rapidly, as they held the boards between their toes and planed away with tools which we had thrown into the discard centuries ago. Not a single modern tool is to be had, and no such thing as a ruler, but only a piece of stick, which they seem to understand. Yet there is virtually nothing that they cannot turn out and, surprisingly enough, with a polish which no modern tool could improve upon.

Then we visited the Lamas who had come to live with us until the job of classification and indexing was done. The three of them were with great care going over every page of the books, which lay scattered all over the large room of about twenty-five by thirty feet. They worked from daybreak until far into the night, but at the end of each day they showed very little progress. I was beginning to doubt if they would ever finish it.

In all I had over forty persons in my employment and under my supervision, and the indications were that double that number might have been employed to advantage. But no more workers were available, and coolie labor was out of question here.

I had my own work to do, too. I was experiencing a feeling of guilt about not using every instant for my studies, which had suffered so many interruptions. I got down to working between times. I was particularly concerned about my progress in the language, to which hours of constant drill were so essential.

The system is too complicated to explain here, and it is quite beyond the difficulties of our Western languages.

On this particular evening I wished to do some studying, which I generally did by lamplight. But something went wrong, or they ran out of oil, so I contented myself by taking a short stroll in the darkness of Tsarong's lovely garden. In typical Lhasa fashion the electric lights did not come on, though they have electric power in the city. At best, it is a nice toy, for the light it provides is no better than to be found in an Indian hotel or in one of our closets. It is hardly bright enough to attract the bugs. There is no telling any day whether the lights will come on, or at what hour.

4

Well it was for me that I finished my studies very early the next morning, for by nine o'clock we were off to a dance at the Regent's, not to return until six that evening. Moreover, I was to discover that my next two days would be similarly occupied, as the Regent's invitation, which I could not refuse, extended to a three days' festival. To sit in the same place for three days in succession, and to watch the same dance for three days, unable to understand what they are singing, and all the while stuffing on Tibetan food, becomes a bit of a bore, even if in this instance it was very much of a privilege and gave you a chance to see high-class Tibetans entertaining and being entertained.

Dressed in the Tibetan regalia of gold, I plunged into the mud and filth of Lhasa with my escort of five. I did not know where this bodyguard came from, but it being one of the requirements of the country I always found it at hand, and there was no reason to give it undue thought. There are times, however, when servants are something of a nuisance. I may be in a hurry, too, and want to do things myself. Here they are yours to command, and that does not always please me either; for it seems to me they have as much right to their leisure as I have. This may not be the right attitude to hold, but having observed the lack of consideration paid to servants during past years and at the same time having some understanding of their feelings, I find it difficult to behave toward my servants according to form; in consequence of which they take more or less a holiday and then we all have a good time.

It was a twisting ride through the streets of Lhasa. I vow that God must have been watching me, for at one instant, while passing close to a house, out came a bucket of slops or something worse, and it missed me by scarcely half an inch! Had not the horse under me taken a sudden lurch forward, I should have been drenched properly. And I was perhaps unduly proud of my new Tibetan costume. In any event, I was aware that I could not possibly return with this costume in its former immaculate condition. The rain and the mud would see to that. Indeed, when we left the party at five-thirty, it was thundering and lightning, so my servants and I made a dash for home, scattering men, women, and children, along with donkeys and dogs, which always lie in the middle of the street and will move on no condition except when they are stepped on, which is frequently the case, when they scamper away howling and yelping at the top of their voices. They are thicker here than flies in a Mexican village, and their sole sustenance seems to be the fæcal deposit of the natives. On the whole, we did not do badly. We did brush aside one old man wobbling along on his stick, too lazy to move to a side when he heard us coming and saw every one else scattering. Then, again, in rounding one of the corners in a hurry, there was a girl who appeared deliberately to run to the middle of the narrow lane, where she paused to have a frontal view of us. She got an upward view as well, for we left her lying in a puddle of mud looking up at the horses who were quickly passing over her. She probably learned her lesson, and is still talking about the episode. At times I felt more exasperated with the populace which always persisted in clinging to the middle of the road than with our own pedestrians who insist on crossing the path of your car against the signals when you are in a tearing hurry. This probably all denotes a very cruel heart, but one who has never experienced the meaning of life in these parts will never understand the feelings with which this is written. This, be it remembered, was the land of the Gods, not of men.

But I am anticipating. On our arrival at the patio of the Regent's house, we found it packed with humanity and the dance well under way. I hurried up to the third balcony, where a special tent had been arranged in the center of the stage. I scarcely reached the gate when the dancers lost the attention of the onlookers, whose eyes were focussed on the bearded head projecting out of a body draped in gold. It is really extraordinary the excitement a European in Tibetan apparel may cause out here.

The setting was the precise counterpart of a Chinese theatre. It consisted of a large slabbed pavilion in the center beneath a high canopy, surrounded on three sides by two tiers of verandas, which were crowned with a row of tents specially erected for the honored guests. The English Mission and I seem to have rated first place; our seats were right in the center, opposite that of the Regent himself, who had a tent set up on top of the temple which, as it were, formed the fourth tier. The Prime Minister's place was beside the Regent. Beneath them sat the Shapés, and below the Shapés were the fourth-rank officials, with all the lower officials occupying a tent on our level, but situated on the side rather than in the front, where we were. The Regent's place was bordered in front with a long row of flowering pots, and the interior of his tent was decorated with yellow silks of a regular pattern along with draperies adorned with immense dragons. The whole setting was the pavilion in front of the Regent's monastery.

The women were in their showiest attire, save for the seething mass of rags sitting on the ground below. It is these contrasts that stir the soul of one in Tibet, for above are the representatives of God on earth, while below is poor starving humanity huddling together for warmth in such tatters as they have been able to find in garbage heaps. We in the West have our slums and the like, but the contrast this offers to the wealth of our capitalists is trifling when compared with the contrast these poor folk of Tibet offer to the dignitaries and the potentates. In our country there are a few, with their numbers growing ever greater, who put forth some effort to bring about a change; but here there are the Perfect, and not for them is it to think of those in Hell, for such is the judgment because of their past lives. There is nothing that fires the heart to such a temperature as does the religious racket in this part of the world. I imagine that if I were an integral part of this society, I might be filling the rôle of the person who is now incarcerated in the dungeon of the Potala, with his eyes gouged out, while his son, apparelled in yellow silk, is sitting among the ranks of the minor officials in the presence of the Regent. They don't seem to have as much valor in Tibet as there is in a Negro running through a graveyard on a dark night. And the reason is Religion—the deepest-rooted evil of mankind—the sooner it is done away with, the more quickly will humanity begin to rise. When I say Religion, I mean this organized control, this dictating of sainthood. There is that latent religious feeling in the heart of every man, and this aspect is the richest part of every man's life; but there is scarcely a thing to be found on any organized religious system today which we could not do better without. So it might be better for a while to turn our course in the opposite direction and call it by another name, so that there will not be any reversion to this faithful path of ignorance. It well-nigh drives me to rage because there seems to be so little that can be done about it—nothing but to let it ultimately destroy itself by deadening the hearts of men as it has deadened mine; and then when the group of rebels is large enough it may find a way to disseminate the right spirit.

5

The performance was of a play put on by the Aché Lha-mo, whose dancing in recent days I have already touched upon. This particular play enacted the bringing of the Chinese Queen to Tibet. Its story briefly is as follows: Delegates from the most powerful countries in the Eastern world were sent to the Chinese Emperor to request his daughter in marriage. As there seemed to be some difference of opinion within the Court as to whom the Princess should be given, the Emperor decided to set the candidates a test of skill and to award the Princess to the winner. So there was no end of devices, such as mixing up large groups of mares, chickens and other creatures with their young and requiring the candidate to select the parents of the young. Again, the candidate was given a stick and was asked which end had come nearest the root of the tree. All the candidates were called upon to drink *chang*, which made them drunk. The wily Tibetan among them, before drinking, made an offering to the Gods. Many girls were fetched; they all resembled the Princess, and each candidate was permitted to keep the girl he chose. The Tibetan, having gone to an astrologer, got tipped off that there would be a turquoise fly about the face of the real Princess. In the circumstances, it was a walkover for him. The Emperor had no alternative but to send off the Princess to Tibet, with the sacred image, which is reputed to be the same which sits today in the famous Tsug-lag-khang, the holiest place in Tibet. In return the Tibetans brought presents to the Emperor. This simple little tale was performed during nine hours or so, which meant that we had a chance to consume two complete meals and, heaven alone knows, how many cups of tea!

The dancing was rather monotonous, relieved now and then by rapid twirling by individual dancers. One dancer excelled in this. On a back cartwheel he leaves the ground entirely, never once touching it with his hands, but maintaining his equilibrium by a series of quick thrusts with his feet, and so all the way around the pavilion.

It comes with something of a shock to see one of the dancers stop and blow his nose on the ground and clean it with his hand, then wipe the hand off on his lovely silken apparel. Still worse is it to be sitting at a dinner table next to a Lama and have him pull out his striped Tibetan handkerchief of woolen cloth lined with silk, into which he blows his nose all the year round, and yet another year after that. Even without being squeamish, it is almost too much to watch him pull out this folded article and, after stretching it apart like something glued together with untreated rubber, and filling it up a little more, and rolling it up, wipe off his face with it, only to repeat the process ten minutes later as a preliminary to sniffing in a dab of snuff, which is used by all the Lamas; high and low.

While I was standing on the edge of the roof, the Chinese official came over to say Hello to me, he having the tent next to ours, and shortly Rai Bahadur Norbhu told him the latest news from London about the Japanese attacking Nanking, whereupon the Chinaman flew into a rage and began to drool and froth at the mouth, and members of his armed escort drew their guns—Heaven knows what would have happened next. Fortunately, Norbhu said nothing more but retired, and I had to make a private call on the Chinaman, by which time he had more or less returned to a normal state. But it would have been fatal to mention the Japanese again; he would have surely wiped me off the face of the earth. It had been a tense moment, and we all thought there was going to be a killing, and the crowd was gathering rapidly. You could hear him shouting above the drone of the beating drums, and all eyes were focussed in our direction.

6

This was the second day of the great festival given by the Regent. Tsarong said it was to be the biggest of the three days. The place was to be packed more densely than ever.

Not being in a hurry to get there any sooner than was absolutely necessary, at ten o'clock I once more plunged through the mud and the slop of Lhasa streets. When your own pony was not bespattering you with mud, the one in front or behind was doing a good job of it. Indeed, a wad hit me on the back of the neck with the force of a well-packed snowball. Tibetan women, lavishly apparelled and bejewelled, not one of them with less than 25,000 rupees' worth of ornamentation, were holding up their skirts and clinging against the wall as we passed to avoid being bespattered with mud by our ponies. The contrast of women so beautifully dressed and wading through such incredible filth is perhaps to be found nowhere but in Tibet, and it goes against the grain with an onlooker like myself. Not that the Tibetan would understand my attitude any more than I understand his. Right or wrong, I myself follow the accepted line in my garment of gold and silk, and twitch every time a speck of mud strikes me.

I found the dance well under way. The English Mission, however, did not arrive until round eleven-thirty, which gave me the idea that I would do a bit of tarrying myself on the morrow. By now the performance assumed something of a routine air, with an occasional diversion from mirth-makers in animal dress. Little wonder they have a real fondness for Charlie Chaplin, for there is nothing that brings down the crowd as quickly as the sight of some one being chased, having a fall and being hit with a whip or a club. They appear to have their jokes and their wisecracks, but from the two or three I've been able to pick up I shouldn't say they were highly exciting. At today's performance they had more deer, elephants, dogs, hunters and clowns than at the show of the day before. The costumes of the regular actors were very much the same. The reader will have guessed that I did not think very much of this Tibetan show. Perhaps, this is due to my training. But whether or not, only sheer necessity would ever bring me to the experience of witnessing a show such as this.

The crowds came pouring in from the street, which was nothing but one large puddle of water that had been kneaded down to a nice oozy mud. Along the sides of the street, in the middle of small ponds, small native shops were temporarily erected beneath umbrellas, very much after the fashion of hot-dog stands at our large public gatherings; but in this case the smell was somewhat different, waves of warm air wafting our way a mixture of human filth, accounted for by the fact that just in front of the temple was a small blind alley of about sixty feet in length, at the end of which men, women and children, to say nothing of some Lamas, were squatting together, with the dogs almost knocking the small children over before they could finish their task.

Such is the land of mystery, next to the filthiest place on earth. If it ever got hot in this country—which God forbid!—the sewers of Paris would be clean in comparison.

Not that I care to go into the details of the necessities of nature. Yet one's experiences in this part of the world are often so singular that it is hard to resist. Having sat long in one place, the time at last arrived when something had to be done about it.

So when one of the servants came in, and in all politeness asked us if we would like to go out, I acquiesced only too willingly, and with actual glee. I followed him below to join a queue of about twenty of the loveliest Tibetan ladies waiting for the same purpose as myself. So there we stood all together, watching the ladies lifting their beautiful silk skirts from the ground, which was flowing over from the effects of poor marksmanship. As one finished, the next in line stepped forward to occupy one of the three slits in the floor of the filthiest room that I ever hope to stand in as long as I live. It was not without its humorous side, for they would look up at me with strained faces broken by grins of amusement, while I tried to hold my ground without batting an eye. I must confess, however, that it gave me a queer feeling to be attending to the wants of nature in such intimate association with the élite of Lhasa. Thus, I had a rather personal insight into things feminine. It was not one to inspire pleasant reminiscence.

7

So I returned to my tent satisfied to stay on for weeks if necessary before making another attempt at anything outside of returning home. Then, of course, there was still the play of the day to watch.

It was the story called "Zug-gi-nyma Namthar," and here is the gist of it:

There was a King who suffered disappointment in not having a son. So one day one of his hunters came in and reported that while he had been hunting in the woods he saw a beautiful maiden. He advised the King to pursue her and make her his Queen. The King indeed already had several hundred Queens. The girl was the daughter of a hermit, who did not want to give her up, nor did she wish to go. (It must be explained here that the girl's mother was supposed to be the Tibetan deer, the *Sha*, and the story goes that when the hermit was washing his clothes in the stream, the deer came along and drank the water, and the child followed in due course.) The King pled that he would die if she did not come, and she yielded to the plea. As might have been expected, the King's espousal of the girl caused a lot of jealousy among the other wives, to whom he no longer showed the same attention. So they planned a trick to get rid of her. After many lies had been told the King about his new Queen's actions, he sent her back to the forest, where it was thought she would surely die. But instead she became a nun and wandered about the country doing the good work. This went on for about twelve years, during which the King repented of his action and spent his time in grief, thinking as he did that she was dead.

In the course of time, one of the Queens came to this nun to confess her sin of having told the King the evil things that had caused him to dispose of the hermit's daughter. On hearing the story the nun invited her to come to her regular quarters, and to go through a certain ceremony and make her repentance, whereupon she would be forgiven. One of the Knights of the Court recognized the nun, and told the King about her. The King refused to believe that the Queen was still alive. So the Knight went to the nun and told her that he knew who she was; he also told her about the King. Then together they made a plan that the King should come to this place at a certain time and hide while the confession was being made by the other Queen. This was done, and the King on learning the truth more than ever regretted his error. After considerable persuasion the nun was induced to return to the Court and to become the favorite Queen, and every one lived happily thereafter.

It took them nearly nine hours to unfold this tale, which did in fact have some funny spots. The actors, however, spoke so rapidly that I found it almost impossible to understand them. Indeed, the Tibetans themselves find it hard to catch some of the words.

8

Next morning, with my work out of the way, clad in my yellow *namsa* (Tibetan robe), I left for the play at the Regent's. It was the first time I had seen the sun in days, and, in consequence, I felt in good spirits. The roads were still filled with muck, but because it had not rained in the night there was a little consistency to the road under my pony's feet. Apparently, the villagers thought it was going to be a good day, for they all had their shops set up in the middle of the large square, where they held their daily bazaar. They were deceived, however, for around four it rained as usual; nevertheless, they had the start of half a day's takings, which might have brought them enough to buy a cup of butter tea for dinner.

On my arrival I found only a very sparse crowd sitting on the slab floor of the patio. The truth of the matter is that there was little enough room for them even if they had wanted to come. So much of the place was filled with expansive puddles of water, so that they had to find the high dry spots, which did not leave much room for a crowd. After a couple of hours an effort was made to remove the water, which appreciably increased the sitting space. About two in the afternoon there were as many people as there had been on the previous two days. One wonders how on earth some of these poor devils can see anything at all; they are always required to sit on the ground, which means that a short fellow in the rear is just out of luck. And there is little chance of cheating, for there are about half a dozen guards who saunter up and down all the while with their long ten-foot poles made from the thin branches of trees

with the green leaves still on the end. Moreover, they are the regular Lhasa police, who have strong canes, with which they rap any one not conforming to the custom; some of them too have whips with long leather thongs, with which they strike the more persistent offenders, who must stay down, whether they can see anything or not. Then, again, there is some custom as to the wearing of hats. I had not ascertained what exactly it was, but on one occasion I saw a woman's hat knocked off. She was apparently not wearing the regulation headdress, and had put on a felt hat very much like the felt hat we wear here in the West. Today this is the hat commonly worn by all Tibetan traders. Then there was a Lama who put his shoulder coat up over his head, as the Lamas were wont to do when walking in the sun, for they never wear hats and always shave their heads. No sooner had he covered his head than a guard knocked it off with his stick. Again, I observed the magistrate making a terrible fuss about some one who was doing the wrong thing in the matter of headwear, but I could not make out just exactly what it was.

The magistrate, it may be worth while to note, was one of the boys who had spent five years studying in England. What would his old school friends think of him now? Among his duties was to walk around in a red cloak at such functions as this and to see that everything was properly conducted. These boys were sent by the Government, which practically has full control over their lives, as it does over every one else; indeed, the Government's control over the sons of officials is supreme. The children as they grow up must take their positions under the Government, and if one of them has an inordinate amount of luck he may find himself ultimately a Shapé. On the other hand, there are four Shapés in all at any one time, and such plums usually fall into the laps of the most influential families.

9

Once more I arrived ahead of the British Mission, in time to see the Shapés, the Regent and the Prime Minister take their usual places around eight o'clock. They moved from their seats only twice in the course of the day, and that was when food was brought around. They, like the rest of the crowd, seemed to enjoy the performance, for there was no end of light laughter, though you seldom heard a good hearty laugh. Again, I observed that there was no such thing as the clapping of hands in response to a good performance.

This day's play, which began about eight o'clock, had this story to unfold:

There were two Kingdoms, one in the North, the other in the South. They had been quarrelling and fighting for some time. The rulers of the South tried to find a way to defeat their rivals, so they consulted the sorcerers, who promised their help. The first effort proved a failure. The next time they advised throwing poison into a neighboring lake, which the people of the North were wont to frequent. The Gods of the lake were distressed and incensed. The Goddess of the Lake, addressing herself to a fisherman from the North, promised him a reward if he would kill the sorcerers. After he had accomplished this, the Gods took him to their place below the water, where they gave him a wishing gem, which would make any wish he had come true. Dubious of its value, he consulted a couple of great repute. They directed him to a hermit of the upper valley. This Lama had been meditating in his cave for one hundred and sixty years without any one disturbing him, so he felt this visit must be of some import. He told his visitor that some ceremonies would have to be performed first, but that he had an important affair to attend, as the fairies were assembling at a certain spot and he had to be there. As the fisherman, being of the butcher class, could not attend this gathering, he advised him to wait until his return. The fisherman, impatient, chose a point of vantage to watch the fairies' gathering, then conceived the notion of capturing a fairy in order to present it to the King. The Lama hermit read his thought, and told him that one of his class could not do that, for the fairy would disappear. He advised him to return the gem to the Goddess of the Lake and to ask for a certain net with which he might catch a fairy. The fisherman did this, and returned with the net to find that all the fairies had returned home, save two, who had some ceremonies to perform before becoming fully purified. He captured one of them. To frighten the fisherman, she transformed herself. But the fisherman, being an incarnation of Chan-dorje, likewise reverted to type. On discovering the nature of her captor, the fairy yielded, and he took her and presented her to the King of the North, who duly rewarded him.

But this was only the beginning of an interminably long and involved tale about the King of the North who had a hundred wives, jealous of the new Queen (the transformed fairy), and about a sorcerer whose aid they invoked to dispose of her, and about dreams, and about the old Lama hermit . . . and of course it all ended in the King and the Queen living happily thereafter.

And thus the three-day festival came to an end. Just before the final act the servants began to clear away the flowerpots which decorated the center of the stage. And at the very end the Regent and the Prime Minister sent down their sacks of *tsampa* with their scarves. The servants of the Shapés, along with the Mission, myself, and other guests, presented our gifts with the sacred scarves. All of the guards, watchmen and others, who managed the show, passed by in line and each received a scarf from the Regent. We sent our scarves to the Regent, who returned the courtesy. So there was no end of scarfing. Then followed the rain of manna from heaven, for at the end of this as of the previous days the Shapés flung down small coins wrapped in a *kata*. As soon as those below gathered up their gifts, they took a large canvas and walked with it beneath the balcony of the other guests and caught the gifts like so much ripe fruit falling from a shaken tree.

CHAPTER XIII

GATHERING UP THE LAST THREADS

I

I HAD never realized what a holy room I had been occupying until one morning I had a visitor with some books to sell. His partner, on entering the room and observing the complete set of *Kangyur* and *Tengyur* next to my shrine, immediately went forward and began mumbling off his *mantras*, which took several minutes and made the room hum for a while. Afterwards, he stepped back a short distance and, after placing his hat on the floor in the customary manner, he thrice prostrated himself, all of which would bring him considerable merit—some day—at some place, but no one knew when—or where. They did not worry about this aspect of things in this country. They were going to store up virtue, and let the rest take care of itself.

While this chap was going through with his short ritual of devotion, his partner was doing his best to drive a bargain. As a matter of fact, I already had the volumes he was offering, but as they were difficult to obtain I thought I ought to buy them, provided I could get them at a more reasonable figure. These sellers are never the actual owners of the property they offer for sale, but only middlemen who do it on a commission basis; so they could not give us an answer until they had consulted the owner.

With the booksellers gone and the Lamas well under way with their job of indexing and Tharchin off to the city to do some things for me, I retired to my study to enrich my mind with matters for which I had come here. The rainy weather, which had been keeping up for some time, was actually an inspiration to work indoors. Yet on the score of the rain I was getting a bit nervous, I had yet many pictures to take in and about Lhasa; I had been waiting for good weather for almost a month. I heard it said that it would come within a week or so. Indeed, I hoped so; as I did not want to nurse any lifelong regrets. This morning it looked as if I should have a nice long stretch of work, but there were endless interruptions. There was a stream of visitors with articles I had been trying to get for a month and had given up hope of ever getting. I took a few objects off their hands.

Tsarong had expressed the hope that I would remain in Lhasa long enough to see a part of the great feast which he would be giving shortly. He puts on the finest show in Lhasa, being in a position to do so. Since I was now planning to leave earlier than I first anticipated, he came forward with the suggestion to give me a farewell party, to which he would invite all the friends I had made during my stay. He said that all the lower suites of the house would be decorated for the occasion and that he would erect a huge tent in the garden in which we all might have a grand time in order, as he put it, that I would have such pleasant memories of Lhasa as to create the desire in me to hurry back as soon as possible. He added that he would be heart-broken if I did not return before he died, which touched me deeply.

And, indeed, the very next morning I could hear the rap-tap-tap and the buzzing of the saws breaking the air in the midst of singing hearts, for now the carpenters were preparing the cross beams for the carvers. These are used on the outside of the shells to decorate Tsarong's new temple room. It is impossible for Tibetans to work without singing, so the house was full of music for the greater part of the day. Even the littlest chap,

whom I judged to be about twelve, was amazingly skilful with the sort of saw that we haven't used since the fifteenth century.

As soon as the beams were ready, a couple of fellows with planes smoothed them; then they were turned over to the carvers. Three of these stencilled their designs and commenced work with their crude tools, which, however, were as sharp as razor blades. They worked so rapidly that they completed their job in less than no time and the hall was quickly back in its original state of quiet.

In Tibet people start work at the break of day and if you ask to have something brought in the morning, it is assumed you mean the morning and it arrives at five o'clock! This time it was another large collection of books, and I spent some time coming to terms. In this country one never buys anything the first two or three trips, but by the time the seller has dragged them back and forth a few times his ardor for high prices cools down considerably. It seems to me to be a poor way of doing business, but as it is the custom of the Orient there is nothing to do but to fall in line.

2

This was the fifteenth of the Tibetan month, which is a special day for making offerings. On such days the Government performs a large ceremony at Tsug-lag-khang and minor ceremonies elsewhere. This is truly a theocratic country. The streets were full of devotees going to the holy shrines with their butter and *chang* to make their bimonthly offerings, in order to store up virtue for the next life, whenever and wherever it might be. They surely go to a lot of trouble to rig themselves out in their best to struggle through the mud and filth of Lhasa; presumably the difficulties make their effort count the more.

From the Rammoche, where I went, I returned to the market place, because there was a chap there who, having committed murder, was wearing a large three-foot-square board around his neck, which was very reminiscent of one of our colored boys at a circus with his head thrust through a screen ready to dodge your ball, which you buy five for a quarter. At the top of this contrivance was a long hand-written statement of the crime which he had committed; and now for the rest of his days he would remain in confinement, with the privilege of wandering from place to place after a stay in the public market-place. To my surprise, he was very willing to have me take his picture, and as often as I chose. I rewarded him with a few coppers, since he had to depend on the bounty of the passer-by for his livelihood. The market-place is situated in front of the Tibetan court building. On one of the neighboring walls were pasted various notices which gave the latest news of the Chinese-Japanese situation, and there was a large crowd gathered reading them with strained necks.

Even quite apart from the rainy season, Lhasa is not a comfortable city to live in. Conveniences simply do not exist. Living conditions are more primitive than our own centuries ago. Since all Tibetans live on the floor, their furniture is anything but elaborate, and by no means conducive to the comfort of the Westerner. It would kill the average European to double up on the floor hour after hour. Indeed, he cannot do it, unless he has learned to fold those legs of his in early childhood, or happen to be an adept at acrobatics. Again, there is the Tibetan food, which is no substitute for the European food, and one must learn to dispense with our table implements and master the more difficult chopsticks. As for the personalities the European will encounter here, he would consider them boring if he should try to hold them up to standards of his kind; to enjoy life with them is impossible unless one learns their ways and acquires sufficient knowledge of their language to join in their fun.

My own deep attachment to the place is due precisely to my having overcome every one of these difficulties, so that if needs be I could live life here as at home. A profounder reason is that, as a result of the last year's experience connected with my Tibetan visit, I have been able to gain some knowledge of myself. In Kalimpong I prepared the physical aspect, and sounded depths which I had not known to exist outside of fiction. Since then I have been able to carry on and meet all externals of life in the faith of this deeper feeling toward life in general. It is truly beyond words to express the rhapsody of life when one is able to sense the rhythm which lies beyond all the externals of life. It is not to be denied that form can offer its own glimpses of pleasure, but that which lies behind the form holds untold joys for one as long as he lives. After such an experience as mine one begins to see the world as smaller and smaller, instead of, as with us, more complex and infinite; at the same time one sees it deeper and deeper, for sooner or later all forms begin to bring one back to the same thing; so it matters little what one's environment is, and the all-important thing is to have that uninterrupted solitude which will permit one to penetrate deeper and deeper into the mystery of life. These depths are not those of understanding, but those of feeling. And that is why it is so incredibly difficult to convey to others your meaning. So-called rational men quite sincerely think you are "not all there," and you as sincerely can return the compliment—and with good reason, too!

It has been by no means a singular experience. Thousands down the countless ages have tapped the same source of joy. They have tried in vain to find words for these feelings. The truth is, we must sense it for ourselves. The words of others can only point the way. It is very much like a father trying to tell his very young son the meaning of love. The child will never come to know that passing ecstasy of adolescence, of the first embrace, until he has experienced it; all the poems of the earth cannot reveal it. Now that joy of which I am speaking is very much the same; for the personality gains the embraces of every form of nature, and he lives in perpetual ecstasy as long as he remains thrall to his passion. But as he comes back to the surface, he still has all the forms of the outside world to stimulate his return.

Considering the little tangible knowledge we possess on this aspect of life, the way to these joys is long and arduous. Yet I am strongly under the impression that the way can be made much easier, so that great multitudes may have a sip of these spiritual joys in the same way that every man living can taste of the pleasures of love without having to read Havelock Ellis or some equally renowned authority. But even in this, only those who have the greater understanding ever come to know the lasting joys of love and are able to penetrate its nuanced depths; for it is not instinctive with man to sound the bottoms of this fountain.

3

Now that the day of my departure was growing ever nearer, all sorts of matters, social and otherwise, pressed thick and fast upon me. There were parties, visiting and receiving visits, filling out gaps in the library and objects I was taking with me, studying, packing, taking pictures and moving films. I was gathering up the loose threads. I could dwell upon my activities at this time for pages without exhausting the voluminous diaries I faithfully kept. I must content myself here, however, with the high points of my experience or with trivialities of general interest, and at all cost avoid the repetitiousness inevitable in the life I lived in Tibet.

In particular, I indulged in an orgy of photography, anxious as I was to make a complete record of an experience in many ways unprecedented.

Among other things I paid a visit with my camera to the medical-temple of Chak-po-ri, which is situated just outside the city gate and is built on the high peak which forms the upper end of the small hill on which the potala stands. If anything, the Medical College is a trifle higher than the Potala, and forms the point of the pinnacle which magnificently rises heavenwards. The trail zig-zags back and forth, and at a certain point we were forced to leave our horses behind and begin a stiff, steady climb. The only point of interest was one small, square building, which housed the chief medical deity along with the usual deities to be found in all shrines. There was nothing distinguished among these, except possibly one Chen-re-zi, which was entirely covered with small seashells. This was quite out of the ordinary for Tibet; but this in itself is no merit. On the contrary, the impression was quite distasteful. There was also a small *chorten* entombing one of their high medical Lamas. The science must have died with him, for medicine seems to be a lost art here.

A later episode was my visit to the Rakashas, a famous Lhasa family. The Lacham had been at our party, and I observed her arrival in a beautiful Tsang headdress. When I went into the tent to ask to be allowed to take a picture of it I suffered a disappointment, for she had already removed it. I was perplexed as to how to overcome my difficulty, being most anxious to have photographic records of the two principal types of headdress used in Tibet. Here had been my chance, and I had missed it. I put it up to Mrs. Tsarong, and her response was that she would arrange everything. Indeed, there was the prompt invitation to tiffin at her house—and to take the pictures. It was most generous of her to go to the infinite trouble of rigging herself out in all that elaborate finery—and to make a party of it.

The house being rather near, we decided to walk over, even though we did have to wade through a small pond which had not yet receded from the rain floods to permit a path. The Lacham met us at the head of the stairs adorned to the last word in Tibetan grandeur. Truly it is impressive, this arrangement of a large bow up over the head, which is a solid mass of pearls, as is the crown which goes over the forehead and out to the ends of the bow about a foot on either side of the head, where all the hair is arranged to hang in a long braid down alongside the shoulder. There are enough pearls, corals and turquoise inlaid in the headdress to keep many a family going a lifetime. This is not to mention the rest of the paraphernalia, which consists of a solid breastplate of pearls, a very costly prayer-box and a long necklace of large amber which reaches down far below the waist.

The whole pattern was simply perfect for color photography, as was also the day, full of brilliant sunshine, which however made it rather difficult to handle the blacks and whites; for the pearls and the other jewels were literally dazzling in radiance. I found a very small corner which had just enough shade to cover the Lacham's face, and I tried a few shots there in the hope that I might get something besides the grim face seen in the glaring sunlight. They do not have a courtyard at the Tsarongs', as their house stands in the middle of the city and is built in the typical Tibetan fashion of a large stableyard for an entrance in front of the large three-story building which is their home. The only place out of doors is a small protected enclosure on the roof, where the flowers are so arranged as to give the illusion of the out-of-doors—just a Lhasa penthouse.

After I photographed to my heart's content we retired to the sitting room, where we were served with heaps of Tibetan food under the name of a small light lunch. It was enough for "all the King's men." This, as I more than once indicated, is one of the oldest and most important families in Tibet, and of the royal line, the Lacham being the eldest daughter of Raja Tering, brother to the present Maharajah of Sikkim. Jigme is her brother. Rakasha is the brother to the present Maha Rani of Sikkim. There are many ancient houses in Lhasa, but this seems to be one of the purest lines to be found; they can trace theirs back in a more direct course than any other house, and at the time of its inception it seems to have been very powerful. Indeed, the Rakashas are the only ones who have the divine privilege of erecting a *chorten* to entomb their dead instead of cutting up the bodies and feeding them to the vultures in the characteristic Tibetan fashion. As far as I have been able to determine, no other family in Tibet is permitted this privilege. The Tashi and the Dalai Lamas, and a very few other high Lamas, may share in this right.

4

The evening was spent in our regular long philosophical discussion with my *Geshe*, providing me with a yet deeper insight into the training of the monastery. He happened to be telling me of the effect of the ceremonies in which I had taken part and what the Lamas had been saying about me. He told me that the T'ri Rimpoche had gone to his own monastery some four days' journey east of Lhasa and that whenever he went into his meditative chambers it was possible for him to know everything that was happening in Tibet. Indeed, he went so far as to say that the T'ri Rimpoche could even read my thoughts, could tell the impression the various ceremonies had had on me, how well I was progressing with my early morning meditations according to the instructions which had been given me, and it was because of this mysterious knowledge that he was able to determine what step should be taken next toward my initiation.

What the *Geshe* said filled me with a strange hope. I had become aware of my discovery of those deep joys that I had never before dreamt existed in this life, and I felt that all my effort gained for me a reward altogether overwhelming. But I still longed for the opportunity of receiving that mystical initiation. It is only possible in this land, which is the only place left on earth for such masters as yet living who can pilot one over its precarious course. I feared to ask questions appertaining to this desired goal; it is not the sort of thing one dare talk about here. I had been told that the only thing for me to do was to continue my meditations and as soon as I should be ready for the next step the teacher would appear. So there was nothing to do but go on working and to rest unswerving in the faith that a guide would always be with me.

I must confess that after the evening's talk I retired to my meditative corner and reflected upon all that had happened to me, and tried to determine if I had worked hard enough. I knew that I had put all of myself into my effort, yet I resolved to work harder, bearing in mind that the chief prayer taught by the great masters in this country was one which exalted action, the basis being that nothing happens without a cause. To convey a full comprehension of this statement would require several volumes, which would permit a vast expansion of the endless manifestations of this law. All that I can mention here is that such a law exists, and that this law had been given me as a guide.

The following day—September 6—marked what was to be the beginning of my last week in Lhasa. When I reflected that originally I had expected to be back in India many months before this, I was truly overcome with amazement. Yet, in reviewing my accomplishment during these months, I experienced a deep feeling of emptiness, for it seemed to me that I had done too little. No end of problems faced me, answers to which were to be found here; but with such limited time at my disposal I found it necessary to gather in factual material for the purpose of future study. I wished I could have found it possible to box up a few of the Lamas and store them away with the books until such a time after my return to the world beyond that I could use them. So much time had been spent in gaining their confidence, in discovering those who were well trained and eager to impart of their knowledge. After that, there was so little time left for serious discussion. As it was, I probably drove not a few of them crazy with my endless questions. They thought, not without cause, that there was something wrong with me. In the absence of any rational explanation, they attributed my state to the driving spirit of a past life trying to assert itself in the desperate effort to make a contact with my conscious self.

5

A mere triviality perhaps, but I cannot help noting a disappointment I experienced at this time. The fact is, the Regent presented me with a new pair of official boots, which had been made to order for me. They were beautiful specimens of their kind, but the wrong color. The exasperating aspect of it was that there had been a whole month of endless discussion as to the kind of boots I wanted, and then this! I had stipulated in a very precise way that the boots were to complete a Shapé costume I wanted to show in America, while the boots I received, if all right in their way, were worn by those of the rank just below the Shapés. This meant another private talk with the Regent to see if I could not have him prevail upon the bootmaker to do the job all over again. The result of the interview was embarrassing, for he concluded by making me a present of the boots! A gift from the Regent, of course, could not be refused. But I realized that I should have to set my wits to work to get the desired boots somehow.

From the look of things, I was now going to take up the rug

business. Tharchin brought a number for my inspection, and the temptation was great to acquire some. But for Tharchin I should have hardly thought of it. Most of these rugs were made at Gyantsé. I could not get around the fact that the rugs procurable at a reasonable figure were not of the best workmanship; so I played with the idea of obtaining a representative set of each class. Rugs in Tibet are sold in sets of two. The best, I understood, came from Eastern Tibet, and Tsarong promised to have some one bring a few specimens on the following day that I might see the difference, and choose those which struck my fancy.

On the next day Tsarong came in with a beautiful rug which he presented me as a gift in harmony with the Tibetan custom of friendship. I was elated, for it was the very thing I had been trying in vain to obtain, and now to have it drop on me out of the blue as a gift was almost too much for the emotions already overstrained with the revelations of friendship so abundantly shown in the house in which I was a guest. This last gesture touched me too deeply to express my gratitude in words and I was left with a profound desire to recompense my host in some way commensurate with the spirit that moved him again and again to do me kindness.

5

It was the *Kashag* that would decide the exact day of our departure; it would also supply us with the Arrow letters which would provide us with places of shelter and the necessary pack animals. It had been my plan to leave on Monday, September 13, but I discovered that it was a very inauspicious day in the Tibetan calendar for starting on a journey; so I requested to be allowed to leave on Wednesday, Tuesday of any week being considered a bad day when going on a long trek.

I spent part of the day in photographing as many street scenes as possible, and, having done the Tibetan bazaar up brown, I found myself just outside the Tsug-lag-khang. I entered and visited all the shrines by now so familiar to me. This temple lost none of its fascination for me, even though there can be no doubt about its being the blackest religious dungeon in existence. Half the time you are following a small butter lamp, which is carried at your feet, while your head is bent almost to the ground in the effort to follow the low passageways. It is a queer feeling to be walking down into the blackness of hell to the tune of an ascending torrent of weird chanting and musical effects, which are trying to find their way to the heavens above and beyond.

And as I ascended the stairs leading to the deities of the upper floors I became aware, as on a previous occasion, of the sickening sweetness of the five thousand generations of mice, which are still running over the same time-worn trail. So thick were they that it was hard to avoid stepping on them, and if you happened to be lost in devotional abstraction you were shocked back to reality by the sudden squealing chorus on their part or by the darting of a rodent across your lap or up your leg. I was sorry I could not take a picture of this view; it is about the only picture that I would lack. As soon as the rounds had been made I began to take flashlight pictures of anything that held the slightest interest. And, to finish up the day, in finding myself out of doors again, I added no small number to my photographic collection of beggars.

I was more and more impressed with the need of packing everything as quickly as possible, the chief reason being that Tsarong was making preparations for his official entertainment which would begin on the seventeenth and go on for a week; and he would need to utilize my quarters, indeed every bit of available space.

It was on the day following my visit to the Tsug-lag-khang

that Tharchin dashed into the room, all out of breath and apparently worried. I could not imagine what had gone wrong, so I sat calmly by and waited for him to recover his breath and his speech. He announced that the Prime Minister had just sent word that he and his associates were waiting for me at Norbhu Linga. There was nothing to do but to send word back that I was on my way.

The horses were quickly made ready, while I had three attendants about me to dress me. I wondered what I should do when I no longer had these three persons to dress me and a couple of attendants next to me all day to see that I remained intact. As a matter of fact, I knew it would be the greatest relief to me not to have these people fussing about me; indeed, nothing irritated me more than to have them trying to dress me.

At Norbhu Linga I was greeted by servants galore, who promptly began to sputter like a flock of chickens, to bring in chairs, tables, and what not, for my comfort. I must admit that I had yet to sit on the front porch of the Dalai Lama's palace and not feel a flow of romantic rhapsody, as I looked out across the open expanse of flowers at the height of their glory. Shortly before everything was hollyhocks, and now they were all gone, and yellow dominated the scene, with a heavy growth of grass to let one's emotions slide into the shaded thunderclouds among the incomprehensible blue above. I could stand going there every day for breakfast, tea, tiffin, and early dinner. There was hardly anything I would not give to be imprisoned in any of these exquisite chambers of sacred gold.

Soon I was served with tea. It is in eating that one wastes one half of his lifetime in Tibet. I should have gladly foregone my tea to get down to the job of photographing while the sun was at its best; but apparently tea was more important. The daily ceremony which is conducted before the throne of the Dalai Lama began in the midst of my sipping; so presently I went inside to meditate while arrangements were being made to take photographs of the complete set of their medical *thangkas* in the patio above. It is always interesting to watch them puff and blow their horns, their cheeks bulging out and drawing in like those of a croaking frog. The drummer marked time for them, while the rest of the monks either chanted or beat cymbals or rang bells. The ceremony was a short one.

The Prime Minister appeared and greeted me. Then, leading his servants to the secret chamber, which was under his personal lock and key, he had them bring out large carved blocks of the thirteen Dalai Lamas, of which he was giving me the privilege of having some prints made. Never before was any one allowed to take a print of these sacred blocks out to India; the privilege accorded me was of the rarest. Indeed, the very existence of these blocks was a mystery hitherto known but to a few. In all, there were thirty-two blocks. Thirteen of them were large and revealed the likenesses of the thirteen Dalai Lamas; then there was a set of seven, and another set of twelve small ones. At this time I had not yet been furnished with detailed information about them, and I had to remain content to wait. The printers were ready, and endless servants came out of the darkness bearing the heavy forms on their bent shoulders. A former bodyguard of the late Dalai Lama supervised the work; he was a hefty chap standing six foot six, and he made me feel like a pigmy. The place was buzzing with activity like a beehive.

Presently the message came that the Prime Minister, who by the way is the brother of the late Dalai Lama, had the *thangkas* out for me and ready for the camera. There were dozens of them, and I was kept busy right up to four o'clock, when it was decided that we should stop and eat again. I had time to learn that the Prime Minister himself was a camera enthusiast, and had several very good cameras of his own.

Another day. I was busy with packing things in my desk, wholly oblivious of what any one else was doing, until all of a sudden I got a whiff of yak skin. I knew exactly who had arrived and what was being done. The skin was used to wrap the boxes of books. I did not envy the workers who handled it as their job, at which they would be busy for the day. I do not see how they can stand the odor. They get used to it, I suppose. My *Geshe* was working very hard trying to finish the last set of books, so that they might be packed in the boxes by evening. He had almost finished when the Regent sent word that he had ordered some men to cross the river and return with a set of *Sum-Bum*, which I had been wanting but which I had given up hope of securing, owing to the fact that the river at this time was next to impossible to cross. The Regent's command, however, is law, and life and death mean nothing; so there was hope I might have my books yet. In all there would be another thirty volumes, which meant that my *Geshe* would have his work cut out for him until it was time for me to leave. I must admit I was getting a bit nervous, and wondered if I should have to delay my departure a day or two.

6

Life was not offering me much sleep these days and nights. On this particular day I rolled out of bed around three-thirty, after a single hour's sleep. I made for the "graveyard," for I heard that three persons had just died and I went out to see them cut up their bodies and feed them to the vultures. It all sounds rather low in contrast to our own customs; nevertheless, I felt it to be worth while to make a record of it as a part of my chronicle. The graveyard rested at the edge of the Sera hill. Every one is required to pay a small fee for the use of this spot, as well as to donate to the monks whatever clothes the corpse happens to be wrapped in. I understand the monks sell the clothes.

It was quite a trek getting there, the rainy season having left effects which made travel difficult.

The process of disposing of the bodies to the vultures takes place a few hundred feet up on the side of the great disintegrating sandstone hill; we were forced to dismount and lead our ponies. We reached the rock on which the ceremony, if ceremony it can be called, was carried out. It was a high flat rock, slightly on the incline, and at the top end was another large boulder, which had been obviously carried there. Around it many pieces of rope were securely fastened, and in a long row were six deep well-formed holes, into which some of the ropes led. These holes were filled with water from the heavy rains. The body is tied down with the rope to prevent the vultures from carrying it away in the process of stripping the skeleton of its meat. The birds have to be beaten back from these long strips of flesh until they have first disposed of the bones; these are pulverized in the holes I have just mentioned, and the vultures will not touch them if they have had a chance at the flesh first. The greatest delicacy of all is the crushed skull, well moistened with human brains. This is always kept until the end, for once the birds have had a taste of it—so at least I was told—they will not eat anything else. Quite apart from this, I never visited a "graveyard" which showed fewer tokens of death than this.

Only a single member of a family is disposed of on this site. Should there be any small children, their material forms are rubbed out of existence on another rock several hundred yards removed, and the mother has a place of her own on the other side of the valley. In all, there are four such disposal grounds in the vicinity of Lhasa. The family may request any place they wish. If they happen to be very poor, it is all done according to the whim and way of the man who has been assigned the job. The way of the poor is hard in Tibet—as elsewhere.

7

Everything was confusion about the house, adding unaccountably to my inner excitement. Tsarong's large house was nothing but one stack after another of things which would be used for his party. There was scarcely room left to walk. I now began to understand what he meant when he said that it took a lot of trouble to give a large party to which all the high officials of Tibet were to be invited. In all he was going to have over 300 guests, 200 of whom would be the servants of the other 100. The ground of the entrance would be lined with carpet so that no one need put his feet on the ground on arrival. There would be the most lavish decorations. His private temple surpassed any other private temple I had seen, and I had seen a good many. His images were superb, entirely covered with gold and radiating with the finest jewels. The silks in evidence here were also of the best. There are few persons who know their silks better than Tsarong, and, indeed, what little I know about silks I learned from him. As for Tsarong's sitting rooms, they make as perfect a museum of Chinese antiquities as any I have ever seen. He has objects of art which even the Museum of the Forbidden City of Pekin might regard with envy. And in this respect the entire house is of a piece. Yet, quite apart from this, and in spite of his wealth and power, Tsarong dresses very simply and there is no ostentation of any kind in the matter of daily living. It is only when he gives a party of this kind that you begin to realize the high place he holds in Tibet. I have heard it said that he set the pace for Lhasa. Everything he did was regarded with respect, and his ways regulated the ways of others.

8

In the afternoon a couple of Lamas from a monastery called to have a long talk with me. And again I must note how truly mysterious it is that they are able to keep track of one and to know of one's every act—I might almost say, thought. I sat with them while they told me how I had been spending my early mornings in prayer and what progress I had been making. More than that: they told me the precise developments in my attitude of mind, the contacts I had been able to make, and why I was able to experience that which I did experience when participating in the various ceremonies at the great monasteries.

I was dumfounded at what they told me, and perplexed as any one could possibly be. There was not the least doubt of it: what they told me about myself was quite accurate, and I really had the feelings which they ascribed to me.

Then they came out with the astonishing statement, that all that now remained for me to do was to take the last step, to go through with the ultimate initiation ceremony, which would make it possible for me to become conscious of these inner processes in me, would enable me to contact my inner self at will, and to the end of my days.

They said that word had come from the great monastery east of Lhasa, that the T'ri Rimpoche had returned, and that preparations were being made to receive me there for the last ceremony and to inculcate in me some knowledge of the ultimate native mystery.

It will never be possible for me to convey the fervor and ecstasy of my feelings on receiving this momentous news. Nor could I get over the wonder of their knowledge concerning me. They revealed to me every thought I had since my arrival in Lhasa, the precise nature of my reactions to the various ceremonies, and the depths I had sounded in the course of them.

I thought that this life was all my own, but they seemed to have some mystical power that gave them an insight into the understanding of others.

It was not a question of whether I would go or not. It was a question of how quickly I could leave. There was no time to be lost. I had come to Tibet for this, and here it had come to me on the day before my departure. Prompt plans were made that I might leave on the following morning. It was a four-days' journey east of Lhasa, to the third largest monastery in all Tibet, the sacred abode of the most divine soul of this mysterious land. That very night a message was sent to the monastery by runners to tell them that I was leaving on the morrow. The actual distance was not very great, but there were no roads to speak of, and the physical obstacles to overcome were considerable. It was necessary to ford the large river, and many of the trails had been washed away by the heavy floods. Full of emotional fervor because the privilege of a lifetime had been granted me, I was hoping we might make the journey in three days. Little time had been wasted. Everything was now about ready to leave for India. It was just a question of putting things in their corner and of leaving the order so that everything could be moved at a moment's notice.

Long before sunrise everything was helter-skelter in the effort to get the last-minute details taken care of before leaving for the Ganden monastery. The rains were still with us, and everything was discouraging, for the sky was black with very low clouds; we were anticipating the worst kind of weather, and as usual the transport arrived late. The only thing that interested me was to get there myself.

9

It was scarcely more than half an hour before we arrived at a point at which it was necessary to cross the river in a small yak-hide boat called *kowas*. On the sandy banks there were three of them trussed up on end in order that they might be drying out while not in use. The riding ponies had to be swum over. At first we had planned to use donkeys for transport and take them along with us in boats, but arrangements were finally made to secure more ponies on the other side; so our party broke up into small groups and joined a couple of other parties who had arrived shortly before. All the boats went over together. It provided something of a thrill to hear the echoing voice of a coming boatman around the bend of the river and then see a group of them winding their way down stream. It is possible to travel for many miles in such boats down these large streams. Considerable transporting is done, and often a large quantity of timber is lashed together, and a party will ride it to the other end. The current is by far too strong and swift to allow going upstream; so it is a case of ride down and walk back. I assume that all the boats accumulate at the other end, and are then carried back. They are very light. Indeed, one man can carry a boat; yet a single boat will hold many men including their transport. Just before reaching the far bank we had the thrill of rolling over the dashing waves of a small rapid.

Ponies were waiting for us, so it was not long before we were off, to ride only about five miles, when we were to change transports. While waiting for the servants to go to the fields and bring in the ponies for the next day, I talked to a few of the traders and sheepherders who were hanging around. There was one chap who dragged heavy iron shackles around the ankles. With no prison system to speak of, when any one commits a crime he is simply put into fetters and allowed to roam at large. This fellow had devised some sort of automatic device for killing foxes and, as luck would have it, a man became his victim instead of the stray fox; so he was arrested and punished

in the manner described; he would wear these shackles until the end of his days.

One of the men was carrying a large sling-shot, the sort of weapon that David must have used to slay Goliath. This one was woven out of yak hair. I simply had to look at it and see how well it worked. It had been many years since I had heard the hum of a rock projected by this device, but it was only a matter of putting it into my hand to be tempted to make use of it. So we all had a little fun, and they were truly astonished to find out that the sahib could handle their weapon with the same skill as themselves; indeed, could send a bit of rock a little farther into space.

After our exercise we went in and had several cups of Tibetan tea with their *tsampa* bread, and thus nourished the soul before covering another several miles, stopping only to receive another set of transports. I had to change horses no less than five times that day. Our packs could not expect to catch up with us, for as soon as we arrived at another station and had a few cups of tea we were promptly off again.

I think I have already explained that travel in Tibet requires a governmental pass, which is an order to the headman of each village to furnish the holder with all the necessary animals, for both riding and transport, as well as his supply of essential food, and a place to spend the night. On arriving at a village you go to the house of the headman with the letter stating your requirements, and everything receives the most gracious attention. Indeed, the hospitality offered is beyond anything you expect. Now without this letter it would be impossible to secure anything. They do not even see you, the very good reason being that if it is ever found out that they have given any sort of aid to one not holding a passport, the penalty would be death. If not, it might just as well be death, for you are thrown out of the social scheme of things without ever a chance of finding your way back. There is an instance of a very high family, whose head was above the fourth rank. He was persuaded by an Indian scholar to help him, which he did, and when it was discovered years later, his entire family lost the prestige and the power of the rank, while the head of the family, who did the helping, was imprisoned for life; only through the fates of the Gods was he released at the time of the 1904 Mission, which requested it. As far as being of any value to himself, however, he might just as well have been left in his dungeon of blackness, where he had been for years, for his eyesight was sadly impaired and in his effort to keep alive on the rations given him his body had wilted away to a mere shadow. I heard this story from Sir Francis Younghusband himself, who ordered the release. There is a book on Tibet whose author goes to considerable extremes of denouncing the Tibetans as an unmerciful race, with absolutely no consideration for human life. He has come to this conclusion because of the tragic results of his experience in virtually having to crawl from Kashmir to Gyantsé. If he had an Arrow letter and was not trying to steal his way through the country his story would have been wholly different. Speaking for myself, I found the Tibetans the most gracious people on earth, and never before had I such friendship extended me by foreigners.

All day we rode up the Lhasa Valley on the opposite side of Lhasa River. It was one of the loveliest outings that one could wish at this time of the year. Everything was ready for the harvest. There were endless fields of flowing wheat, which formed one of the colors of Nature's beautiful patchwork quilt of hues which she had laid across the valley. Perhaps the most outstanding delight was that of riding along for miles through air delicately scented with the fragrance of the brilliant yellow mustard fields which cover a vast expanse. At times we were travelling on the brink of the river, where a very narrow trail cut into the sheer, overhanging precipice looming immediately above the water. Then there was always a passing panorama of human interest in the Lamas, traders, sheepherders, women and children on their way to Lhasa. There were many *chortens* marking sacred spots. And in one of the narrow passages I passed the first white yak which I had ever seen. I also met with new types coming in from Kham, loaded to the ground with guns as well as with their heavy skin clothing. The arms varied from the old matchlock to the modern rifle. I also noticed that one group carried the bow; it hailed from the southeast corner of Tibet on the Bhutan frontier.

Due to our hurried pace, the transport was left far behind last night, for they had not arrived at twelve o'clock, when I decided to call it a day and give the body a chance. Weighing on my mind on awakening was whether or not they had come in during the night, and much to my disappointment I found that they had not yet arrived. About six o'clock, however, we heard their bell coming down the road, so we gave the matter no further thought and simply directed them up the hill to Ganden.

Dressed in a Tibetan robe, and accompanied by my bodyguard, I headed toward the sacred monastery of Ganden, situated on top of the mountain, below which we spent the night in an old house of the past potentates of Tibet. It was a three-story structure of solid rock, and I was made very comfortable in it and provided with a repast as usual three or four times more than was necessary; I suppose they thought I needed all that to sustain me until I reached the top.

The lift from the floor of the fertile valley was somewhere between two and three thousand feet, which means that Ganden is between 14,000 and 15,000 feet above sea-level. The stark barrenness of the hills reminded me of similar hills in our own West. It was a continuously ascending, zigzagging trail worn in loosely thrown limestone. At all times we had an excellent command of the surrounding valley formed by the knife-like tongues which ran out from the main ranges. The trek was not long, for Ganden was at the very top; it was a steep, quick climb, with soaring eagles for company.

Just before reaching the top our trail went through a narrow cut in the rock ridge. At this point there was a Lama who apparenty guarded the spot all the time and warned every passer-by to be sure and remove all bells from his animals, for the Most Precious One was at the monastery, and nothing should disturb his meditation. This is done only for the T'ri Rimpoche, and the Dalai Lama, when he is alive. I held a great deal of anticipation of being able to come in contact with this divine soul and realized that it was he who would act as my "guide into Heaven."

Here, to my mind, was the ideal monastery, tucked away as it was in a hidden corner in the bend of one of the higher ridges which juts out into the valley. For could there be a more ideal place for a monastery than among the gathering clouds of heaven yet remain completely hidden from every one passing up and down the valley? Below it the mountain drops straight down for a couple thousand feet. Could one ask for better protection and isolation? In appearance it recalled to my mind any New York array of small apartment houses, for it consisted of many three-story buildings stacked up on top of each other; but from the distance you lost the true perspective, as they appeared merged in a single crowding structure dotted with small windows, a structure which filled the uppermost tiers of this amphitheatre of the Gods, where its inhabitants while away their time preparing for the hereafter. And I vow that any human being dwelling in a like place would be unable to think of anything else; the country hereabouts surely awakens all the religious awe that any soul might possess.

Ganden Monastery, third largest monastery in Tibet, officially supposed to have 3300 Lamas

10

We had to descend a few hundred feet in order to reach the level of the trail leading to the main temple, where they had made arrangements for me to live during my visit. The clouds hung very low; indeed, if we had jumped, our heads would have plunged into them. It was out of question to take pictures. Monks met me to conduct me to my monastic cell, where I should be living the life of a Tibetan Lama, and learning to contact the consciousness in the manner taught by them. I knew I was being honored, for I was permitted to live in a sacred chamber in the main temple building, where the great ceremony would take place on the following morning at the break of day.

I need scarcely say that there was tea when I arrived and that from the moment I occupied my cell a tiny acolyte came running in every five minutes to refill my cup. And, of course, there was food. I got so filled up with tea and food that my reaction was a desire to throw both in the face of the faithful attendant; but what I actually did was to smile graciously and accept another swallow. There is just as much privacy here as in a hospital, with attendants who go in and out, and others who remain to look you over. I was, of course, a source of intense curiosity to the Lamas. And I was equally curious about them.

Beside the shrine in my quarters were the *Kangyur* and *Tengyur* which had been read and studied by Tsong Khapa, the founder of this monastery and the organizer of the Gelupa sect. This is the oldest and most sacred of all the Gelupa monasteries. Two of Tsong Khapa's disciples built Drepung, Sera and Tashi Lunpo. There are two sets of small platforms in front of the monastery. On the high one the Dalai Lama dismounts from his palanquin when he comes to visit the monastery; while the lower one he uses to make the three devotionals to the monastery. The other set is used by the T'ri

Rimpoche, the head Lama of this monastery, who is next in rank to the Dalai Lama of Tibet.

II

As later I sat in the dark cave of solitary confinement the last thing I recalled was my drifting into sleep that first night in the monastic cell, having previously reviewed all the events of my Tibetan and pre-Tibetan experience which led up to this, the ultimate mystical initiation and the instructions from the divine head of this monastery which conferred the power and the authority to pass on something of my experience to others, after they had prepared themselves sufficiently to take the steps as they were revealed to me.

I already sent out a message from my cave that I should be finishing my reflections late that evening, and word had come that the T'ri Rimpoche would be ready to receive me in his private meditative chamber at the break of dawn. Subconscious forces were flowing too rapidly for me even to think of sleep; so after I had finished the review of my entire life I spent the rest of the night meditating in the manner I had been instructed, thus preparing myself for that which was going to be passed on to the following morning.

It was like being reborn to emerge back into the world after an absence of three days and four nights spent in the cave; not a single moment had I lain down to sleep, having spent the entire time in contact with the inner force. Not a word was spoken to me by the monks who had been sent to conduct me to my teacher. No one else was allowed to enter his meditative chamber but myself. The vibrations of the room were very peculiar. A strange mood possessed me as I stepped into this private shrine, and took my place beside him. Not a word was exchanged between us, but only an understanding twinkle of the eye, which told both of us how we felt.

Gathering Up the Last Threads

The sun had not yet come up, and the light within was very dim; there was but the dull flicker of a few small butter lamps before his altar. I arranged myself in the customary meditative posture, and the two of us remained in dead silence to greet the new day, symbolic of a new world for me. Thus we remained for three hours, like two frozen images, but the light and the speech within were more illumining, more eloquent, more active, than anything I had ever experienced before.

Our silence was broken at last by the repetition of a few sacred syllables. A short conversation followed, during which he explained the meaning of everything that had taken place. He pointed out to me that now I had gained contact with an old soul that was within me; this was, he said, the reason for my pilgrimage, that I had by no means come as a disciple to acquire learning, that I had, indeed, previously possessed this knowledge, and that it had been only a question of making the contact. Now, having brought consciousness into it, he said, it would be possible for me to continue my development throughout life.

For my part, I said in response that I would be willing to remain here for the rest of my days, to which he said that this was not the way for me. It was essential first to permit the past existence to fulfill itself; it was this that had caused me to be born in the Western world, that there was some predestined purpose in it, that it was necessary that I fulfill it; having done that, I should be free from all the shackles of the past. Then, again, the soul had chosen this body, which is only an instrument of the soul. It was important that I should perfect this instrument by a process of maturation. Therefore, it was essential that I should live the life into which I was born, but continue unceasingly this process leading to the fullest maturation. Although my soul was old, my body was still very young, but notwithstanding the age of my soul it was required of me that

I continue in the life given me and add new experience to it, that now having made the contact with my inner self I should have the fortitude to withstand all the sorrows and adversities of life and be able to transmute them into blessings.

The Lamaist teaching is that every person should spend a certain number of years of his early childhood in gaining contact with himself, which should provide him with a philosophical outlook on life and enable him the better to face it. This is the opposite of our Western method of education. We feel that we can fit the individual into the prevalent scheme of things by first providing him with the facts and with an understanding of all the externals of life. This is our idea of the equipment he needs in the facing of life. It is not until he has been battered back and forth along the path for forty or fifty years that he is able to gain, if he gains it at all, the first inkling of a philosophical understanding. At this juncture his one attitude of mind is: "If only I had known about life when I was a child just starting out in life! How much easier it would have been for me to pass through all of these experiences! How much more they would have meant to me, how much more I should have been able to gain and do!" The Lamaist teachers contend that the individual should be provided with the philosophy first, after which he may acquire the necessary facts and pass on through the endless experiences of this life with some means at his disposal, provided by the philosophy, to enable him steadily to grow and evolve, which is the only purpose of his existence.

Secure in my knowledge that I had a way of communing with this mind from any corner of this earth, it had now become possible for me to return to the world of affairs. And my own land, America, suddenly beckoned to me, and my return to it, I was aware, would be fraught with meanings which I had not even suspected when I left it for my wanderings in India and, above all, Tibet.

INDEX

INDEX

Index

Index

Lightning Source UK Ltd.
Milton Keynes UK
UKHW010954241118
332888UK00001B/46/P

9 781406 744279